# Pon My Puff!

# Pon My Puff!

## A Childhood in 1920s Isle of Wight

Peter Stark Lansley

Edited and Annotated with an Introduction
by Charles Morris Lansley

PARTNER PUBLISHING

BEACHY BOOKS

First published by Beachy Books Partner Publishing in 2021
(an imprint of Beachy Books Limited)
www.beachybooks.com

1

A CIP catalogue record for this book is available from the British Library.

ISBN: 9781913894023
(Also available as a hardback - ISBN 9781913894016)

Set in Adobe Caslon Pro
Cover photo ©rparys - stock.adobe.com

# DR CHARLES MORRIS LANSLEY

Dr Charles Morris Lansley has strong connections to the Isle of Wight through his father's side of the family who lived on the Island, his Stark and Morris ancestors having had grazing rights in 1425 in the reign of Henry VI. He still maintains his connection to the Island through his home in Shanklin and his interest in Island family and social history. Charles Morris Lansley's other research interests are in eighteenth and nineteenth century natural history, science and literature. He was awarded his PhD by the University of Winchester in 2016 for research into Charles Darwin and his book *Charles Darwin's Debt to the Romantics: How Alexander von Humboldt, Goethe and Wordsworth Helped Shape Darwin's View of Nature* was published in 2018 by Peter Lang. Prior to his research on Darwin, he worked in education and training before retiring. He is a Fellow of The Linnean Society of London.

Also by the same author:

Lansley, Charles Morris (2018). *Charles Darwin's Debt to the Romantics: How Alexander von Humboldt, Goethe and Wordsworth Helped Shape Darwin's View of Nature*. Oxford: Peter Lang. ISBN 978-178707-138-4 (print); ISBN 978-1-78707-139-1 (ePDF); ISBN 978-1-78707 (ePub); ISBN 978-1-78707-141-4 (mobi).

# ACKNOWLEDGEMENTS

I would like to thank the following for their help in locating my family's headstones, obituaries and providing other family background enabling me to edit the book as accurately as possible: Friends of Newport and Carisbrooke Cemeteries, in particular Tony Barton; Isle of Wight Family History Society; Isle of Wight Society and East Cowes Heritage; and Isle of Wight County Records Office, in particular Simon Dear. Also my cousins Jane Smith, Eve Ward, Anthea Nex and Derek Stewart for family tree information and photos. Thanks also to Hilary Lloyd for permission to use postcards from the Hilary Lloyd Collection and for providing additional historical information; also for her invaluable research in providing so much background information to the characters in the book. Many thanks to my wife Claire Lansley for providing editing suggestions and help with proofreading. Also thanks for help and support from my publisher, Beachy Books, in particular from Philip Bell.

# CONTENTS

# INTRODUCTION

This is the story of my father, Peter Stark Lansley's (1919 – 1999) childhood memories of Wootton Bridge in the 1920s. In particular, it is about his very special loving relationship with his grandfather, 'Gramp', William Stark (1857 – 1929), and his grandmother, 'Granny' Harriette Stark (née Morris, 1854 – 1943), known by their friends as Bill and Harty. It also tells the story of his adventures with his childhood girlfriend Victoria. Like Laurie Lee's *Cider with Rosie*, the story is told through the eyes of a child. No exact dates or ages are given in the book but events, together with my father's outline chapter notes, suggest that the period covers the years 1924 – 1929 when my father was between the ages of five and almost ten, up to the time his grandfather died in March 1929.

*William & Harriette's children, Millie (14), Adolphus (Uncle Will) (22), Harry (Uncle Harry) (17) & Annie Ethel (Mummy) (19) 1902 © C M Lansley*

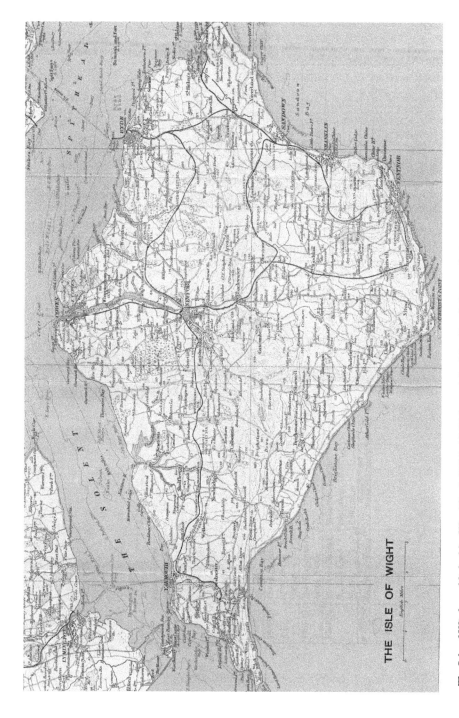

*The Isle of Wight published by Ward Lock 1926-1927 (copyright John Bartholomew & Sons Ltd Edinburgh). In the Public Domain.*

My father's father, my grandfather, Percy Lansley (1886 – 1970), was a Chief Engine Room Artificer in the Royal Navy, who consequently spent a lot of his working life at sea. It therefore seemed a good idea that my father and his mother, my grandmother, Annie Ethel Morris Lansley (née Stark, 1883 – 1959), a school teacher, should live with his grandparents who would help with his upbringing as well as that of his older brother Percy Morris (known as 'Morris'). Annie Ethel is referred to as 'Mummy' in the book.

The stories centre around their home at Woodside Villas, Station Road, Wootton Bridge. Records from the Isle of Wight Records Office are some-what confusing as they show that some of the family members lived off and on at 1 Woodside Villa (now 8 Station Road) between 1924 and 1937 and 2 Woodside Villa (now 6 Station Road) between 1926 and 1952. The records also show that some of them also lived at Carlton Villa, Station Road, be-tween 1924 and 1929, but this house cannot be located on any maps.[1] Station Road,[2] as the name implies, is named after the location of Wootton railway station[3] which still exists today and is one of the four stations on the Isle of Wight Steam Railway line (the four stations being Smallbrook, Ashey, Havenstreet and Wootton). However, in the 1920s steam locomotives linked Wootton to Ryde and Portsmouth and the world beyond until the end of the steam era on 31 December 1966. But in the 1920s, the Starks and the Lansleys lived near enough to the station to know when uncles, aunts and cousins had arrived from Portsmouth from the sound of the engines and the sight of the steam. This was the age of the railway but not yet of the car, where it was still considered safe for young children to wander down the road to the

---

1  To add to the confusion, the electoral rolls for October 1931 and 1932 show that my father and his parents Percy Lansley and Annie Ethel Lansley and his grandmother Harriette Stark lived at 32 St. John's Road, Newport. This probably coincided with the start of my father's first year at Newport Grammar School. As Harriette died at Woodside Villa in 1943 it suggests that the family might have rented the St. John's property and owned the one at Woodside Villa.

2  Beech Lane, Wootton, was the Victorian name for Station Road in 1866 (Wightpedia, 2019, p.1).

3  The original station opened in 1875 and closed on 21 September 1953. The new station is located about two hundred yards to the south east of the original station and was opened in 1986 (Disused Stations: Wootton, 2019, p.1).

creek unaccompanied by adults. This was also the age when not all houses had electricity and oil lamps and candles were still used for illumination.

The stories in the book show how all the family members valued the importance of family life and this is brought home by their get-togethers at Christmas time with carol singing (with children allowed a sip of Guinness) and the presents that mattered—perhaps even more than a trainset—such as my father's proud ownership of his very own watering can for the hens. The book is not just about love and family life; it is also about growing up and learning about life, but within a sheltered and protected environment. This is about childhood between the interwar years. My father knows about the death of his Uncle Will at sea in 1917 but the nature of war and death is seen from a distance and the Second World War is still some way off. Yet the notion of death is not taboo and Peter and his grandfather talk openly of death and where 'Gramp' will go—to Mount Joy Cemetery at Carisbrooke where he will continue to play his whistle[4] in heaven. Through questions and answers, 'Gramp' opens up the world to Peter, even exploring graveyards with quotes from Tennyson's[5] Maud and a visit to Elizabeth Wallbridge's grave (the Dairyman's Daughter) at Arreton, like Legh Richmond's[6] musings, linking the soul to the beautiful countryside of the Isle of Wight. Throughout this learning process, though, there is still the innocence of childhood making for literal interpretations of the adult world and its adult language. It creates a delightful charm in softening the harsh realities of the real world and of war and death yet to come. For the moment there is a lull and any shocks or surprises are restricted to soft, pleasant, almost cuddly, surprises expressed through Gramp's 'Pon My Puff!' (thus the original name my father gave to the book) or Granny's 'My Godfathers!'

---

4   William was a well-known performer on the penny whistle. According to family anecdotes, on Saturday nights when the pubs were shut, he would play his whistle leading a file of men all around Cowes singing 'we won't go home till the morning'. He was also known to be a singer of popular songs.

5   Alfred Lord Tennyson (1809 –1892) was the Poet Laureate of Great Britain and Ireland during much of Queen Victoria's reign. Tennyson and his wife, Emily, lived at Farringford House, Freshwater, Isle of Wight for thirty-nine years from 1853 until his death in 1892.

6   The author of *The Dairyman's Daughter*.

*Edmund Morris's Store, Newport. From Remembering Newport: Marking the Changes (2010). Published by Terence Westmore. Unknown copyright. In the Public Domain. Author's permission given.*

It should be noted, though, that this very cosy life with no shortage of food on the table at Christmas time and money to go to Ashey races over the Bank Holiday was hard won. William Stark (Gramp) had been employed as a coach wheeler by Higgs the coach building firm in Southampton but in 1887 he was made redundant at the age of about thirty. Harriette was about thirty three. William and Harriette then moved back to the Isle of Wight to live at 2 Cypress Terrace, Adelaide Grove (now 69 Adelaide Grove), East Cowes, where Harriette converted the property into a Grocer's store with help and support from her brother-in-law Benjamin Redstone who was a grocer at 3 Albert Street, Cowes. It is likely that she received encouragement and support from her father, Edmund Morris, who was a cabinet maker and upholsterer by trade. He had established Edmund Morris and Son in Mill Street, Newport, as a store making and supplying furniture, mattresses and blinds. His son, Edward Morris, developed the business in Newport selling china, curtains, carpets and other household items at the premises he built at 28 High Street opposite the Town Hall and at 39 High Street on the corner of St. Thomas' Square.[7] He eventually renamed the stores Edward Morris's Stores and expanded the business to Cowes and Freshwater. So it is very likely that Harriette could also have received advice and support from her entrepreneurial brother Edward. Harriette was a dedicated grocer and astute business woman who held family values dear to her heart. She not only used the proceeds of her work to look after her family but also paid for her two sons Adolphus William (Will) and Harry to be apprenticed as engineers at J.S. White and Co's Shipbuilding Yard at East Cowes which enabled them later to join the Royal Navy as officers. Sadly, Adolphus William lost his life at sea off the coast of Northern Ireland in 1917 aboard *HMS Drake*. This was devastating for the whole family and it is touching that in the book we are told they remember him at Christmas time and that a photograph of him in his splendid uniform was still on proud display. His name is recorded on the Rolls of Honour in the chapel at Carisbrooke Castle, at the Isle of Wight War Memorial, Newport and at the Portsmouth Naval Memorial. His brother Harry served aboard HM Submarine. William and Harriette's children were either in the Navy or were married to someone in the Navy. Their daughter Annie Ethel was married to Percy Lansley, a Chief Engineer, who served aboard *HMS Caledon*, and their other daughter Mildred was married to Jackson Stewart who served on *HMS Encounter*. Harriette not only worked hard to pay for her two sons' apprenticeships, but also provided financial support for Annie Ethel to go to Salisbury College to train as a teacher (having passed the King's Scholarship Examination to be accepted in 1902). Prior to this she was trained as a pupil teacher at Blue Coat School in Crocker Street, Newport. Harriette continued to provide support for her

---

7 The building at 39 High Street, known as Emor House, was rebuilt in the 1970s becoming in turn the Army and Navy Stores, House of Fraser and Laura Ashley. His original mosaic logo was incorporated into the brickwork of the new building and can still be seen today. Edward became a Liberal town councillor and Justice of the Peace and was a devoted member of the Board of Guardians of the Poor. When he died, the Town Hall flag flew at half-mast and many shops closed for the day. There are headstones for both Edmund and Edward, along with other members of their family, at Newport Cemetery.

*Peter writing at his desk late 1950s, early 1960s, about 40–42 years old © C M Lansley*

family in this way until ill health prevented her from running the business and in 1907 they converted the shop back into a private dwelling. My father and his parents, Annie Ethel and Percy, also lived there until they all moved to Woodside Villa in Station Road, Wootton in the summer of 1924, when my father was five years old.

My father also went to sea and served as a Radio Officer in the Merchant Navy. One of the ships he served on was the *MV Wandby* which, like his uncle Will's ship, was torpedoed by a German U-47 submarine and sank off the Teesside coast on 19 October 1940 on its way back from Victoria, British Columbia, Canada. Fortunately all the crew survived. After the war he served as a Telecommunications Officer for the Civil Aviation Authority and worked at Eastleigh Airport (now Southampton Airport), Birdlip Radio Station near Cheltenham and at West Drayton serving Heathrow Airport. During this time he was posted to other airports such as St Mary's on the Scilly Isles and to Alderney airport on the Channel Isles. No doubt during these postings while away from home he had time to think and write about his childhood. I remember my father talking about his book in the 1960s and sometimes he would read out extracts to my mother (Ruth Lansley, 1922 –

*Peter's Woodside Villa Suitcase showing Wootton Address and Notebooks © C M Lansley*

2013). I was under the impression that she was in the process of typing out the manuscripts for publication, but I never came across a completed version. Upon my mother's death in 2013 and during her house clearance, I looked everywhere for any typed-up copies but could not find anything. Finally I looked in the garage and saw an old trunk in the corner. Inside I discovered my father's handwritten notebooks along with some family tree scrolls. I was so relieved and happy at rescuing his book. It contained many revised versions and it does seem as if some chapters may be missing. But at least I have saved the bulk of it to be able to shape it into the book about his much loved childhood memories of his grandparents at Woodside Villa, Wootton. And hopefully this will be a memory that others will delight in.

Apart from being a book about my father's memories of his childhood, it is also a book based on nostalgia. His nostalgia may reflect a longing to return to the innocence of childhood. Peter's childhood came before the horrors of the Second World War and he wrote this book having lived through that experience and having married a victim of the Holocaust. One senses a yearning to return to the safe unthreatening nature of his games with his friend Victoria and his cousin Barrie[8] and the delights of Christmas. This is of course a personal interpretation, but it could also be seen as an unconscious wish for these same memories to be a substitute for his wife's lost childhood. My mother Ruth's parents, Rudolf and Ida, sent her and her sister over from Germany to escape Nazi persecution and sadly her parents, my grandparents, died as a result of the Holocaust. My mother experienced this when she was sixteen and she never saw her parents again although fortunately her two brothers were later able to join them. Well before leaving Germany in 1939, she had the humiliation of being put in the corner of her classroom wearing a yellow star and had to suffer the distress of her parents' shop window being smashed in during Kristallnacht. Like my father, she too had loving memories of her parents and family life but this was all destroyed by the Nazis and the Holocaust. Her parents' last letters from home came in 1943. She knew they had been sent to the ghettoes but never knew exactly where and when they died. It is likely they ended up in Auschwitz as most of the Jewish residents from her hometown of Leipzig were transported there. My mother and her siblings were haunted by this throughout their lives. This is a story for another day. But it is easy to see the two childhood memories as opposites representing light versus darkness, loving protection versus persecution and

---

8    Donald Barrie Stark (1917-2005). His mother named him after J.M. Barrie the playwright.

murder. As a youth I remember my father reading out passages of the book to my mother and I can imagine how these might have brought back the happier memories of my mother's family life. It is true, as David Herman points out, that 'many things can bring back memories of our past. A childhood song, a favourite dish, small objects, images of home [...]. All of these can bring back powerful memories for those driven from their homeland, fleeing for their lives' and it is no wonder they can be 'haunted by the past, by the dead' (Herman, 2020, pp.1-2). For my mother, certain childhood songs and dishes no doubt brought back memories of loss. For my father, his idyllic memories must have strengthened his faith in how wonderful childhood could be. Hopefully listening to my father retelling these stories helped her rediscover the sanctity of childhood and faith in humanity. I hope that the delights of the idyllic side of childhood prevail in future generations.

My interest in my father's book made me even more curious about my great-grandparents and where their remains were located. Through the Isle of Wight Family History Society and the Friends of Newport and Carisbrooke Cemeteries, I was able to find them. William Stark and Harriette Stark are at Carisbrooke Cemetery (Mount Joy[9]), section Y, plot 160. So William Stark really did go to Mount Joy where he told his grandson Peter he would go to upon his death. But it seems as if William referred to it as more than just a cemetery and more a physical representation of heaven. The outstanding views from the top of the hill overlooking the Island certainly give that impression. In September 2019 I commissioned a stonemason to clean the headstone. I have to say this was a second attempt, as the stonemason initially cleaned the wrong headstone—he mistakenly cleaned William Henry Thomas Stark's headstone on plot 149. But never mind, he was still a relative (he was William Stark's father's brother's grandson). I am sure if he had known, Gramp would have said, 'Pon My Puff!' Sadly my Grandparents, Percy and Ethel, were cremated off the Island and there are no memorials for them (Percy at Cheltenham Crematorium and Ethel at Bournemouth Crematorium). My parents' ashes were scattered in their garden in Alverstone Garden Village.

---

9   Also written as 'Mountjoy.'

So at least my father's remains came to rest on the Island he knew and loved so well and not too far from his childhood memories of Wootton. I have placed two memorial plaques for my parents on the memorial wall at Ventnor Botanic Gardens.

I heard childrens voices. I slipped on my mask. I waited. I heard several voices. Too many I thought. Why must they all walk home together.

The last group of voices had died away, and I was about to give up when I heard a faint footstep. Black hat, mask, sword at the ready, I held my breath. Someone alone. Through the bushes I could just see the top of a little head. I pounced: "Your money or your life", I shouted. And then I saw my victim. She was a little older than my self and obviously quite frightened. She didn't seem to know what to say or do, so waving my blood stained sword I shouted again, "Your money or your life."

"I think", she whispered falteringly, "I, I think I'd rather give my my money if you don't mind."

"Thanks mam", I said, in best highway fashion, "I see you're being sensible. In my hat please." She obliged by dropping the half penny into my hat. "Now mam' any twinkets, necklaces broaches..."

"My mummy ha had a bean beautiful broach once but she she lost it on the beach. If I ha had it I would ge give it to you."

"I see you're telling the truth mam'" I said, "you may go..."

She turned and walked away down

*Extract from manuscript – Chapter 19, The Highway Robbery © C M Lansley*

# 1

# SETTLING IN

Settling in to Woodside Villa was a wonderful experience of discovery.[10] It was an abundant fruit year. There seemed as many apples, pears and plums on the ground as on the trees. Mrs Jones,[11] during those first days, was a frequent visitor, and in such company I helped gather this wonderful harvest, somehow escaping the stings of wasps that seemed to be under every grounded fruit. Granny and Mrs Jones collected the fruit in their aprons as they marched slowly, their aprons held in front forming huge sagging basins which I filled to overflowing with rolling fruit. We walked back to the house to fill Granny and Gramp's bedroom with apples and pears wiped to a shiny green or a glossy red, and others such as yellow and toffee-burnt-brown of 'not quite William' as Gramp said. They were all placed side by side on newspaper around the skirting boards until in the end there were apples and pears everywhere with just room for Granny and Gramp to walk to their bed between hedges of sweet-smelling fruit. The plums, because of 'mind the stones,' were constantly referred to as 'stone fruit.' They were bottled while the others were made into jam. The days were breathtaking with everyone working non-stop. My bouts of sickness during these days were accepted as part of the settling in process, with Granny, loving her fruit, being a fellow companion in over indulgence.

On one bright breezy day I swung on the wooden gate making it go 'creak, creak' with Gramp saying I would swing it off its hinges if I wasn't careful and that he would oil it with a feather. From the big conkers scraping against the shiny tin summerhouse roof, the small trees in the garden, and the giant

---

10   This was the autumn of 1924 when my father was five and a half years old. During the move to Woodside Villa, Peter's older brother 'Morris' spent the first week with friends in Newport.

11   Mrs Jones was the Starks' housekeeper and home help. Her Christian name was Jessie and her husband Harry was killed in WW I.

*1 & 2 Woodside Villa, 6 & 8 Station Road © C M Lansley*

trees from the wood opposite, came the sound of some great sea. The wind shook their branches and tore the end of summer-tinted leaves skywards as if they were particles of spray crashing over the sea wall during stormy seas at Cowes. My world was wonderful as I stood in my smallness by the gate, now and again leaning backwards against the wind, using him as a resting place for my back, and talking to him as a living person instead of a sea noise taking away fading summer leaves. I splayed out my hands and felt the freshness glide through my fingers as I watched the leaves soar upwards against a background of white seahorse clouds under a bluey canvas sky. Suddenly I felt as if there were raindrops on my face. Gramp was bent over by the gate dipping a feather in and out of the neck of a browny beer bottle, dripping oil onto the hinge. As he did so some of the drops got carried in the air with Gramp saying, 'Look, oil on your face, oil on your pants[12],' taking my hand and moving me from range. Then he oiled the other hinge with the same

---

12   Pantaloons.

*Annie Ethel Stark (Mummy) & Percy Lansley's (Daddy) Engagement 1908*
*© C M Lansley*

'flip, flip' of the feather, telling me to swing again, which I did to his obvious satisfaction. As I swung, without so much as a squeak, the oil ran down the red painted gate in dark wavy lines.

As I played the gate game, I saw a little figure coming down the road, now level with the summerhouse and soon to be passing my gate. She held her hands in front of her, clasped around a blue bag, which, as she came nearer, I knew was a sugar bag. I stopped swinging on the gate, keeping my feet still on the bottom crosspiece as I watched her waiting to gather her breath against the wind. She wore little white socks and little white shoes and was wearing a white dress with tiny flowers. They stood out of the material, becoming clearer as she approached. She was now nearly level with my gate. She had dark hair with a fringe above large brown eyes that met mine as she stopped at my gate. Pausing again for breath and half turning, she said, 'Hallo.' She was, I thought, about three or four, perhaps a rather old-looking three. Age was most important, so I asked, 'How old are you?' I had the great satisfaction of being older, as she would not catch up with me until nearly Christmas,[13] or so she said, and to both of us, at that moment, Christmas seemed a lifetime away. So far away, in fact, that we couldn't say what we were going to have for Christmas, so we talked about what we had last Christmas. I boasted of last year's camels, eleven in a brown smelly cardboard box. Her farmyard brought us closer together, as I too had a farmyard, but from her glowing reports of her farm stock and wagons, she was a big farmer: she had seven grassy-greenie fields, and seven white gates. But I had rail lines with carriages and one coal truck. She had no lines or carriages, though her brother, five years older, had Meccano, but I could see I had impressed her with my railway. She had a large doll, so she said, almost as big as herself that opened and shut its eyes with 'real, real' clothes both underneath and on top. She could see now that I was most excited because I had never seen a doll so big, or heard of one so dressed, and so we became enchanted with each other. During this excitement she dropped her precious sugar bag in the road. The bag lay burst open with bits of gritty road looking through the glassy sugar. Our hearts

---

13 My father, Peter, would have been five at this time, so Victoria would have been four, becoming five in December.

*Harriette and William Stark (Granny & Gramp) 1913 © C M Lansley*

quickened and our hands melted towards each other as we surveyed this calamity, forgetting farmyards, dolls and engines, as we together understood its full significance within the world of grown-ups waiting to use the sugar.

Not far away, ever watchful hedge-clipping Gramp had observed the mishap and came quickly to the rescue as we moved up the path. We each claimed a hand as he guided us into the kitchen, surprising Granny peeling apples, as Gramp announced with pride, 'Look what I've brought you.' Granny said, 'Pon my word, you are a lovely child. What's your name?' Before I could say, 'It's "Victoria," Granny,' Victoria said, 'It's Victoria,' with both Granny and Gramp expressing their delight at what a lovely name it was, and how it suited my friend.

This made me feel very, very important to have such a friend to make Granny and Gramp so happy. Gramp called from the door for Mummy to come downstairs. He had something very special to show her, something, he said, the wind had blown in, which of course I knew to be true as I thought of the bluey sugar bag and gritty white dust in the ocean wind.

Mummy was just as enchanted with Victoria as I was. I tiptoed with pride when Mummy said that I would have been called Victoria if I had been a girl. Granny asked where she lived. With a toss of her fringe, Victoria said, 'Four houses down the road, not quite at the corner.'

'The house with the green tiles,' Gramp explained, making me feel even more important; for once on passing the green-tiled house, Granny had remarked, 'I wonder who lives in that house?' and Gramp had replied, 'Whoever it was must be well-to-do to say the least of it, pon my puff!' and so I was prouder still, my only regret being that Mrs Jones was not present to add her sniff of pleasure.

Granny shook the boat-like apple slices within the colander, asking Victoria and then me if we would like sugar-apples, causing saucers to be produced filled with browny sugar. We helped ourselves to raw boat apples from the colander, dipping their pointed ends into the sugar. Crunching away at these beauties produced forever-golden-brown memories of friendly kitchen smells of apples in the stewing pan, and memories of the bright copper of the recently installed kitchen range[14], with the pleasantest of sounds as hot cinders escaped to fall with a 'ping-ping' into the ash pan, and the sounds of coals rearranging themselves within the grate.

I shared the sugar-apples with Victoria. We cast shy glances at each other as our mouths performed the same delightful tasks, and tongues enjoyed the same tastes as we became linked within this physical bond of common enjoyment. With the sugar-apples finished, sticky fingers were washed over the kitchen sink by Granny. This was followed by Mummy saying it must be time for Victoria's lunch and wouldn't her Mummy be worried. Victoria's fringe was propelled by her head saying, 'No, no,' as she asked what time she could call in the afternoon, saying she '*would* stay for tea.' Granny and Gramp laughed and with a chuckle Mummy said how nice it was for Victoria to want to come for tea. Of course she would be very welcome to call a little after three, and, 'Yes, Linda could come as well,' in answer to Victoria's repeated question. I then discovered that Linda was the doll with the open-shut eyes with real, real clothes.

This was followed by Gramp singing a song which went, 'Here's to little Linda, here's to little me, and here's to Lady Victoria dancing on my knee,' ending with a tune from his brassy whistle-pipe, bouncing a laughing Victoria on his right knee as the not-to-be-forgotten me clung to his left, with groans from the old kitchen chair on its age-worn unbalanced legs rocking sideways like the old cow in the field. At the end Granny said, 'Pon my word Father, haven't you anything better to do cluttering up my kitchen.'

With Gramp's 'no peace for the wicked,' we departed as we had arrived, with Victoria proudly clutching an even bigger sugar bag, waving our goodbyes from the oil-stained gate where we had met, as once more I swelled with pride hearing Gramp say, as we walked away, 'They must be somebody to live there. Pon my puff they must be.'

Hand in hand with Victoria, walking towards her green-tiled house, I enjoyed the aftertaste of sugar apple, reliving our side by side long glances and our dips of apple-boats into the golden brown sugar of lasting sweetness.

---

14 'Victorian and Edwardian kitchen ranges were coal-fired cookers that existed in many old houses until the 1960s and 70s and even later' (Cryer, 2020a).

# 2

# VICTORIA COMES TO TEA

The Cuckoo 'cuckooed' three times from its little house as I played with my camels on the un-clothed, white-scrubbed dining leaf table, made by Gramp long ago. It was always longer at Christmas and other occasions and was pre-announced by its sudden bigness. The door opened and thinking it was Mummy I continued to move my camels across the white-scrubbed desert until 'Hallo' told me it was Victoria. 'Sh,' she said, 'or you'll wake Linda.' Hardly daring to breathe, I admired the sleeping Linda being rocked gently within Victoria's arms, her eyelashes quivering with each forward movement as if she might awake at the minutest sound at any moment. 'Put her on the couch,' I whispered, leaving my camels and arranging Gramp's after-lunch-time-snooze cushion for Linda's head. Ever so gently, Victoria placed the sleeping beauty on the couch, folding the after-lunchtime-snooze travelling blanket carefully over Linda's beautiful dress of Maltese lace, which, explained Victoria in whispers, had been given by a much-travelled uncle and made up by her grandmother for Linda's first birthday. This had been given with a doll's tea set for that occasion, a set that was almost grown-up because the doll was so big. With Linda safely asleep, protected by a chairback in case she rolled out with her dreams, we tiptoed from the scene, Victoria leading the way 'to see over the house,' as she put it. In every room she murmured her approval, saying, 'This is a nice large room,' as I showed her one after the other until at last we came to Granny and Gramp's bedroom. Victoria started to say 'This is …,' but the sight of all the apples and pears surrounding the bed, with Gramp busy wiping the fruit with a cloth, defeated her approval.

'A job for you two with nothing to do,' Gramp said. 'Come and wipe the sticky sweet apples with this rag, only handle them ever so gently, or they won't keep until Christmas.' We began to wipe the fruit, Gramp playing tunes on his brassy whistle-pipe, sometimes first singing and then playing, and sometimes first playing and then singing. Finishing each tune he looked as if he wouldn't play another, but Victoria clapped her hands, and we both said, 'more, more,' until Gramp, in his rich voice, sang again. Then ending suddenly, his brassy whistle-pipe leapt into life like a golden snake in his hands. He moved his fingers over the holes like the picture book Indian snake charmer while we wiped the same apples again and again with happy contentment. This continued until, in the middle of *Five and Twenty Black-birds*, Granny called from the kitchen, spiriting Gramp away, leaving us to our wiping.

'Ugh! An earwig,' said Victoria, as an earwig emerged from a crack in her apple, falling with a thud on the newspaper protecting the floor.

Unconcernedly, Victoria planted a finger on the earwig's middle, its reddish-brown body bending back on itself in one last desperate effort for life, its pincers opening wide in its struggles.

'You are brave,' I said, as Victoria, flushed with pleasure, released her finger.

The earwig moved sluggishly sideways leaving a light trail of life-substance upon the newspaper as it came to a stop. Although now dead, it quivered, surrounded by all those sweet-smelling apples and pears of an earwig's world with the afternoon sun casting dancing fruit-shadows against the skirting board. Yesterday, I considered, the earwig was alive, exploring other cracks in other apples, maybe even a pear.

'You killed it,' I said, adding, 'Poor thing,' and 'Perhaps it has a brother somewhere.'

Victoria laughed, rocking on her white stocking-heels, sitting cross-legged on the floor. 'Whoever heard of an earwig's brother. I'm glad I killed it. If they get in your ears they go right through your head to the other ear. That is,' she mused, 'if you don't hook it out in time. And if you don't, and it reaches the other side—then—you die. It's true—Baker said!'

The sound of a tinkling bell with Granny's voice at each pause calling, 'Tea,' interrupted my meditations, but as we left the room I looked back at the earwig's broken body. Was the earwig now in heaven, if he had lived as a good earwig, or was he in hell, or did earwigs just stay dead? I would ask Gramp one day.

The best cups were out in honour of Victoria. They were decorated with little flowers from a fairy field that pinpointed their gleaming whiteness. When drinking from one, the rim gave the impression of a circle around some magic lake. I knew the 'Floral Set' was something very special as I remembered Granny often saying that Gramp had bought it on their honeymoon. How nice, I thought, it would be to be 'grown-up' and visit a honeymoon with Victoria. Perhaps in a honeymoon I could buy a white floral set like Granny's. Honeymoon must be a very special place, I thought, as it seemed there was nothing you couldn't have from Honeymoon Land.

With tea over and my magic cups cleared away, the special tablecloth centred upon the scrubbed snow-white table was put away underneath. Gramp then produced his brassy whistle-pipe from the 'all things' cupboard that was fixed between the window and the living room fireplace.

'What shall I play?' Gramp asked, running his fingers swiftly over the holes, producing a melody from 'your boots to your head,' and then 'from your head to your boots.' Thinking of 'Honeymoon Land,' I said, 'Where the bee sucks, there suck I, in a cowslip's bell I lie'[15]. Enchanted we both listened to Gramp's brassy whistle-pipe. Between the melody every now and then he would pause to sing, with a 'merrily, merrily,' to which I would join in followed at first by a shy Victoria and then by a vivacious Victoria singing 'merrily' in all the wrong places!

Slowly the darkness of the day claimed us. The 'early for the time of year' firelight made Gramp's brassy whistle-pipe show huge against the wall.

Granny's voice said, 'Come on you night owls, light up time.' Gramp finished his playing, knocking his brassy whistle-pipe against the palm of his hand, and 'drops of spittle', as he called it, made hissing noises on the bars of the living room grate which had an Adam surround.[16] I often marvelled at

---

15 'Where the bee sucks' is a song taken from Act V of *The Tempest* (1611) by William Shakespeare (1564-1616). It is sung by Ariel, a spirit, when told that soon he will be freed from the service of his master Prospero: 'Where the bee sucks, there suck I: / In a cowslip's bell I lie; / There I couch when owls do cry./ On the bat's back I do fly / After summer merrily. / Merrily, merrily shall I live now / Under the blossom that hangs on the bough' (OU, 2019).

16 Adam fireplace surrounds were named after Robert and James Adam who set the neoclassical style for domestic interiors for the latter half of the eighteenth century after their

this, to think Adam had actually made our old grate but grown-ups laughed when I told them our grate came from the Bible.

Gramp returned in a moment, carrying the brass lamp[17] which he placed on the centrepiece pattern in the middle of the table, carefully removing the lamp-glass. He seemed to draw his finger and thumb over the wick, saying, 'Always light the wick when it's just showing,' which he did, 'and then place the glass over it. Wait a bit before turning it up, because if you rush things and turn it full on the glass will break. That's life,' he said, playing a little tune on his pipe. 'Take a little care and you'll always get there, rush if you must and you're sure to go bust.' I always loved the 'bust' bit, as I imagined people going off with a loud bang like the balloons at Christmas time. That was the reason I decided why Gramp never hurried because he feared going 'off' with a 'bang.'

The friendly glow of the paraffin lamp was now complemented by the pulled curtains which Gramp had drawn with his 'fruit-branch-pulling-down walking stick', as he called it. He moved each ring over the mahogany curtain rod, until dying day and born paraffin light were parted. Then I sat on Gramp's knee and listened to *Hey Diddle Diddle the Cat and the Fiddle* and other nursery rhymes which Gramp played on his brassy whistle-pipe until he ended with the *Home Sweet Home*[18] of the music box joy. This must have given Gramp a cold, for while he was playing he blew his nose many times and Granny would say, 'Pon my word father, you're a sentimental one,' whatever that was. With the ending of *Home Sweet Home*, Mummy appeared

---

Italian tour in the 1750s (Biography, Your Dictionary, Robert and James Adam Facts, 2019, p.1).

17   The oil lamp. See Cryer, 2020b.

18   *Home, Sweet Home* is a song adapted from dramatist John Howard Payne's (1791-1852) 1823 opera *Clari*, or the *Maid of Milan*. This was first performed at Covent Garden, London in 1823:

Mid pleasures and palaces though we may roam / Be it ever so humble, there's no place like home / A charm from the skies seems to hallow us there /Which seek thro' the world, is ne'er met elsewhere / Home! Home! / Sweet, sweet home! / There's no place like home / There's no place like home! / (Lewis, 2020).

wearing her fur-collared, fur-cuffed coat to take Victoria home. It was now quite late and wouldn't be good for Linda.

'You may kiss Linda if you like,' said Victoria, holding the quivering long-eye-lashed Linda close to me.

I kissed the rose-marble cheek of her hot face, not once, but twice! Then, with candle-guttering Gramp,[19] I watched from the back door, until footsteps and voices became a part of the silent village.

---

19   A guttering candle is a candle flickering and spluttering and about to go out when it is near the end and the wick is not burning properly. Here Gramp is holding a flickering candle by the back door as they say goodbye to Victoria.

# 3

# HILLGROVE PRE-SCHOOL[20] VISIT

Soon after I met Victoria the word 'start' crept into my life. Soon I would 'start,' Gramp said, and 'Bless 'is little 'art,' said Mrs Jones on one of her frequent visits, 'the young master will soon start at school.' I was told the Rector's two children were already at Hillgrove School. The oil man[21] showed us Hillgrove from the crossroads. It had long since been decided I should attend, if they would take me, though what was likely to be extra special about me to make me not 'takeable' I didn't know.

---

20    Although there are no official records of a school called 'Hillgrove School' in Wootton in the 1920s, unofficial records show that Hillgrove House was used as a nursery school from around 1921 to just after 1945. The 1921 Census shows that Edith McKerchar was registered as living at Hillgrove House, Whiterails Road, Wootton Bridge. According to various news reports in the Isle of Wight County Press , Edith Sarah McKerchar (née Bryer, from Surrey, 1865 – 1954) was the widow of Dr Robert McKerchar (1847 – 1915) whom she had married in Lewisham in 1889. They then moved to Dalbeattie in Scotland where they had five children, one son John (b. 1890) who was a doctor, and three daughters, Edith (b. 1893), Janet (1895-1986), Kathleen (1897-1967) and Christian Robina (1900 - 1955). Edith moved to the Isle of Wight with her children to set up the nursery school after they had received their School Leaving Certificates and after Robert had died in 1915. Janet, Kathleen, Christian and their mother Edith are buried at St Edmund's Church, Wootton. Kathleen remained unmarried, like her sister Christian, while her other sister Janet married Lieutenant Douglas Gordon Brodie, the only son of Major C. G. Brodie, M. C. and Mrs Brodie, J.P. of Fernhill (also buried at St Edmunds's Church). The wedding reception was held at Hillgrove House. Kathleen McKerchar and her mother ran the nursery school from their home from around 1921 until sometime after 1945. Kathleen would have been 26 years old when Peter Stark Lansley first went to her nursery school. She must have been comfortably off as she was seen driving a car in 1932 when she was thirty five. Unfortunately she received a summons for driving with a faulty rear light and was fined five shillings (McKerchar Index, 2019; Isle of Wight County Press Archives, 1928, 1932 and 1967).

21    The oil man was Barney who always delivered the Starks' oil on Mondays. He was also a barman. This could be Noah Barney listed in the 1939 Register living at 1, Rose Cottage, Littletown. This is not far up the lanes by the Woodman's Arms so he could have been a barman there. He was listed as a hawker so he could also have gone around calling at houses with items including oil. He was with his wife Priscilla and sons James b1921 and George b1924 who were also hawkers. He had another son Noah b1929 at school.

Nightly I prayed, 'Please God may Hillgrove not take me,' and 'Please God make me too old-fashioned for school,' for Mrs Jones had said with a laugh, 'He's too old-fashioned for school,' whatever old-fashioned was. And Gramp had said to me one day, when I'd mixed up my letters, 'They won't take dunces at school.' So I added to my prayers, 'Please God make me a dunce,' with second thoughts, 'so long as a dunce isn't very bad.' If a dunce was something very, very bad I thought, I'd rather go to school. The harder I prayed the nearer the prospect of Hillgrove became, and one day I knew at last God had not answered my prayers or he was leaving it very, very late, because the visiting day had arrived.

It was a windy blue-and-white-clad day. Dressed in my fawn pants and coat and white socks, that always slipped down to the tops of my little white boots, I waved goodbye to Granny and Gramp and started the mile-long walk with Mummy to visit Hillgrove. I remembered now the first time I had walked this way, only then in the opposite direction when I had visited our new old-house for the first time. I remembered especially my engine driver friend. He would understand me being afraid, I thought, if he knew I was about to start school. Nearing the station at Wootton, I could hear the puff-puff of the train—the Newport and Cowes train—from Ryde.

'Let's wait,' I asked Mummy.

With a dirge of smoke and steam hissing from both sides of the road bridge in all directions, the engine and its few carriages pulled into Wootton.

'Wootton, Wootton!' shouted the office boy porter in a shrill voice.

Mummy's hand tightened on mine as we walked down the steep path towards the platform. Suddenly the engine driver saw us—the same driver I remember of sweet long ago, of grown-up talk and manly lavatory smells. Jumping down from his cab, wiping his hands with a rag, the engine driver lifted me under the arms to my giggles of delight, rubbing his huge nose from side to side against mine with bullseye[22]-breath, saying over and over again, 'It does me 'art good to see you both—fair good it does.'Ere,' he added,

---

22 Bullseyes are hard boiled black and white peppermint sweets like humbugs but are spherical.

*Original Wootton Railway Station 1900s.*
*Unknown original copyright. Assumed in the Public Domain.*

fumbling in his pocket, ''ave a bullseye,' popping it straight into my mouth as Mummy said, 'Mind you don't choke.'

In a moment we both crunched our bullseyes with shared delight, hands clasped together, pacing alongside the engine.

'We must be away,' said the engine driver, opening the carriage door, before Mummy could say we were not going to Newport, explaining we were on a visit to my intended school.

A look of understanding crossed his face, and tickling me under the chin he began, 'Sorry to 'ere it, real sorry, strike me I am, fer when I be at school I got the …'

While he was speaking, Mummy gave him the kind of look she would give Gramp when he forgot he was saying something 'not for young ears,' as Granny called it.

'What did you used to get?' I asked.

'As I was saying,' the engine driver continued. 'I used to get the bullseyes every day on the way to school. "Appiest days o' me life,' adding, "Ere take the bag for luck,' pressing the bullseye bag into my hand.

With a friendly pat on the top of the head and a too-near blast of the whistle, the train moved on its way with much waving from the rolled-up sleeve arm of the engine driver. With cupped hands to his mouth he shouted, 'Tell Gramp and Mrs Jones I've a good 'un for next year's Derby—out of Captain Cuttle. I've also got a couple of dark 'orses for next Ashey.' And with two more blasts on the whistle, the last carriage vanished from view with the line curving for the next stop at Whippingham.

'Who's Captain Cuttle Mummy?' I asked.

'A very great horse that won the Derby. Steve Donoghue rode him,' Mummy answered, straightening herself, which was always a sign of some personal connection. I repeated slowly to myself the words of the engine driver's message to Gramp and asked Mummy why the engine driver said 'out of' Captain Cuttle.

'Because the horse the driver says is going to win next year's Derby is a son of Captain Cuttle. He must be good if he is,' Mummy explained.

'I wonder who old Markwick's[23] horse's father is,' I replied. I could see in my mind Mr Markwick, our Tuesday afternoon greengrocer, and his grey horse. He always wore his helmet[24] because he was proud of the Navy as I was of Daddy.

'Why is it that old Markwick's horse can never run fast like Captain Cuttle, Mummy? Am I "out of" Daddy?'

---

23 Joseph Charles Markwick (1876-1945) was a greengrocer and fish salesman residing at 1, White Houses, North Fairlee (Racecourse end), Newport. He married Esther Lydia Coughtrey at Brighton in 1902 and they had two children, Grace (1907) and Charles (1909). He moved to the Isle of Wight on the opening of Osborne Royal Naval College in 1903, probably in a training capacity. He is buried at Newport Cemetery, section H, plot 83. He served in the Navy for twenty eight years, was in the *Princess Royal* at the *Battle of Jutland* and witnessed the sinking of the *Queen Mary* on 31 May 1916. He retired with the rank of Petty Officer and was the proud possessor of six medals, including those for the South Africa War and Persian Gulf campaigns (Isle of Wight County Press, 1945).

24 The Navy also wore Brodie type steel helmets in WWI as in the Army.

Mummy stopped walking, rather breathless and I knew she was gathering her wits. It must be wonderful to have so many wits to gather, I thought. After gathering their wits grown-ups seemed to be very, very wise. Once I had heard Mrs Jones say she was nearly at her wits' end which must have meant she had used her wits too often.

At last Mummy's wits were gathered and she said, 'There are too many questions in the world and not enough answers. One day you may ask a question that no one in the whole wide world knows the answer to and if you study hard enough to find the answer you may become a very great man. But even if you become a very great man, one day a little boy like you may ask you a question and you may have to answer that you don't know. But we don't say you are "out of" Daddy though.' Mummy then added thoughtfully, 'It would be really true as you know to say you were from the seed of Daddy, but we don't say it that way. We only speak like this if we are horse breeders. So you see I can't tell you why Captain Cuttle's son is said to be 'out of' Captain Cuttle but I can answer your question about old Markwick's horse. When you are grown-up I expect you will love the sea like your father and you will be lean and as about as tall as him. And from me you may love literature and from us both you will love this land and fight for all that is honest and true. This will be you because your father, grandfathers, grandmothers and their mothers and fathers have been similar. So it is with horses. Racehorses are bred with racehorses—they are slim and strong in the flank whereas horses like Markwick's are bred from similar horses that for hundreds of years have pulled carts. Each has his part; the racehorse for man's pleasure and the other for his labour. So it is with us. Some of us are quick, some slow, some strong in limb but throughout the world we all need each other.'

Through the half-open white gate, which separated the gravelled station path from the dusty road, it was not long before we passed Chatfield-Clarke's lodge.[25] Next came the great house itself by the muddy lane with its stable

---

25 'On the left side beyond the station is a big house and in its grounds is a little lodge where the chauffeur lived with his family [...]. The house was owned by Sir Edgar Chatfield-Clark and his brother Edward. Sir Edgar was an MP and he wore a monocle and kept nodding his head as he talked [...]. Every Christmas he came to the school and gave all of us children a

clock forever stopped and then the Woodman's Arms.[26] 'The Pig and Whistle,'[27] I said, pointing to the Woodman's Arms, for Gramp had the same name for all public houses.

'It was wonderful Mummy. Gramp took me in with the oil man the day we moved in. They all talked of horses too and drank beer. I had a lemonade.'

'Whatever next, I'll ….,' Mummy was saying when a tall man in a dusty-white flour apron appeared, pint in hand at the door.

'He works at the mill, Mummy,' I whispered.

'Hallo Mr Bill,' I said as magically a lemonade glass appeared in my hand.

''Ow about you Lady,' asked Mr Bill.

'Oh!, no thank you Mr er Bill. It is kind,' Mummy replied smiling, adding, 'It's a little early in the day.'

'Quarter to eight Wootton Bridge time,'[28] said Bill. 'Never alters. But just as ye say Lady.'

'I'm just taking Peter to Miss McKerchar's. He's going there to school soon.'

'So 'is Gramp was saying tother day. 'Tis a good school. Miss McKerchar is a lovely teacher. Wish she could be a teachin' me! Beg yer pardon Lady, if I was yer boy's age,' and Bill's face grew quite red, as touching his cap we went on our way.

---

new sixpence […]. He allowed the chapel Sunday School parties to be held in his grounds.' (Snow,1986, p.34).

26  The Woodman's Arms has been traced back to circ 1840. The landlords Gramp would have known would have been 1905-07 Robert Clark, 1912-20 John Willie McDine, 1920-21 Mrs McDine and 1921-32 Thomas William Butler (Wootton Bridge Historical: 'The Inns of the Village 1775 – 1985', 2019).

27  The 'Pig and Whistle' is an archetypal pub name. There are various explanations as to its original meaning but the most likely is 'going to rack and ruin' which comes from the Scottish poem Har'st Rig, in 1794: 'For he to pygs and whistles went, And left the land' (Phrase Finder, 2020b). Granny would no doubt have agreed with this definition!

28  'In the days of the coaches, they always stopped at the Sloop Inn. There was a clock in a shop window there which had stopped at 7.45. This was called *Wootton Bridge time*. Time stood still in Wootton. Then some friends would ask 'What's the time?' and we would answer, 'It's a quarter-to-eight Wootton Bridge time' (Snow, 1986, p.25).

*The Woodman's Arms 1900s. Unknown original copyright. Assumed in the Public Domain.*

We paused by the iron church[29] at the crossroads. 'So that's the Iron Church,' exclaimed Mummy. 'I'm not surprised they don't use it anymore, for whatever the reason it looks a cold unlovable place.'

'There are a lot of dead people there,' I replied, moving to the far side of the road, watching Hillgrove appear closer and closer with each step. Once outside the gates of Hillgrove with its drive of blue-like pebble stones, blue garage door and white painted porch, I felt less afraid. I wondered if my prayers to God had been necessary after all. It seemed friendly with the grove of trees rustling in the wind, reminding me always of the sea. Mummy pulled the iron bell-handle. From inside came the ding-a-ling-ling of a bell dancing on its spring.

The sound of the bell died away and with it my strength. I looked behind me. I wanted to run. I quickly pretended I was Sir Richard Grenville in his little *Revenge*[30] facing all the Spaniards. Though the sails and rigging were around my feet with half my men sick, we fought on. The spell was broken by the sound of fairy feet. A door opened and there stood an angel in white with golden hair glittering in the autumn sunlight.

'So this is Peter,' the smiling voice was saying, 'and do come in.'

Entering the large hall, I wanted to say 'sorry' for my past fears, but no one knew but me. Then just as suddenly all my fears returned. 'Say this was not the teacher after all,' I asked myself, 'and this lady was not Miss McKerchar?'

---

29   Mrs Nunn-Harvey of Shanklin donated the land from the Briddlesford Estate and paid for the building of the church and Sunday school which opened on Wednesday 13 September 1885. The church was sited at Wootton Common on the Whiterails/Briddlesford Road junction and faced the Woodman's Arms. It was constructed of corrugated galvanised iron, accommodated 250 people and was named St. Michael and All Angels. With the opening of St. Marks, the church was no longer required and was sold for £55 and taken to Cornwall. It is believed that between 1932 – 1933 the Sunday school was sold for £18 as scrap (Wootton Bridge Historical, St Michael, p1.,2015). 'At this corner there was what was called St. Michael's—the Iron Church and the graveyard. We children often walked there on Sundays and played in the graveyard' (Snow, 1986, p.35). There are similar iron chapels still in existence at St John's Church, Rookley (derelict) and at St Barnabas Church, Blackwater (now a farm shop).

30   Sir Richard Grenville (1542-1591), was a daring English naval commander. He fought heroically against a Spanish fleet off Flores Island in the Azores. After fifteen hours of hand-to-hand combat against a force of 5,000 men, his ship the *Revenge* with her 190-man crew was captured on 9 – 10 September 1591. The wounded Grenville died on board the Spanish flagship a few days later. The battle is commemorated in Tennyson's poem *The Revenge*.

Once again my battle was on, and my ship *Revenge* was listing more and more and soon the water might reach the gunpowder.

Suddenly a voice snatched me from the battle. The sweet face with the golden hair adjusted itself to my height saying, 'May I call you Peter? I am Miss McKerchar and I'm sure we'll be good friends.'

So this was Miss McKerchar. I could have shouted with happiness. Of course we would be good friends. Oh, how I wished now I was grown-up! If only I could catch up with my angel's age and marry her, living the way of grown-ups. How wonderful to be grown-up.

During the time my future was being discussed, I surrendered my heart to the room: the animal skin outstretched on the floor, the snow-white grey-veined marble fireplace, the dark, browny piano in which you could see the reflection of your face, and the miniature framed pictures with one larger than the rest on the walls. Then high up on the ceiling were white flower petals making me proud to be a part of Hillgrove. As my wonder grew, my feelings caught my breath. The spell was broken by Mummy saying, 'A penny for them.' My thoughts were too much a part of the room for sharing. My face grew hot like Gramp's forgotten fire poker when he was blazing up the fire. My face became hotter still when I thought how I wished to be married to my golden white-dressed angel.[31] I looked down at my little boots, then up to the magic ceiling asking in a faraway voice if it was not time for us to leave, adding *I had promised* Gramp to help collect the afternoon's chicken eggs.

---

31  Peter really did regard his teacher as an angel due to her love and help with his learning. When he heard of her death in 1967 he wrote a letter to her sister Janet Brodie, a copy of which I found in one of his notebooks: 'Dear Mrs. Brodie, I have just received your sad news and understand so much how you must feel at this time. My thoughts, love and sympathy are with you and yours as I write. Words I know are such cold marks on paper at a time like this and must be such poor comfort. It is so difficult for me to express my feelings of someone I held most dear; someone who gave me so much sunshine when I tried to learn my first poetry and add number to number. In my chapters on "Hillgrove" I called her an angel as indeed she was, for when she smiled her face lit up with the very heaven of love and understanding (where as a child I realized there was no death). In later years, with those all too fleeting meetings, her smile would say, "How nice to see you," and whenever I met her I would feel lifted up, and the world would seem a better place.' It seems Peter had informed Janet of his idea of this book at that time.

42

*Similar chapel to St. Michael and All Angels Iron Church in existence at St Barnabas Church, Blackwater, I.W. (now a farm shop). © C M Lansley*

'Homeward-bound,' Mummy said. We waved a final goodbye from the road and now the great wind beat on our backs, blowing us half-running, half-walking the return journey. It was different now—I was longing to start school. I cried a little when I discovered I would have to wait until after Christmas before entering Hillgrove again.

Clean water and broadcasting a mixture of corn and maize always preceded the afternoon egg collecting. Part of my contribution to Gramp's smallholding was the task of cleaning the drinking vessels and refilling them with clean water. During the procedure I had carried on a non-stop chatter of the virtues of Hillgrove, giving a vivid description of my future Governess which met with Gramp's obvious approval. I could always tell his moments of approval from deepening wrinkles spreading outwards from his blue-grey eyes which would nod caresses in my direction between questions and answers.

'My puff,' said Gramp suddenly, 'I didn't clean out the Rhode Island Reds[32] this morning. Run down the garden and get the scrapers.'

Returning with the scrapers and two dustpans reserved for the purpose, we set about scraping the droppings into the pans. At the end of our labours Gramp sat contentedly on the perch puffing at a medicated cigarette, surveying the bucket of droppings.

'It's good for the garden,' he said, 'but a bit too concentrated. It's better after it's watered down after a year in the water butt.'

A curious Rhode Island Red came through the open hatch and joined Gramp on the perch, looking up enquiringly at Gramp, head on one side, like Granny when she was afraid to miss a word.

''Pon my puff you have a clean house,' said Gramp, stroking its neck, its beak opening slightly with each stroke.

'Always remember this Peter, a dirty hen house is like a dirty house. Nothing good comes from dirt, does it my beauty?' said Gramp, kissing the feathered neck, and in return the bird wiped its beak from side to side on Gramp's trousers.

'Gramp,' I asked, 'how old …,' I thought for a moment, and then continued, 'how old were you when you got married?'

'My puff,' replied Gramp, 'that's set me thinking.'

I watched Gramp think. I watched his eyes as they seemed to go bright, and then they half closed, and then they opened very wide, and then they laughed because all the wrinkles opened out all over his face. And then I could hardly believe it. I saw a tear fall down his cheek, and then he started smiling from one ear to the other as he wiped it away with the back of his hand. Watching Gramp think was a new experience. Suddenly I knew he had stopped thinking because he looked at me, seeing me again.

'Whatever made you think about marriage?' he asked. 'You thinking about little Victoria one of these days?'

'Not Victoria.'

---

32  The Rhode Island Red was developed in Rhode Island in the late nineteenth century and is a first class laying hen, laying throughout the year. They are known to be hardy, active foragers with a sweet disposition and make great companions (Kasandra Smith, 2015, p1.).

'Not Victoria! Why I was kind of hoping it would be. She's a nice one.'

We three sat on the perch. Gramp, the Rhode Island Red with its neck contentedly stretched under the inside of Gramp's coat, and myself.

'If not Victoria, who then?' said Gramp.

'Promise you'll keep it a secret.'

'Of course you can trust your Gramp,' said Gramp, placing his rough hand onto mine.

'It would be a long, long time Gramp, that's why you must keep it.'

'Well of course,' answered Gramp, 'I didn't think you would be one to marry all of a sudden.'

'You will promise to keep it a secret Gramp, won't you, because if I tell you, only we will know about it.'

'You mean you haven't got round to the question,' said Gramp, his eyes going very bright, and his face smiling, and then going ordinary again.

'Whisper,' he said, holding his ear close to my lips.

'It's Miss McKerchar,' I whispered, 'and now you know why it will be such a long time before I catch up with her birthdays.'

'I know how you feel, but if you work very hard when you go to school, and save a heap of money when you go to work, and give her flowers on her birthdays, and buy a nice, nice house with a real motor car …'

'Yes, Gramp,' I said, 'go on.'

'Well, I'm thinking, when you have all that, she'll be ready to be Mrs Peter.'

'You sure Gramp?'

'Sure, and—my!—we must hurry and collect the eggs, it's getting dark.'

We collected the eggs in silence with our important secret, the only real secret of my life. When we entered the kitchen, Granny said, 'Here you are you two. I can see by your faces you've been up to something. I was about to send the Town Cryer out to find you.'

Gramp just grinned knowingly. I realized then that he was the finest Gramp in the world. After my prayers later, and after Mummy had tucked me into bed, I was happy. Gramp came up and kissed me goodnight, saying as he left the room that I looked as happy as a sand boy. I closed my eyes. One day Granny would bake the wedding cake.

# 4

# SINNERS AND WHAT
# THE BUTCHER SAW

It was decided, as Mummy said, that I was now old enough to attend morning service. Gramp was not enthusiastic about this as he thought a service would be far too long. Besides he would miss me on Sunday mornings helping with the birds. Meanwhile I wondered what the service would be like, and from my game of camels I asked, 'What is a service Mummy and what do I do?'

'It's something which is held in God's house every Sunday to thank Him for all He has given us so that we can pray together and pray for each other and for sinners.'

Just at that moment we were interrupted by someone walking down our garden path. 'There's the butcher,' I shouted.

While wondering what a sinner was, the butcher's head appeared passing above the halfway-up curtaining of the front room window. I knew it was the butcher's head because of his lack of hair. Then suddenly there was a frightful commotion as Granny, holding a towel up to her front half, dashed into the room slamming the door. 'My Godfathers!' she shouted, panting, 'I was just having a wash over the kitchen sink, and that old sinner of a butcher opens the kitchen door without knocking, sees me stripped to the waist and says, "Any orders for the butcher" and all you can do is smile.'

Granny was just adding to Mummy's, 'Well I'll …,' when her words were interrupted by a knock on the dining room door with the butcher's voice behind it.

Granny retreated barebacked towards the window opposite as the butcher said, 'I'm very sorry Ma'am, there's no need to mind Ma'am. I didn't worry Ma'am.'

Granny's face went all rose-apple as she replied, 'But *I did* you old sinner,' and then she began to laugh saying, 'It's the last time you'll catch me like that in the kitchen, butcher.'

'And it's the last time I'll come in without knocking, though I must say it's made my day Ma'am.'

By this time Granny had slipped on her blouse, her flaxen hair falling over her shoulders, instead of her usual bun. Her apple-rose coloured face was deepening, which made me say, 'You look as if you are just off to school Granny.'

'There you are Ma'am,' came the butcher's voice, 'takes an old sinner like me to turn you into a schoolgirl.'

With this, Granny opened the door to the smiling butcher, and from the kitchen I heard much laughter. Later when we were eating a steak lunch, Gramp said, 'This is the best bit of steak I've had for many a day, pon my puff it is.'

'And that's what comes of having an old sinner for a butcher,' said Granny, and for once, as Mummy looked at me, I didn't say anything.

A few days later, after an earlier than usual breakfast for Sunday, Gramp waved from the gate as Mummy and I left for the few minutes' walk to the Station Road New Church[33], to the ding-dong of its one bell.

The bell stopped as we entered. Looking at her silver watch, Mummy said, 'Goodness, a quarter to eleven, only just in time, and Gramp said we had a little bit up our sleeve too.'

Gramp was a wonderful person, as he always stored several minutes up his sleeve, though his watch, on its long chain, was in his waistcoat pocket. Gramp was very clever I knew.

Who else but Gramp kept minutes up his sleeve? Certainly not the old sinner of a butcher, I mused, as you never knew what time of day he would

---

33    The New Church referred to here is St. Mark's Church, Station Road, Wootton. It was dedicated on 29 August 1909 and in 1925 was amalgamated with St Edmund's Church (the old church). 'There is a "new" church [...] opposite the lodge to Fernhill [...]. From the outside, St. Mark's resembles a church hall but the inside is really striking, built of red brick, like the new church at Quarr, very light and spacious with an elegant curved alter rail.' (Sibley, 1983, p. 40).

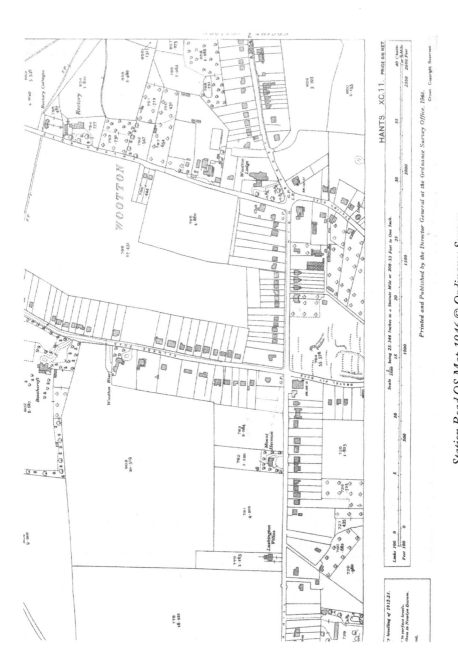

*Station Road OS Map 1946 © Ordinance Survey.*

*Permission to reproduce the image kindly granted by the IOW Records Office.*

call. 'That butcher's late again,' Gramp would say, looking at his watch. The organ was still playing so we knelt on the cushions in front of our polished chairs for a few minutes longer. I hoped Gramp wouldn't forget to give Tiddles, my tabby cat, its bread and milk.

From the cushions we regained our seats and then stood up, which I found more comfortable than sitting, as my bottom kept slipping on the polished wood. To make matters worse, my feet couldn't touch the floor. After a time I knew I was having pins and needles, but once more we were on our feet again. I helped Mummy hold the hymn book but the words were meaningless letters to me. However, as I listened I found at the end of every line everyone made a shrill 'S' sound, so by careful concentration I joined in beautifully. At the end of every line I did an 'S' between my teeth, so loud on one occasion that the lady in front turned in my direction which made me make the 'S' louder than ever. This time when we sat down, the vicar, looking very serious (I couldn't understand why as he was usually very jolly), began to read from a huge Bible. This was just like the one we had underneath the couch in the front room, only this one was held in the wings of a golden bird. It must be marvellous to have a bird like that I thought, though I was lucky as we had a huge green china pig which had come from Queen Victoria.[34] I used to play piggyback on it and it lived next to the Bible between the couch and the piano.

There was no green pig in this church, but at last I could join in with 'Our Father,' making one mistake saying a loud 'Amen' at the end. This echoed backwards and forwards within the lofty church, causing everyone to look at me, until suddenly I had a pain and wanted 'to go.' What should I do? I wished the engine driver and Gramp were here. They would help me. That's

---

34  Peter's mother had purchased the green Weymss china pig at auction. It had been given by Queen Victoria to one of her chamber maids. It was usual for the Queen to give her staff gifts at Christmas time : 'The people on the estate always went to Osborne to a Christmas party given in the house or "Palace" as it was called, and the Queen would sit on her throne in the Durbar room and present them with a gift. Then they would have to walk backwards to one of the Princes […] and then they would take you to the Christmas-tree where another gift was given' (Snow, 1986, pp. 7-8). I too remember the pig as part of my childhood. Sadly, upon my mother's death in 2013 there was no sign of the pig. If there are any sightings, please inform the editor. Its distinguishing feature is a glued-on broken right ear.

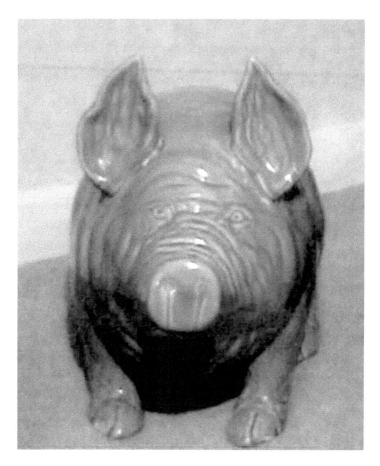

*The missing green Weymss china pig from Queen Victoria 2008 © C M Lansley*

it, I would pray. I prayed, 'Let me save it till I get home' and I repeated it again and again in my head.

At last God answered me and the pain left, but now I had pins and needles again, and Mummy whispered right inside my ear, 'Oh you are a fidget.'

The vicar was now talking about sinners. *Sinners*, I thought. I looked around carefully at everyone. There seemed to be a lot of ladies, all with funny hats. Mummy wore a simple hat with one flower but one of the ladies just two seats in front of me wore a hat with a huge feather which was never still. A fly suddenly perched on it. I let out a little giggle which stopped when I got a quick never-seen-before angry look from Mummy. The fly now settled

*Wootton Bridge, Station Road and the 'New Church' 1925. Permission to reproduce the image granted by Wootton Bridge Historical: Towill Collection ©*

on the almost completely bald head of the huge man sitting next to the feathered-hat lady. It crawled for a moment over that shiny surface, with the head making little movements, until at last the big man's hand came up in a swift movement but the fly was swifter. It flew up and landed again, this time on the big man's ear. Again the hand came up, and again the fly returned to the shiny head. Inside my head, I giggled, fit to burst, my face screwing up with every effort to stop any sounds coming from my lips. I prayed I would stop wanting to giggle. And now I wanted 'to go' again with pins and needles. I prayed harder than ever with my eyes closed, which prevented me seeing the funny side of things, and then I felt better. The vicar was still talking about sin, and being saved, which reminded me again of the butcher and also of Gramp.

One day I remember Granny saying to Gramp, with a laugh, 'My Godfathers, you are a sinner. You'll never go to Heaven. You are past saving.' Past saving, I thought. So that was why Gramp never went to church. What was the use if he was past saving? It would only waste God's time. Then there was the butcher. Granny had called him an old sinner. That *was* funny, I thought, for both the butcher and Gramp had little hair and that big man in front hardly had a hair on his head except for a little at the back of his neck. I looked carefully around the church. Goodness, I thought, the vicar has a lot of hair, all dark and shiny, like a rook. But how about the rest of the men? There were not many men. There were nearly all ladies it seemed, but, yes, I counted eight men, and each one, unlike the vicar, had patches where there was no hair. So this was it, without a doubt. Gramp was an old sinner, and was past saving, as he had lost most of his hair in front. The butcher was an old sinner as his head showed shiny skin in many places. There was also this big man who was almost hairless. *What a sinner he must be.* I should have thought he would have given up trying to be saved years ago with a head as bald as that; but the man in the front row was different. He had only lost a little hair. He could still be saved. One final glance around the church convinced me of the shuddering truth, the real truth. I noticed the choir boys and the men making up the church choir. They all had perfect heads of hair. There were no sinners there. I was determined to be very much on my guard in future.

We would be having chicken for lunch today. I felt quite hungry, only sorry, because one of the birds would be missing from the runs. I expect Gramp had killed the Wyandotte[35] hen that didn't lay many eggs. *Poor thing.*

The vicar cleared his throat. 'And unless you can become little children,' he paused, 'the kingdom of heaven will be like a closed shop.'

I then made a ghastly scraping noise with my chair as I slipped on the polished seat having to be rescued by Mummy. I consequently missed the vicar's closing words but I felt I would be safe as I was a little child. But why was heaven a shop anyway? It would be nice if they had bullseyes. Bullseyes, wings, what fun!

We were on our feet again. Everyone was singing except me, though I helped a lot as before with my sharp 'S' at the end of each verse.

'Let us pray,' the vicar instructed us.

---

35   The Wyandotte hen was established as a breed in America in 1883 and introduced in the UK in the 1890s. It is known for its brown eggs and yellow-skinned meat, is a popular show bird and comes in seventeen colours (Andrews, 2019, p1.)

We knelt on the cushions.

I wondered if we were going to have the Wyandotte or the feather-plucker for lunch. Gramp had said there was no cure for a feather-plucker so perhaps it would be the Rhode Island Red feather-plucker.

The service was over.

Outside on the gravel path the big sinner stopped and spoke to us. He moved nearer, I moved back and he gave me sixpence. *Sinners were not so bad after all, I thought.* He might even be saved one day if he continued to go to church and didn't stop going like Gramp or the self-confessed old sinner of a butcher who 'never set foot in the place.'

# 5

## ALL-OVERS AND HANGOVERS

'Dark days before Christmas,' said Granny, drawing the huge curtain rings with the walking stick.

It was late November, and the oil lamp lit by Gramp a moment before cast a 'round plate,' as I called it, on the white ceiling. I used to play the plate game when left alone, turning down the lamp wick, making the plate on the ceiling smaller, and then turning it up making the plate bigger. I had just turned the wick up, when the door opened before I could turn it down. The flame was a little too high now being slightly up at one side.

'My Godfathers,' Granny said, 'Father hasn't made a good job of that wick.' I said nothing, and just then there was a slight 'ping' sound. I knew what it was. Turning up the wick too quickly had broken the glass through overheating.

'My Godfathers,' Granny said, 'I can't think enough of Father. He's forgotten to trim the wick, and turned it up too far. That's what comes of thinking about horses and easy money. It's cost a lamp-glass. Well I…'

Just then Gramp came in. 'I did trim the wick, and I had it burning low to warm the glass before I turned it up,' said Gramp. 'There's something wrong with the oil. You want to see the oil man next week. I'll tell him! Not only that, the last winner he gave me was down on the course. I lost a couple of bob,[36] and this is the second lamp-glass we've lost in a week.'

I felt quite uncomfortable thinking of the second lamp-glass, and thought it a good idea to be helpful so I disappeared into the 'Odds and Sods' cupboard, as my father called it when he was home from the sea, and returned with another lamp-glass. Gramp was still saying things about the oil man and his inferior oil.

---

36  A bob or shilling would be about £7.00 in today's money, so he lost about £14 on the horse (see http://www.concertina.com/calculator).

'That's it,' said Gramp, 'I wonder if he got his funnels mixed up.'

'Funnels, funnels Father!' said Granny.

She always called him Father in a loud voice when she was very, very angry, or Father in a soft voice when she was very, very pleased. This time she was very, very angry.

'Funnels,' she repeated again, 'It's not funnels that's the trouble, but your trouble of following four legs and a tail with a weak head. Always 'as been. Can't think what I *hever* saw in you!'

'Mother,' said Mummy from the door, 'I wish you wouldn't drop that aitch[37] and add it on.'

'Drop the aitch?' said Granny. 'Sometimes your father gives me the all-overs.'[38]

'And when your Granny has the all-overs,' said Gramp, addressing me, 'that's when I make myself scarce, pon my puff if I won't,' and with that Gramp left, pulling the door to with a jerk, causing the oil flame from the lamp to spurt up suddenly, with another 'ping' from the glass.

'If you want a good job done, do it yourself, that's what I say,' said Granny, as she lit a candle, adjusted the flame to very low and replaced the glass.

Once again everyone was happy. I sat on the rug in front of the blazing fire. The oil lamp produced a smaller plate on the ceiling giving the room a cosy white light. Granny then produced her Singer sewing machine to run up a shirt before she set the table for tea. The rattle, rattle of the sewing machine, with Granny's expert hands moving in and out near the needle, with the now and then hiss, hiss, and little blue flames bursting out from the coal fire, which Granny called 'coal gas,' gave me a feeling of complete contentment. However, I was worried about one thing. As Granny replaced the hood on

---

37   '[There is] a mystery as to why certain pronunciations cause such strong feeling. Take the eighth letter of the alphabet, pronounce it haitch and then look for the slightly agonised look in some people's eyes. One suggestion is that it touches on a long anxiety in English over the letter aitch. In the 19th Century, it was normal to pronounce hospital, hotel and herb without the h. Nowadays "aitch anxiety" has led to all of them acquiring a new sound, a beautifully articulated aitch at the beginning [...]. However, the link between class, voice and status is not what it once was' (Sillito, 2010).

38   The all-overs are a feeling of nervousness or revulsion (The New Oxford English Dictionary).

the machine I said, 'Granny, does it hurt when you have the all-overs?' And as she laughed I asked, 'and what are the all-overs?'

'All-overs,' she said aloud to herself, as the sky-white tablecloth was laid, and the lamp firmly established in the centre of the table, with cups, plates and crusty bread. 'All-overs, why, I've suffered from all-overs for years. My poor mother used to have the all-overs as well.'

'Does Gramp ever have the all-overs?' I asked.

This was a fatal question, because Granny said 'Father' in a loud voice, and repeated 'Father' in an ever louder voice, before she said, 'Father; about the only thing I've known 'im to 'ave is 'angovers.'

'Mother,' said Mummy, 'there's that aitch again, and you shouldn't mention hangovers.'

It was Gramp who suddenly gave the answer from behind the pages of his sporting paper, making us jump because we hadn't noticed his return.

'All-overs,' Gramp said, 'are something we men never get,' placing a kindly hand on my shoulder, 'and hangovers are something we have if the ladies get the all-overs. And once more,' Gramp added with a glint in his eye, 'I'm going out tonight and shall come back with a hangover. It's no place for me when Granny has the all-overs.'

Granny gave the tea in the brown teapot a terrific stir, and then began to pour Gramp's tea into his moustache cup with an up and down movement.

'All-overs, all-overs,' said Gramp again, 'all because of a lamp-glass, and that oil man's oil.'

My thoughts bubbled inside me like a boiling kettle. I wanted to cry. It was all my fault. I had given Granny the all-overs, and now Gramp was going to have a hangover.

'It's all my fault Gramp,' I choked, climbing onto his knee. 'I've given Granny the all-overs; please don't go and get a hangover because I turned up the oil wick, and,' I repeated with tears running down my face, 'I did it before. Each, each time I, each time I turned it up, the door opened before I could turn it down.'

Gramp produced his red spotted handkerchief and blew my nose.

*Gramp, Mummy and Granny © C M Lansley*

Granny said, 'Here's a special lady's slice with honey,' putting the slice of bread, butter and honey into my hand, kissing Gramp on both cheeks, and then everyone was happy and laughing.

But Gramp said afterwards, and very seriously, 'Promise you won't play with the wick again, as you could turn the lamp over and we could have a fire.'

'Oh goodness,' said Mummy looking very worried.

'I promise Gramp,' I said, 'but don't have hangovers. You promise too.'

'Hangovers and all-overs are all forgotten,' Gramp answered, kissing Granny 'a smack on the lips,' as she called it, while making a great fuss of wiping her mouth.

So hangovers and all-overs were forgotten for a long, long time.

# 6

# FIRST DAY AT
# HILLGROVE SCHOOL

At last the great day arrived. This was the first Monday in December when I was going to start at Hillgrove School. This day had been arranged in order for me to 'settle in.' What magic words these were. This would help me get used to school when beginning the January term.

No longer, I thought, as I brushed my teeth in the cold, cold bathroom without hot water, would Gramp say, 'When you start school,' as I would now be a schoolboy. One day when I was old enough, I would go to my big brother's school and captain the football team and maybe the cricket team too.

'Hurry up you slow coach,' called Granny from the kitchen, 'it's time for your breakfast. If you don't hurry you will be late for school.'

I hurried, sniffing the bacon smell from the kitchen. Never in all my life had bacon smelt so good or the start of a day felt so good; for this was the day when I was going to see my 'in love with' teacher again.

With my teeth finished, I opened my mouth wide for Mummy to inspect followed by an inspection of my hands, knees and face. I brushed my hair until it shone in the old bathroom looking glass like 'pure gold', as Granny would put it, or as Mummy would say, 'not all the money in the world could buy.' This was followed by a 'my puff, you do look smart,' from Gramp.

I entered the breakfast room to begin the hurried task of a school breakfast in the same way as my brother always hurried. This was all part of going to school, I thought. So I put half a slice of bacon into my mouth all at once, drinking my tea in huge gulps rather than sips, with great-day impatience. Now I had to leave.

'Have you got everything?' asked Granny, knowing full well I had, as Granny had packed my satchel the night before with slate, pencils, coloured chalks, ruler and a paper bag full of bullseyes from Gramp to be eaten during my break.

'Yes, Granny, I'm ready to start,' I replied.

Mummy looked very pleased as we walked to the gate of pleasant swings and feather-oiled hinges, accompanied by Granny and Gramp. At the gate Gramp said, 'I know you will like school, Peter. Work hard and one day, you know what will come true.'

Wonderful Gramp, I thought, still keeping the secret of my one day marriage. Gramp pressed my hand with his 'work-never-killed-anybody' hand that Granny would rub with olive oil from a bottle, repeating, 'My Godfathers, your hands are rough.' Now I felt their friendly roughness join up with mine.

For a moment I wanted to stay at home as he said, 'I shall miss you helping with the birds this morning,' and when I looked at Gramp's face it was all fixed. My face was fixed too, as we looked at each other. I thought I would cry and then I didn't because Gramp said, 'But I'll keep the Rhode Island Red house for you to clean Peter, and of course you'll be here this afternoon to help me with the eggs.'

We were both happy again, smiling at each other. I felt the happiest boy in the whole wide world as I kept looking back, waving to Granny and Gramp, until they were lost by the bend in the road.

I had just passed the New Church's early morning service with Mummy, when there was a noise like a motorboat going down the creek, followed by a 'honk, honk,' and a large red car suddenly stopped beside us. The car was all open and the man at the wheel looked down on us from a great height. I would have been very frightened, but I could just see the faces of three children, one a boy and two girls smiling greetings from a shared back seat.

The man removed a very funny-looking hat, which Gramp explained afterwards had something to do with fishing. He bowed towards Mummy, then replacing his hat said, 'I was asked to look out for you. Can I give you a lift to Hillgrove?'

*Hillgrove House, Wootton © C M Lansley*

'Oh yes, thank you, that is kind of you,' Mummy replied, and I noticed Mummy was speaking very slowly, and very clearly, which made me know this was a very important gentleman.

'I'm Captain Moore,' he breathed, turning the brass handle and opening the door to the front seat which was very long and leathery.

I gazed up at his face, expecting to see scars of battle, for he was a real live captain, but all I saw was a round smiling face with creases round his eyes like Gramp's. I tried to think of him cutting off a head in one blow, but he seemed to me more like a man who would put a head back on again, if it was off, just like I would when my soldier, with his matchstick-stuck-on-head, lost his in battle, and I would press it back on again. I was introduced as Peter, with a big smooth handshake but I had a lingering disappointment at the lack of scars.

Mummy was helped into the front seat, and the captain said, 'I'll put this consignment into the back.'

This must have meant me, because with those words, I was lifted without opening the brassy handled door, 'up and over' onto the large seat, all leathery and button-backed, with hurried introductions to Tom, Mary and Ann.

With a spluttering from the motorboat-sounding engine and a rocking movement as the captain pulled out a wire from under the steering wheel, we started off.

Soon the engine was not spluttering and the captain sounded very pleased, saying, 'She goes very well when she's warmed up' to Mummy, including us with a huge smile.

I felt very important, waving to our sixpence-an-hour 'now-and-then' gardener help, as we motor-boated our way towards Hillgrove. My three companions seemed very bold. In low voices they were saying funny things about the captain's hat. Every now and again I wanted to laugh but didn't. I felt that to laugh at a real live captain's hat might be very dangerous, but their whispered remarks were getting louder and louder and any moment I expected him to hear. Even if he was the kind of captain who would stick a head back on again, I thought he might not stop at other things.

Tom and Mary's father was the vicar of the early morning services held at the New Church. Picture-book-looking Ann was the daughter of a village shopkeeper. You could have lunches and teas at his shop, if you were too tired and lazy to look after yourself according to Gramp. As none of the village people were tired and lazy, the shop was empty during the winter. However, in the summer it was full of visitors who were all tired and lazy.

One thing spoiled the excitement of this first ever car journey, and that, of course, was the meeting with Tom. He proudly informed me he was eight years old. He had hair the colour of Granny's beads, all shining and black. If Tom wanted to marry my teacher, I thought, he could marry her sooner if he wanted to as he was older than me. 'How could he not want to?' I asked myself. Oh dear, say our teacher wanted to marry Tom instead of me. I would soon know of course if Tom received more smiles than I did, or if she was cross with me and not with Tom. I didn't feel she could ever be cross, but if she could, I hoped she would be cross with Tom, because if people got really very cross with each other, Gramp had told me, they wouldn't marry. I must be very good, then she would never be cross with me, and if she gave me a penny for sitting still for five minutes, like Gramp did sometimes, I would be very still.

Suddenly the motorboat engine stopped, and the captain was one big smile. 'Here we are boys and girls, safe and sound at Hillgrove,' the captain said, raising his hat to Mummy, helping her down from the front seat, and lifting us one by one from the back seat onto the blueish pebble stones of Hillgrove drive.

The captain, still smiling all over his face because he thought everything very funny, gave the high glass front of his car windscreen a wipe with his window leather. Meanwhile, my new friends joined with me on seeing how funny our faces looked in the brass car lamps. They looked first long then fat and, to our giggles, the captain joined in, with his face and funny old hat going long, then short and fat.

At last, still laughing with a reddened face, and much hand waving, his car motor-boated away towards Newport with a last honk, honk on its big rubber motor horn. With one last wave at the retreating sound, Mummy said, 'The captain is a very nice man, very kind and gentle I should think,' and again I wondered more and more how the captain could ever be a captain in the Army, and if he had ever killed anybody. How could he, with such a funny-looking face and funny old hat?

'I knew I heard fun,' said a voice with a smile in it, and there stood Miss McKerchar, my angel teacher I had met at my first school visit. I took several deep breaths. She was not dressed in white now, but in my favourite blue, mixed with her golden hair and grey-mist eyes into a loveliness which was almost too much for me, so I hid behind Mummy's skirt. For a moment my absence was not noticed, but peeping from behind my skirt hideout, much to my concern, Tom seemed to receive a special smile. How could you measure smiles, I wondered, and then I was discovered. Mummy turned around and my angel saw me.

'Why Peter, how nice to see you. I hope you'll be very happy at Hillgrove.'

All I could do was to look down at my shoes, then up in the air, and then sideways, moving first one way then the other and then down at my shoes again watching my toes move under Gramp's shined leather.

Suddenly her head came very close to mine and her golden hair touched my face. With a smile a hundred feet long, or at least much longer than the one she gave Tom, she said, 'Come on little Peter, there's no need to be shy,' and holding my hand, we all walked up the steps into the hall of Hillgrove School.

Within the hall a tall lady dressed in a black shiny silk dress, longer than Granny's, advanced towards me. She placed a pair of reading glasses on the end of her nose, different from Gramp's because they were all glass with just a piece of gold pinching them on, and a mauve ribbon attached.

'So this is Peter,' she said, bending slightly, looking at me, from my head to my feet, and then back again.

I felt a little fear inside me going up and down with the movement of her head, but in a moment the fear was gone forever when she said, 'You must all come into the kitchen later, and then Peter can meet Robin.'

Then she left disappearing through an exciting-looking door covered in red cloth. We were taken round the garden. The others had seen it all before, but it was wonderfully new to me. We saw where the coal was stored in a very dark place down some steps. I was told we were not allowed to play on that side of the house because it was dangerous. *Not to play*, I thought. So we were allowed to play as well. I must tell Gramp. He'll never believe we go to school to play.

From the dark cold place we reached the kitchen garden, 'And this is the Bramley Apple,' said my angel.

'Yes,' I answered, 'Gramp has one at home, and you wouldn't believe it last summer—we picked twenty bushels!'

This remark more than made up for the few extra smiles Tom seemed to be getting. My angel, with hands resting on her sides, gave whistle-pipe laughs like Gramp playing the scales.

At last she said, holding her smiling face close to mine, 'Yes, of course I believe it, but you must have a lovely Bramley.'

I was about to repeat Gramp's words, 'Not another Bramley like it for miles,' but noticing her little Bramley again I said, 'Yes, it's a lovely big Bramley, but when your Bramley's grown-up there won't be another Bramley like it for miles,' adding quickly, 'Except Gramp's.'

Now her face looked wondering, and for a moment we were all silent with only the garden bird voices. *Had I said something wrong?*

Then my angel stretched out her hand and touched the little Bramley, resting her fingers on the branches and I heard her say softly to it, 'When you are grown-up.'

We moved on to the brick-built woodshed with its half-open door. An end of an old tree trunk was on the floor with an axe sticking in it.

'Your chopping block is bigger than Gramp's,' I said.

'Are you quite sure,' she laughed.

Again I looked at the block. Could she know, I asked myself? Had she ever seen Gramp's chopping block? I so wanted her chopping block to be bigger than Gramp's. My face was feeling all hot. 'Never tell a lie,' Gramp had said more than once when we'd been working together in the chicken runs. And now I'd told a dreadful lie for I knew all the time Gramp's chopping block was much bigger than hers. My face was so hot now, I didn't know what to do and I felt chokey.

'Whatever's the matter Peter?' she asked.

I managed to say, 'When…, when did my, my Gramp show you his chopping block?'

Once again with laughing whistle-pipes, and my face cooling, she answered, 'I've never visited your house Peter so I haven't seen your Gramp's chopping block, but I'd love to see it one day.'

'Would you, would you?' I answered excitedly, adding quickly, 'But I'm afraid Gramp's block is bigger than yours after all.'

'Are you sure?' she smiled bringing her face down to mine.

'Sure,' I replied, 'and when I'm home I'll ask Gramp when you can come.'

'Oh! Please don't worry. Don't worry just yet. Your Gramp might be too busy.'

'My Gramp's never too busy for anything,' I replied. 'You will come won't you? Please come and see it! Promise you'll come.'

'I promise,' she said, squeezing my hand.

I was happy again. What a wonderful thing to tell Gramp when I returned. I could just hear him say 'My puff' when I told him my teacher was coming to see his chopping block, and Granny was sure to say 'My Godfathers.'

Leaving the woodshed, we returned towards the house across the lawn where we would have races in the summer at the end of term. I prayed within my mind: *'Please God may I beat Tom when we have a race.'*

*'I must train very hard like my brother,'* I told myself.

We re-entered the house by some wooden steps to a veranda and then through some large glass doors called French Windows, but it did seem a long way for windows to come. Once again I was in the lovely room of my first visit to Hillgrove, able to meet my silent friends once more by touching the animal skin, feeling the cool, smooth marble fireplace and seeing the paper in the grate because the fire was lit in the living room. I gazed again at the little pictures in their frames, and at the one of a young girl who smiled at me as I looked and looked. And then I dared to touch one of the piano keys of the dark browny-red piano, and the sound was very deep like a ship talking on a foggy day. We would have singing sometimes, I was told, with carols as Christmas neared. How wonderful it would be to sing carols as Christmas neared at Hillgrove.

Now I had to go and meet Robin. Outside in the hall we walked towards the exciting red-covered door. My angel opened the door and we were greeted by the fairyland smells of apples stewing, and the spit, spit sound of a roast roasting with mouth-watering smells. The lady with the black, shiny silk dress stood bending by the open oven door 'basting,' as Granny called it, the white browning potatoes gathered around the hissing meat.

'It's pork today,' said the lady straightening herself, slamming the door of the shiny black kitchen range, with copper pans all hot and gleaming on top with the red fire looking through the bars beneath.

We were given little apple pieces dipped in brown sugar while seated at the large kitchen table. It was then I noticed someone sitting in the corner of a long cushioned seat under the window. She was looking towards us half smiling. I could see she wore a red woollen 'sweater,' as my brother called it, but there was something fighting in my mind as I stared at her. Here was something new. I hoped she would remain in the corner. Yet I didn't know why I felt this way because, after all, she was smiling, and her red sweater was pretty. I was just thinking that the lady had mentioned that I was to meet Robin in the kitchen, when the lady said, 'Come Robin and meet our new boy Peter.' Robin came slowly towards where I was sitting, still smiling, holding out an arm with a thin white hand, and said something which I knew to be 'hello' as I stood up. I pressed the hand ever so carefully, but there was no press returned. Our hands just remained resting together. I looked up at her face. It was the face of a white rose that had been pressed against the other roses when picked. I wanted to say something but I didn't know what. And then I said the only thing I could think of, 'Can you come out to play one day?' Her smiling face altered, and again she said something and slowly our hands parted.

'That was kind of you to ask Robin to play, Peter,' said my angel, 'and Robin says she'd love to when the weather's warmer. Didn't you Robin?'

Robin said something which must have been 'Yes,' holding her hand towards mine. I pressed it ever so gently, looking up. Now her eyes were looking at me. Not like before.

Climbing the stairs to be shown our school room, I thought of the red-clothed door, and of Robin in her window corner. When I next helped Gramp with the birds, I thought, I'd ask him. He would know.

At the top of the stairs we were first shown the lavatory. It was a sit down one like we had at home, looking very funny when the door was open like all the others, which gave us the giggles. The school room overlooked the kitchen garden and the woodshed with the chopping block. Tall oaks stood and waved from the other side of the garden hedge, and the grassy-green grass was tucked in the earth like my good-night top blanket. There were several desks and I sat next to Mary. Mary was not quite five, she told me. Our first lesson was to go over things from the beginning, which was easy for Tom and Ann. I knew a lot of things too, so I could help Mary. Mary's numbers, like her letters, were written as if by a giant. I helped her with the number eight because her first one filled the whole page of the exercise book. It looked like the Saturday Cottage loaf which we always bought on Saturday so we could have a nice crusty Sunday.

'Try and do your eight like this,' I said to Mary, writing her a small one. But she then did one with nearly all bottom and a very tiny top which was very, very funny.

So my first morning at school ended. Mummy came to collect me and we all walked back. From my gate Gramp waved from the top of the garden and I ran to him. I was pleased when he told me how difficult he had found it to manage the birds without me, and we sat down to lunch with much talking as we had so much to tell each other. We were still talking when Granny said, 'My Godfathers, it's half past one, and I haven't cleared the table.'

# 7

## MOUNT JOY AND GRAMP'S SILVER WHISTLE

On the evening ending my first week of morning school, I was alone with Gramp in the living room, with the brass paraffin lamp giving its light to the walls. The plate game on the ceiling and a larger than usual fire, muttering in the grate, made us very warm and comfortable. Mummy and Granny had left for a whist drive, a funny card game played by four grown-ups. Daddy often played when he was home from sea, and sometimes he would throw his cards down on the table and say to Mummy, 'If you trump my ace again, I'll go back to sea first thing tomorrow morning.' But Daddy never went back first thing the next morning after a card game, so Mummy couldn't have trumped his ace again, whatever that was. Once I did manage to stay awake until the morning showed through the curtains in case Mummy had trumped Daddy's ace, because if Daddy was going to leave I was going to ask him to give Mummy another chance.

The whist drive wouldn't end until very late and Granny was very concerned whether Gramp would be able to manage alright with me on his own.

'I don't trust you two,' she said. 'I never know what you two will get up to next.'

Gramp just smiled at Mummy saying to Granny, 'Don't you worry about us Mother. We'll find something to keep us out of mischief, won't we?' Gramp added, turning to me.

'Yes,' I said, and then as the back door closed, I asked, 'Show me the pictures in the big Bible that's underneath the couch in the front room.'

Gramp returned to the living room breathing very hard because the Bible was very heavy. He moved the oil lamp from the centre of the table to give us more room to turn the pages, just in case, he explained, we should get very excited at the beautiful pictures, forget where we were, and knock the oil lamp over.

Gramp turned the pages and sometimes he would read a few words from the lettered print which he could read without his glasses because it was so large. However, whenever he tried to read I would say, 'Let's go on to another picture Gramp.' The pictures I loved the most were the ones showing angels with their lovely white wings. It must be wonderful to have lovely white wings and be able to fly like a bird all over the place, I thought. I then asked, 'Do we always grow wings when we die Gramp, and have we got to learn to fly like a baby bird, or can we fly as soon as we're dead?'

'Pon my puff,' said Gramp, 'you do ask some questions. Now where do I begin?' and with this his face became fixed all over and I knew he was thinking and thinking.

Before Gramp finished thinking, I asked, 'What colour wings will you have when you die Gramp? Are they always white or could you ask for browny-red ones like the Rhode Island Reds?'

I could see this question made Gramp happy because he was smiling, and then I asked something that I had often wondered about and been afraid of, though I hadn't told anybody, and I asked, 'Does it hurt when we die Gramp?'

Gramp got up from his chair, walked towards the curtained windows, turned round, took out his watch and said to himself, 'Pon my puff what have I let myself in for,' and then he sat down again.

I waited and waited. I must know the answer I thought, now that Gramp was alone to tell me, without Mummy or Granny here to say, 'Stop worrying your little head about such things,' which they did sometimes over big questions.

'Please Gramp tell me what happens when you die. If you tell me,' I added, 'I'll go to bed first time you ask me to, and only one piggyback upstairs.'

'Well,' said Gramp at last, 'when I die I'm going to Mount Joy.'

'Where's Mount Joy Gramp?' I asked, thinking it must be a wonderful happy place with a name like that.

'It's the Down overlooking Newport, with Carisbrooke and the castle close by, and as you look around you can see for miles and miles, with the

*William & Harriette's Headstone, Mount Joy, Carisbrooke Cemetery*
*(after clean Sep 2019) © C M Lansley*

Medina[39] going in and out of fields and trees until it reaches the sea at Cowes. And on a clear day,' Gramp continued, 'you can hear the angels playing their silver whistle-pipes if you stop and listen. And on a misty day they have a little sleep until the sun touches their wings, and then they know it's time to get up and drive the mist away. All at once you'll see the mist move as the angels fly around until all the mist has gone. It's then if you stand very still, and listen very carefully, you'll hear the silver whistle-pipes of the angels playing for joy.'

What a wonderful place for Gramp to go to, I thought. Instead of having a brassy whistle-pipe, he would have a silver one. That would make him very happy, but would it hurt to die, I wondered? So I asked, 'But does it hurt when you die?'

---

39   The River Medina rises at St. Catherine's Down and flows northwards through Newport towards the Solent at Cowes.

'Do you remember being born Peter?' Gramp asked after thinking very hard again. And when I said I didn't know, he said, 'That's it, it's the same when we die. None of us remember it. One minute we're here in our bodies, and the next minute we're born an angel. So you see Peter,' Gramp continued, 'if you don't remember dying it can't hurt, can it?'

All fear of death and dying departed from me. The great fear I had of what would happen to Gramp when he died was replaced by a happy feeling of Gramp playing a silver whistle-pipe on Mount Joy as the mist cleared after the sun had touched his wings. And then Gramp said, 'And when we leave our bodies and become an angel we don't need our bodies anymore, and when that time comes I will be taken to Mount Joy and laid deep down in a place cut into the chalk, and it will be like being placed between clean sheets.'

Gramp looked at his silver Half Hunter[40] watch on the end of his long silver watch chain and said, 'It's your sleepy time Peter. Remember your promise.'

'Yes Gramp,' I replied, taking the silver Half Hunter into my hands. Gramp opened the back of the watch, as he did sometimes, for me to see the 'works' as he called them.

'One day, when I'm taken to Mount Joy Peter, this watch will be yours. Take care of it,' Gramp added, tickling my ribs, 'and always remember to keep a little bit of time up your sleeve.'

We were laughing and happy as Gramp did my milk, and I went to bed first time with only one piggyback.

---

40   A hunter-case pocket watch has a lid on the front which you have to open to see the watch hands. It also has a lid on the back which you can open to see the clockwork. A half hunter has an outer lid with a glass panel or hole in the centre giving a view of the hands without having to open the lid. The name originated from fox hunters who opened their watch with one hand, while holding the reins of their 'hunter,' or horse, in the other hand.

# 8

# AUNT EMILY COMES TO LUNCH

The next day after hearing about Mount Joy, I could help Gramp all day as there was no school on Saturday mornings. With sleeves rolled up I mixed the birds' mash which used to give a lovely dinner-like smell when it was gently simmering on the kitchen range.

Gramp always rolled my sleeves up as high as he could, because when I did the mixing I used to put my arms into the mash bucket up to my elbows. The mash consisted of brownish flaky stuff called 'bran' and all the leftovers from the kitchen such as bits of potato, potato peelings, carrot scrapings and the outside of cabbages. 'Waste not, want not,' said Gramp as he added a few more scraps into the mixing bucket. It was wonderful to put the warm mash into the low, long, wooden V-shaped troughs on a cold morning, watching it steaming into the air. The birds would rush to the troughs with great excitement from all parts of the run. Then you would hear their beaks working like tiny hammers, each racing the other.

My friend Rodie, the big Rhode Island Red cockerel, was very funny. Rodie would rush, with wings outstretched, like the policeman on point duty at Newport market days, keeping his hens back with his wings. He would run so fast that he couldn't stop falling over the trough, landing on his breast on the other side. His hens would seem to chuckle. Rodie would get up, looking redder than ever round his wattles, make a craw-craw sound and then peck very fast, stopping every now and then, moving his beak backwards and forwards in the mash tossing flakes of bran into the air until he found a piece of potato. He would dig this out of the trough with his beak, taking it into a corner of the run to enjoy it 'in comfort,' as Gramp called it. Often as not the potato would have a hot spot, and suddenly Rodie would stop, his head slightly raised, his beak half-open and his eyes half closed, as he gasped for breath. With great speed he would run to the drinking water, dip his beak in, close his eyes with his greyish white lids, and lift his head to the sky as he cooled both his beak and his little tongue. Then with more craw, craw, craws, which sounded like 'don't you laugh at me,' he would rush back to the trough, winging his hens out of the way to show them who was boss, Gramp explained. There we would both stand laughing, enjoying the fun. I felt I would rather help Gramp with the mash on 'mash' days than anything else on earth.

After lunch Gramp said he was going to kill the Light Sussex[41] cockerel for tomorrow, as Aunt Emily[42] had invited herself to dinner. 'We don't need him anymore,' Gramp explained, 'and there's enough meat on him to last us a good three days.'

I followed Gramp up the garden and watched the Light Sussex cockerel scratching for food in his run. He looked down, scratched with his feet, looked up and then suddenly pecked at the ground. As we approached, he spoke to us in the way of birds when contented, like a man clearing his throat. All the birds in the runs were talking and scratching away quite happily, but as Gramp opened the wire netting door to the cockerel's run, everyone stopped talking and scratching and lifted their heads with a 'what's up now?' look.

The cockerel looked at Gramp and Gramp looked at the cockerel, and then for no reason the cockerel started to run very fast towards the bird house.

'We mustn't make a noise or worry the other birds,' said Gramp in a low voice, as he walked slowly towards the cockerel, adding, 'But it's strange, they always seem to know.'

By this time all the birds in the runs had started to talk at us in loud voices, as if to say, 'Don't kill him. Don't kill him. He's nice. He's nice. Don't kill him.'

'You stay there,' whispered Gramp, as the cockerel, wondering what to do, waited by the corner of the birdhouse. Gramp disappeared behind the other

---

41   The Light Sussex were introduced in the UK in 1865. They are known for their striking plumage, hardiness, docile nature and excellent egg laying (Cosy Hen Company, 2019).

42   Emily Anne Morris (1850 – 1928) was Harriette's sister. She was Annie Ethel Stark's Aunt and therefore Peter's Great Aunt. She was married to Benjamin Redstone (1850 – 1924) who had run a grocery store in Cowes between 1898 – 1911 and had given Harriette help and support when she set up her shop in East Cowes.

side of the house. I waited very still as the cockerel stood on one leg looking very worried. It was listening very hard with its head on one side. Then I saw Gramp crouching very low with his hands moving towards the cockerel from behind. Perhaps I gave the game away as I held my breath, for the cockerel started to run. But he was too late. Gramp's hands closed upon his wings. In a moment Gramp's right hand had grasped his legs with his left hand sliding under the bird to support the cockerel's breast. Gramp straightened himself while the cockerel shouted loudly to the other birds for help. Gramp left the run for the old shed where I knew 'killing, drawing and plucking,' as Gramp spoke of it, went on quite often.

At the door of the old shed, Gramp stopped and said, 'You needn't come in if you think it will make you cry Peter, but this is part of keeping birds and you've had a good many chickens for dinner already. It's just as well you start now and learn what goes on, as you'll have to one day.' So we went into the old shed together.

Gramp sat down on the chair.

'Let me stroke him,' I said, stroking the cockerel's head slowly, feeling the warmth through its feathers. Then I said, 'Please Gramp, couldn't we save him, just this once?'

'No,' replied Gramp, 'because it has to be done, sooner or later.'

I felt very sad and would have liked to have cried, but I took a deep breath and said, 'It won't hurt him when he dies will it?' And thinking of Gramp becoming an angel one day, I added, 'And what happens when he becomes an angel?' As after all, I thought, the cockerel already had wings. Perhaps, I wondered, he would be given bigger ones.

Gramp sat looking very thoughtful while we took it in turns to stroke the bird. 'He won't feel anything,' he said after a time. 'You might think so Peter, but I just give a sharp pull on his neck, and it's over and then he's an angel bird with a beautiful place to scratch in with all the other angel birds that go every day to bird heaven.'

'Will he really be happy Gramp, and will he have bigger wings?' I asked.

'Of course,' Gramp replied.

'Let me give him a little kiss,' I said, pressing my lips onto his neck feathers.

'You can look away if you like,' said Gramp.

I turned looking at the door, thinking how happy the cockerel would be as an angel bird, with bigger wings, and a lovely, lovely place to scratch in.

'It's over Peter,' Gramp said.

'But he's still fluttering Gramp,' I exclaimed, as I noticed the bird's wings and neck making little movements, as it dangled neck downwards in Gramp's hands. 'That always happens,' Gramp said, 'Just as a bird becomes an angel. The next thing is to pluck the bird.'

With the cockerel between his knees, Gramp began to pluck the bird. The feathers fell quickly into the plucking box. I was allowed to pluck a few feathers pulling them slightly forward towards the neck, and then towards the tail, with an up and down movement of the fingers so as not to tear the flesh, Gramp explained. With all the feathers gone except those around the neck, the bird was hung neck downwards over a bucket.

'Afraid he's going to be a bit tough,' said Gramp. 'It would have been better to have hung it another day, but Aunt Emily will talk so much during lunch, pon my puff, she won't know if it's chicken or beef.'

'I like Aunt Emily,' I said, from where I sat on an upturned bucket. 'Last time she came she gave me sixpence.'

'Oh, Aunt Emily's alright,' said Gramp. 'In her way, her tongue's not forked, and her heart's in the right place.'

The next day I was up quite early and met the milkman coming up the garden path. 'Mornen young Master,' he said.

'Good morning Mr Cooper,' I answered. Mr Cooper placed his heavy milk cans on the gravel path and stood looking at me, gaining his breath. What I could see of his face was all wrinkles and the dark greyness of his beard sparkling with morning dew.

'Mr Cooper,' I asked, using my Granny's words when she wanted Gramp to do something at an awkward time, 'Would you do me a favour?'

'Depends what and if I can.'

'Mr Cooper, please show me your tongue.'

Mr Cooper sat down on the lid of one of the milk cans, disbelieving and wondering what he had just heard, until suddenly smiling all over said, 'Must be playing doctors,' and then popped out his tongue ever so quickly touching me with it on the end of my nose.

At any rate, I thought, as I walked up the garden path, Mr Cooper's tongue wasn't like a garden fork. I didn't have the courage to ask him about his heart, but I would find out more about tongues and hearts later.

When we sat down to lunch, I asked Aunt Emily, 'Where is your heart, Auntie?'

'Just here,' she replied, placing her hand in about the same place where I knew mine was.

I repeated the question to Mummy and Granny. Gramp looked at me without speaking, wondering. Then I asked Aunt Emily, 'Can I see your tongue, Auntie?'

'Oh dear,' Auntie replied, 'I know it's bound to be dirty,' sticking out her tongue. It reminded me of the Rhode Island Red going into moult, but it certainly wasn't shaped like a garden fork.

After a moment Auntie asked, between mouthfuls of chicken, 'Why ever did you want to see my tongue and know where my heart is Peter?'

'Because,' I replied, 'just after we killed the bird yesterday, Gramp said your tongue was not forked and your heart was in the right place, and I just wanted to make sure.'

'Oh, you are a funny boy, Peter,' Auntie said, and turning to Gramp she said softly, 'That was a lovely thing to say Bill.'

When Auntie Emily left that day, she gave me two kisses and a half a crown[43], which Gramp said he knew she couldn't afford. I never saw her again, but I was quite happy for her when Gramp told me she had gone to Mount Joy[44].

---

43   A half a crown was two shillings and sixpence or twelve and a half pence in decimal currency. In 1924 this would have been equivalent to about £18.00 in today's money (see http://www.concertina.com/calculator/).

44   She died in 1928 a year before Gramp died.

# 9

## STIR-UP WEEK[45]

The kitchen was filled with the smells which I knew was the beginning of Christmas. 'My Godfathers,' Granny said, 'I've never been so late with my puddings for as long as I can remember.'

'It's this 'ere moving, wot comes of settling in that's caused it. Can't expect anything else,' said Mrs Jones. But Gramp reminded us of the touch of flu we'd had that had run through the village like wild fire in early November by saying, 'Pon my puff Mother, you ain't the only one that's late with puddings this year. The grocer was telling me only yesterday at the Sloop that people are only just getting round to it on account of the flu.'

Granny was busy preparing the fruit, chopping up lemon peel and other exciting things on a wooden chopping board. Every now and again she added to my pleasure of watching, by saying, 'Open your mouth Peter,' and a lovely piece of sugary peel would slip between my teeth. Later came the delightful part when the pudding mixture was ready for mixing. The large mixing bowl made its appearance with top-shelf pantry dust, to be cleaned to a gleaming nut-brown on the outside and a shiny snow-white inside with Granny re-

---

45    Stir-up Sunday is a tradition that goes back to Victorian times when the family would gather together to stir the Christmas pudding on the last Sunday before Advent, five weeks before Christmas. The term 'Stir-up' comes from the Book Of Common Prayer used during the service on this day and reads: 'Stir up, we beseech thee, O Lord, the wills of thy faithful people.' The Christmas pudding would traditionally contain thirteen ingredients representing the thirteen disciples of Jesus. While making a wish, each member of the family would stir it from East to West to represent the Wise Men who visited Jesus. A garnish of holly would represent the crown of thorns. Adding coins would give you luck if you found one. They were silver threepenny pieces and later silver sixpenny pieces. Prince Albert made the Christmas pudding fashionable (Chandler, 2019). Sadly this tradition is disappearing as home-made puddings are replaced by those purchased at supermarkets and as busy working parents have less time to spend making them. As the pudding stirring at Hillgrove School (mentioned later) took place during morning school, it is likely this took place in the week before Christmas as with the other households in the village rather than on Stir-up Sunday itself.

peating, 'My Godfathers, that's dusty,' and Gramp saying, 'So would you be if you'd been on that shelf all this time. Pon my puff!'

Granny mixed everything dry at first. Then came the part I'd been waiting for. 'Go and get a bottle of stout,' adding to Gramp, 'and don't come home late and say "fancy who I met," because I won't believe it.' Gramp winked at me as he left the kitchen singing, 'I don't care what you used to be in days gone by, but I know what you are today.'

When Gramp returned with the stout, Granny gave me a sip to taste before the rest was poured into the mixing bowl. The first thing I would do when I was grown-up, I decided, would be to buy a bottle of stout all for myself and drink it by the fire like Gramp did. Nothing could be nicer to look forward to, I thought, after a busy day with the birds.

Meanwhile Granny mixed away with a large wooden spoon, the stout becoming a part of the pudding. Gramp watched, and I could see he was enjoying it when he said, 'I thought I heard Ethel call from the living room.' I listened very hard and then he said again to Granny, 'That's Ethel calling you,' taking the mixing spoon and adding, 'I'll go on with the mixing.'

I was just going to say I hadn't heard Mummy call, when Gramp gave me a wink twice, behind Granny's back, as she left the room. As the door closed, Gramp took a small bottle—'brandy' he called it—from his coat pocket and emptied it quickly into the mixing bowl, stirring all the time.

'You must have been dreaming Father,' Granny said as she returned and continued mixing. Gramp looked at me very wisely and said, 'Can't expect my ears to be always right after all these years. Pon my puff, you can't.'

Then I helped Gramp wash and polish the silver threepenny pieces, remembering last Christmas when I found two in one piece of pudding. Perhaps this time I would find three!

Granny handed me the large mixing spoon. 'Give a good stir,' she said, 'and make your wish, but you mustn't tell anybody or you'll break the spell.'

I was going to wish Daddy home for Christmas, but I knew that would be wasting a wish because one day Mummy had explained that Daddy was posted to Malta for two years. Everyone had looked very important when

Gramp said, 'That's what comes of being in the Navy.' So I started to stir wondering very hard what to wish.

'Haven't you finished wishing yet?' Granny asked.

'I'm still trying to think very hard what to wish,' I replied, 'and now I've got to start thinking all over again!'

Gramp took his brassy whistle-pipe out of his inside pocket and started to play *O Come All Ye Faithful*. Then I wished very, very hard thinking about what Gramp had told me, how one day he would play silver whistle-pipes. 'Please God,' I wished, 'let Gramp be with us this Christmas, and next Christmas, and the next, and the next…,' stirring faster and faster with each 'next,' until Granny said, 'That's enough Peter, you must have wished by now.'

Mummy asked, as she entered the kitchen, 'Penny for your wish,' and I replied, 'It's a very, very important wish, and I mustn't break the spell ever.'

'Quite right,' said Gramp, finishing *All Ye Faithful*. 'And now you must wish,' he said to Granny.

'I've already wished,' said Granny, 'and that's no secret. I wished I hadn't put in so much stout. And that's a fact. I've made the mixture too moist like I did last year!'

I sat on the kitchen chair with a bout of the giggles, thinking how Gramp had poured the brandy into the mixture without her knowing.

'What are you giggling about?' Gramp asked me, smiling.

'I just thought of something funny,' I said.

'And I think it's funny too if your Granny doesn't know how much stout to put in after all these years!' said Gramp.

'That's enough of that,' Granny answered. 'You stick to your birds and I'll stick to my puddings.'

'Pon my puff I will!' retorted Gramp, giving my face a friendly pinch.

The Christmas puddings bubbled on the kitchen range with Gramp saying every now and again, 'Christmas is coming, the pigs are getting fat. Christmas is coming, put another penny in the old man's hat[46].'

---

46  *Christmas Is Coming* is a nursery rhyme and Christmas song: Christmas is coming, the geese are getting fat. / Please put a penny in the old man's hat. / If you haven't got a penny, a ha'penny will do. / If you haven't got a ha'penny, then God bless you! (Carols, 2017).

The sweet happy time of anticipation made the days for me: crossing off the numbers on the calendar as quickly as possible before Uncle Harry, Auntie Flo, and cousins Len and Barrie joined us for Christmas from Portsmouth. Dressing quickly in the morning to cross off the next day, I would long for each passing hour to bring me nearer to crossing off another day.

'Ah!, bless 'is little 'art,' said Mrs Jones, who had just arrived to scrub the scullery floor, holding me to her big breasts with kisses of carbolic soap. ''Ow wonderful to cross off the days of the month on purpose.'

Christmas carol time, which I longed for so much, was here. Once again the magic music room at Hillgrove School was in its Christmas dress of holly-green, with bright red berries peeping out from every railed picture. A huge log fire was burning on frosty mornings in the grate, making wavy sunsets on the white blue-veined marble. My angel played the dark browny-red piano, joining in the singing until we had it just right, and then we started all over again, with another, and another. Each time the lid of the piano was closed, we chorused 'more, more,' until at last it was time for our break.

Later we were taken in through the red cloth-covered door to the kitchen to stir the pudding and make a wish. I explained I had already stirred and wished at home, but I could stir and wish again, I was told, as this was a different pudding mixture.

Robin and I stirred together, her thin hands resting on mine. I made round movements with the spoon, wishing very hard for a railway tunnel which I could place over my rails. Then I could be in the engine with my engine driver friend, sucking bullseyes, swaying from side to side as we rushed into the tunnel, with dark white-blue smoke and then black smoke following us into the daylight, until the frosty morning sun would make rivers of light upwards to the sky. *That was it!* I could make my tunnel black with a candle. It was going to be a wonderful Christmas. How lucky I was to have had a second wish. Suddenly this magic was broken.

My angel's mother[47] spoke to me, and I noticed the lace of her high-necked blouse moving up and down with her soft cushioned voice. 'Do finish

---

47   This is Ethel McKerchar, Kathleen McKerchar's mother.

Peter, you are making Robin quite tired, though Robin is so happy to wish with you.'

It was then I heard Robin's breath for the first time, like running-at-play breath. I also saw for the first time that her face was not like ours, not old or earthquakey like Aunt Emily's, or Granny's, yet not firm like mine or Tom's or Mary's. It seemed like the cotton wool in the blue paper package, which Mummy always kept in the house for some emergency, whatever that was. I didn't want the silly old tunnel anymore, though I still *hoped* for it. I just wished ever so quickly for Robin. But what would Robin want for Christmas? And then I knew what Gramp would do if he was me. Only the other day, when the butcher said it was his birthday, Gramp and the butcher drank each other's health with some of the specially 'ordered in' Christmas beer. Gramp had said, 'Here's wishing you, all you wish yourself.' Afterwards Gramp had explained to me that if you wish for people what they want for themselves, though you don't know what they want, you are always bound to be right in your wish. I would ask Gramp later, I decided, what the butcher might have wished. *That would be fun*, and perhaps Gramp would have guessed and he could tell me. But now with one last stir I made a wish for Robin: 'Please let Robin have all she wishes herself for Christmas.'

Finally, after everyone had stirred and had their secret wish, many gleaming white silver threepenny pieces were scattered into the mixture. We were then all allowed one little extra stir with the promise of a piece of pudding each to welcome the New Year in after Christmas.

Morning school ended. I walked the long mile home with Tom, Mary and Andy and we sang all the Christmas carols over and over again until we reached my gate. I rushed up the garden path to Gramp telling him the good news that I had had the second Christmas pudding wish. Gramp looked very sad around his blue eyes when I told him of Robin, and how her hands had not really stirred. But his eyes smiled with his face when I told him my wish for Robin. He quickly told me not to worry when I remembered it should have been a secret wish. He said it wouldn't break the spell this time. I then asked Gramp what he thought the butcher might have wished for himself on his birthday. Gramp laughed, then said, 'Bet my puff he wished for the winner of next year's Derby.'

Now Gramp often had a secret bet of a penny each way on a horse for me, but he only told me when the horse had won so that I wouldn't become too excited. Sometimes I would win as much as sixpence, so I knew all about horses and prices. I knew that Steve Donoghue[48] was the greatest jockey in the world. Steve had won me many a sixpence. I made up my mind that the next time the butcher called, I would walk with him to the gate. I would give him twopence from my money box to back next year's Derby winner for me, the one he had wished for himself on his birthday. It would be wonderful to see Gramp's face after the Derby when the butcher paid me my winnings! It was such fun to know I was going to back next year's winner all on my own, though with a little help from the butcher. As Granny often said, we are all here to help each other and that's what it meant. It would surprise Gramp when the butcher paid me my winnings but I knew it would make him very happy too.

While I had been stirring the puddings and making my wishes, I had thought that if I could have a wish with every different pudding mixture, all I had to do to make my wishes stronger was to find other pudding mixtures to stir and make another wish.

After lunch that afternoon, I set about my plan. First, I thought, I would try Mrs Bright up the hill. I knocked very hard on the side door which I knew to be the kitchen.

'I'm sorry my dear,' she said, 'but I can't do any washing this week as I'm busy with my puddings.'

'That's alright Mrs Bright,' I said, 'I've called to know if I can have a stir at your pudding.'

'Why, of course Peter.'

Mrs Bright removed a cloth from the mixing bowl and I set about stirring and wishing. My wish was for Gramp, and after a long, long stir, and a long,

48   Steve Donoghue (1884 – 1945) was a leading English flat-race jockey in the 1910s and 1920s. He was Champion Jockey 10 times between 1914 and 1923.

long wish, I said, 'Thank you Mrs Bright, that was very kind of you, and now I must be going.'

Mrs Bright looked rather surprised as she waved from the door and I walked to another little cottage higher up the hill. I knocked several times as hard as I could using my fist upon the kitchen door. At last the door was opened by a lady with no stockings, and brownish round marks on her legs. She didn't speak and her face was the colour of bonfire ash.

As she didn't say anything, I asked, 'Please may I stir your Christmas pudding?'

Then she smiled and said, 'You lovely, I wish we 'ad a pudding fer you to stir but my 'ubby's been out of a job since 'e broke 'is leg playing footer.'

'No Christmas pudding!' I said with great surprise.

'No luv, an' ain't likely to be a pudding.' She closed the door with a smile and I walked out of the gate with my head down walking slowly along the road to the next pair of cottages.

Would there be a pudding to stir here I wondered? If there was, what should I wish, because my second wish was going to be for Robin and there was this lady without a pudding. I knocked several times and an old lady opened the door just wide enough for her face to appear.

'Please,' I asked, 'please may I stir your Christmas pudding?'

'Stir my Christmas pudding! Well that's strange because I was just going to mix it.'

The door was opened and I followed her into a very tiny kitchen, which was very hot from the kitchen range. On the white kitchen table was a large dish and in it was the pudding mixture.

'What's your name?' she asked.

'Peter,' I replied.

'And why, Peter, do you want to stir my pudding?'

'Please, please, because I want to stir a lot of puddings and make a lot of wishes, because Granny said I could only make one wish when I stirred our puddings and I have a lot of important things to wish.'

'Bless you Peter,' she said, handing me a large spoon.

I stirred for a moment, thinking very hard about the lady without a Christmas pudding. What did one do, I thought, when you had a lot of things to wish for and only one wish? I could go and knock on a lot more doors but I might find a lot more people without any puddings, and then I would have to make a lot more wishes for a lot more puddings! And then I had to make another wish for Robin for her to get well, which would help the wish I'd already made. Suddenly I had a great idea. Yes! Granny wouldn't miss one of her puddings. After all, I heard her say she'd made more this year than ever. So I stirred very hard and wished for Robin to get well, and after I had wished long enough, and stirred long enough, I said, 'Thank you,' and the lady gave me a penny for two sherbet dabs[49], and a kiss for luck to make my wish come true.

I hurried home. When I entered the kitchen there was no one about and the puddings had been placed on the pantry floor. Putting one in a basket, I ran as fast as my legs would carry me down the garden path and into the road. All went well, and arriving at the 'No Pudding' cottage, I placed the pudding on the snow-white kitchen doorstep, running all the way home. It was my bedtime, and as Granny came into the room, I knew something was wrong before she said it!

'My Godfathers!' she exclaimed, 'Somebody's taken one of my puddings.'

'One of your puddings, said Gramp. 'You must be mistaken.'

'There's one missing,' said Granny, 'and I'd like to know which old crony you've given it to.'

'I'll tell you….,' and then Gramp looked at me.

---

49   Sherbet dips or sherbet dabs consist of a small packet of sherbet with a lollipop.

# 10

# CHRISTMAS EVE[50]

At last the long looked-for day had arrived. It was Christmas Eve. It was night-darkness when I slipped out of my little bed in the morning, down the stairs to the living room, just as Gramp was lighting the fire from wood already dried on the hearth. The wood was soon burning brightly on the hot coals from the night before. Gramp carefully added lumps of coal to the fire until it was more black than bright.

I was handed the bellows which always hung from a hook by the grate. With a few puffs the fire was hissing and spluttering with fairy sparks following each other up the chimney. Gramp turned up the wick of the oil lamp to give us more light as we ate our bacon and eggs with fried bread and drank our steaming tea to warm the cockles of our hearts, before we stepped into the now grey day to feed and water the birds. This morning we were extra early. We had so much to do, for the birds' houses must be cleaner than ever now that Uncle Harry, Auntie Flo and our cousins Len and Barrie[51] were due to arrive from Portsmouth in the evening.

I was very proud of my Uncle Harry from Portsmouth. He had served in submarines and had sailed in one of the first that had left Portsmouth just after the war had started in 1914. I loved Uncle's copper ashtray too. This was the one he had made when they were stuck on the bottom of the sea, and I knew that his copper ashtray would be taken out of the cupboard in

---

50   1924

51   In a letter written to one of his cousins in 1995 Barrie expressed his fondness for his family visits to Wootton as a youngster: 'they were always exciting and interesting, especially the ferry trip. I found it very interesting - the crowds of people embarking and disembarking, queuing to get aboard and the cranes loading and unloading the "cages" of luggage and heavy goods. Nothing like that today. One could go down to the engine room to view the engine, clanking and hissing, smell the oil and hear the telegraph ring its orders. Most interesting; never boring.'

the kitchen. Granny had been busy cleaning it the day before, just for Uncle to use. Once again I would listen to the exciting stories of war under the sea before I went to bed.

Everything was all preparation, which I enjoyed so much, unlike Granny who had said, 'If it was not for the preparation, I could enjoy Christmas.' This was a strange thing for Granny to say, especially when after Christmas she always seemed sad and said it was a pity it was all over for another year, and how much she had enjoyed it.

It was nearly ten o'clock that morning before we had finished cleaning the chicken houses. Gramp said, 'Pon my puff, it must be Christmas for the houses to be so clean.'

What a magic word 'Christmas' was, with its renewed nearness. For a time I had forgotten it in all our busyness. I took several deep breaths of joy. I was all happiness. It was then I remembered the little chicken house near the top of the garden which we hadn't cleaned. Gramp explained we could leave it for another day as the four White Leghorns[52] would be moved nearer to the house for us to look after, though I couldn't quite understand why. Gramp had been busy building this new hen house for the last two weeks. I had been allowed to play my part in the wonderful operation of creosoting the outside and whitewashing the inside. Making our way towards the kitchen door, the now sweet smell of new wood and fresh dark creosote added to my contentment.

Indoors, Granny and Mummy had been busy. Sprigs of holly looked out from behind the family pictures hanging from the picture rails. The draw-leaf table was twice its size, with the Hepplewhite[53] dining chairs that once belonged to Gramp's father.[54] They gleamed mahogany-dark, having been freshly polished and brought in from the front room to the dining room. This was because, as Granny said, 'There were going to be so many of us and

---

52  The White Leghorn originally came from Livorno in Italy (Leghorn is the Anglicised name). They were exported to the USA in 1828 and then came to the UK in 1870 (Happy Chicken Coop, The, 2019).

53  George Hepplewhite (1727 – 1786), cabinet maker.

54  Peter Stark 1827 – 1893.

besides you didn't know how many visitors might drop in as well.' Granny sat in the mahogany carver at the end of the table arranging farthings[55] into groups of four. They had been tipped out of an old biscuit box where they lived between Christmases.

'Hevery year,' Granny said, adding her aitch, which was always a sign of something special, 'Hevery year,' she repeated, 'we seem to have more and more farthings. If this goes on much longer, we shall need another box.'

'That's easy to understand,' Gramp smiled, 'for Harry brought over a hundred of his own last year, and he lost the lot, not to mention silver, with the last card game of Bank.'[56]

'Don't play so late Father, this time,' said Granny, 'or you'll knock yourself up[57] again.'

'It was not the Banker that did it,' said Gramp, 'but Mrs Jones with her cold which she exchanged for at least half a bottle of whisky last Christmas. Which reminds me, it's time for a little drop of what does you good!'

To my surprise Granny sat down and said nothing, which was most unusual at this time of the morning. This was another sign that Christmas was here or almost here. I was given a glass with a little of Granny's Guinness in it, whilst even Mummy had a glass of port. With glasses filled, Gramp stood up saying, 'A toast,' giving his whisky a loving sniff. 'Let us toast,' he said looking at me and then looking across the lawn[58], ending, 'There's nothing I can say, that is....'

We were still standing. I longed to take a sip of my Guinness but I knew it would be wrong for me to begin, but in a moment Gramp's face was all happy creases.

---

55  The farthing was a quarter of the pre-decimal penny. It was taken out of circulation on 1 January 1961.

56  Individual card players play against one player who is the banker. In home games, players often play for tokens such as matchsticks or sweets. In the Stark family household they were playing for low value farthings although it says here some silver was lost. In home games, players take it in turns to be the banker so no one is at a disadvantage (Pagat, 2019).

57  Exhaust or make yourself ill (The New Shorter Oxford English Dictionary).

58  This is the green card table felt.

He raised his glass and continued, 'To Peter, for all he has given me, and to all Peter's Christmases. Happy Christmas Peter.'

'Happy Christmas,' we all said, with my 'happy' being a little behind the others.

The Guinness, with its bitter-tongue taste made me feel quite grown-up. One thing I thought and wondered about, while the last froth from the glass trickled slowly into my mouth, was what I had given Gramp. What could it be? I had always shared my bullseyes with Gramp and he had always shared his with me. Was that it? Then I realised what it was. Of course, Gramp must have meant the other day, which he had said had made him feel so young again. This was the day I had shaken half of my Sherbet Fountain[59] into his hand. He looked so funny afterwards with his moustache all sherbet-white. But he did enjoy it, licking his moustache with upturned tongue until every little white speck had gone.

I planned to slip out to the paper shop on the corner later with a half-penny from my money box to buy a Fountain. It would please Gramp to find the Sherbet Fountain wrapped up with his Christmas handkerchief! Granny wanted two kisses for Christmas and Mummy just one. My big brother Morris had said, 'Save all your money for the Banker.' Last year I had won thirteen farthings. Granny had exchanged them for pennies, making the last farthing into a penny so that I had fourpence. I couldn't wait to hear Uncle Harry say, 'Come on, let's clear the table for the Banker!'

'Would you believe it Ethel,' Granny said suddenly, turning to Mummy. 'There's over thirty shillings in farthings here. Just think of what you could have bought for a farthing at one time.'

'They are handy for the Banker,' Mummy replied, 'but as regards other things I find them a nuisance. Everything you buy has to be one and eleven or two and eleven.[60] It always makes it seem so much cheaper than two or

---

59   The Sherbet Fountain was introduced by Barratt in 1925. The sherbet was contained in a paper wrapped cardboard tube with a liquorice 'straw' stuck in the top (Barratt, 2020).

60   This is pre-decimal money of shillings and pence. The one and eleven of that time is like the £1.99 or £2.99 of today's prices where you get a penny change if you pay in cash.

three shillings, but what a job it must be for the shopkeeper in dealing with all those farthings.'

I noticed Gramp, with his face all fixed with thinking, as he refilled his glass, and then he said, 'Not in our time, I don't suppose, but Peter will live to see the day when farthings will be called in and melted down. He might even live to see them turned into ploughshares.[61]

'And no more war,' Mummy added quickly.

'This is a dismal subject for Christmas Eve, talking about what we won't see,' said Granny, 'but I know one thing, say what you like about the farthing; Tim White made a fortune through them. Nothing was too much trouble for Timothy. He would sell you a farthing's worth of anything. Small profits and quick returns was his motto and now there are Timothy Whites[62] everywhere.'

Mummy was about to say something but was interrupted by a loud banging on the kitchen door, followed by the dining room door opening, and there was the butcher, very red-faced, holding a huge turkey by the legs.

'I would give you a good telling off if it wasn't for Christmas Eve, bursting in like this!' said Granny.

'I know you would Ma'am, but seeing it was Christmas Eve, and your name's Hearty[63], and how you'd forgiven me the last time before, I knew it was safe.'

I noticed Granny's face going a little red as she remembered the time before, but we all laughed. Then Gramp handed the butcher a drop of whisky saying, 'Here's a little drop of "how's your father",' which the butcher finished in one go. He was then handed another which he sipped between many 'Happy Christmases' and 'many of them.'

---

61    A ploughshare is the cutting blade of a plough. 'Beating swords into ploughshares' would turn weapons of war into items of peaceful use. Although the reference was to farthings, as this was the period between the First and Second World War, there was hope for peaceful times to come.

62    Timothy White set up as a chemist in 1848 in Portsmouth and qualified as a pharmacist in 1869. By the 1920s they also sold toilet requisites, photographic materials and household items. It was taken over by Boots in 1968 and the name disappeared in 1985.

63    Harriette was known by her friends as Harty but this play on the word Hearty is an allusion to her warm and friendly nature.

I longed to ask the butcher how his father was. I intended to say I was sorry to hear his father was ill at Christmas, but everyone was talking at once. Then Gramp started to play on his brassy whistle-pipe, with Granny and the butcher pretending to waltz to a tune called the *Merry Widow*[64], and another which was called *The Charleston*.[65] At last the butcher, very much out of breath, his face the colour of the station pillar box[66], said, 'I must hurry, it's half past one. You'll find it a good bird. One from Haters Farm. Always the best.'

'I can see by its colour and the feel of its breast bone,' said Gramp, thumb and finger on the bone, 'that it enjoyed life, and will eat well.'

'Here, have another drop of "how's your father" for the road.'

'No, thank you very much Mr Starks',[67] said the butcher. 'Tell you what, put it by for me and I'll drink it on your birthday.'

'That I will do then,' said Gramp, 'but sure you can't manage it now?'

'No thanks again,' replied the butcher. 'You see, I've got a van full of turkeys and meats. By the time I've gone all round the villages, I don't expect I shall finish tonight much before midnight. I've a long time to go.'

With this the butcher slipped a silver threepenny bit into my hand, kissed Granny on both cheeks before she could get her breath, shook Mummy's hand with a slight lowering of his red face, and was going past the dining room window almost before we'd realized he'd gone.

'He's a good butcher, I must say,' said Gramp. 'He's kind-hearted and a man after my own heart, and I'll see to it he has a drink on my birthday.

---

64  *The Merry Widow* was written by Austro-Hungarian composer Franz Lehár (1870–1948) known for his operettas. One of *The Merry Widow's* biggest fans was Adolf Hitler. According to reports, the first thing Hitler did to celebrate the Anschluss with Austria in 1938 was play a recording of the operetta, and during the last two years of the war, he listened to *The Merry Widow* over and over again in his 'Wolf's Lair' headquarters (Opera North, 2018). This is sadly ironic as Peter's wife Ruth escaped from the German Holocaust unlike her parents.

65  *The Charleston* song was composed in 1923 with lyrics by Cecil Mack and music by James P. Johnson (Secondhand Songs, 2019).

66  The red post box at the station.

67  William Stark was also known as Mr Starks.

By the way Mother,' he added to Granny, 'did you give him his Christmas money?'

'Like I always do, a good week ago,' said Granny, 'for good though the butcher is, greasing his palm reminds him to keep remembering us for another year.'

'And that's a part of human nature that will never change. Pon my puff it won't,' added Gramp.

I was just going to ask Gramp about the butcher's father, and why and when Granny greased the butcher's palm and what grease she used, when I was asked to help clean the silver.

Gramp left to go down the hill to post our Christmas parcel to Auntie Millie[68] with all our Christmas cards so they would be sure to arrive on Christmas morning,[69] saying as he left the room, 'Don't wait lunch for me as I shall pop into the Sloop[70] for a Christmas chat.' For once, Granny didn't seem to mind, for all she said was, 'Come back safe and sober,' giving Gramp a little hug! After cleaning the silver, I slipped out and bought Gramp a Sherbet Fountain, which I wrapped in pretty coloured paper with the handkerchief.

With 'how's your father' and 'greasing the butcher's palm' forgotten, I was made to have 'forty winks' on the front room couch after lunch, which was very late as it was Christmas Eve. I was wonderfully happy as I fell asleep, knowing in a few hours' time Auntie Flo, Uncle Harry and my cousins Len and Barrie would arrive and Christmas would really begin.

---

68   Auntie Millie was Mildred Emily Stewart (née Stark) (1888-1960), who was Ethel Lansley's sister.

69   The General Post Office stopped delivering letters on Christmas Day in 1960 in England, Wales and Northern Ireland, and in 1965 in Scotland.

70   This is the Sloop Inn, Wootton Bridge. The Inn goes back to 1782 when Ann Gumm had a half share. The landlord Gramp would have known would have been George Bennett who was landlord from 1906 to 1933 (Wootton Bridge Historical, 2015: 'The Inns of the Village 1775 – 1985').

*Sloop Inn, Wootton, 1905. Unknown original copyright. Assumed in the Public Domain.*

# 11

# CHRISTMAS EVE VISITORS

I awoke to the familiar sound of a spoon striking a teacup. Blinking my eyes with sleepy dust, this made me think it was morning and time to be up. With delightful comfort I could see the flickering firelight on the ceiling. Yet it was unusual to have a fire in the bedroom unless you were ill. I moved my hands, feeling paper and not sheets to the touch, and then I was really awake.

Gramp said, 'Come on, it's teatime. It's after five o'clock, and here's a cup to drive away the cobwebs and warm the cockles.'

As I drank my tea in one go, Gramp sat beside the couch adding to the friendly flickering of the firelight by puffing at a medicated cigarette.

'My puff, you did catch a nice bird, because when I covered you with newspaper you were already away,' Gramp said. 'There's nothing like newspaper to keep you warm,' added Gramp, tickling me under the chin.

I was sad for a moment thinking of the 'bird' I had caught, remembering Daddy was away in the Navy and wouldn't be home this Christmas Eve. Daddy always called 'forty winks' a 'bird' which must be something to do with the sea, I thought. 'Forty winks' must be something to do with the land, for when Tiddles dozed in front of the fire, Granny said, 'Just look at that cat having forty winks.'

But when Daddy was going to rest after his Sunday lunch she would say, 'Go and help your Daddy catch a bird on the couch.'[71] Though 'birds' and 'forty winks' were the same, I always enjoyed catching a 'bird' with Daddy on the couch. Tucked in by the Sunday newspaper, we would sleep, pretending we were in a hammock at sea. At the end of our 'bird,' Daddy would tell me a great sea story where a tiny British ship would fight a big Spanish galleon.

---

71 This means falling asleep and having pleasant dreams indicating prosperity. 'If you dreamed of catching a bird, your dream is supposed to be a good sign, usually indicating prosperity' (Dream Astro Meanings, 2020).

With the sound of 'Borders, repel borders,' cutlass against cutlass, the Spanish Captain would surrender his sword, striking his colours[72] with the British flag flying proudly from the foretop.

'And what's young solemn sides looking so "thinking" about?' asked Gramp, taking an extra puff of his cigarette.

'I was just thinking of Daddy, Gramp, because I know if we had caught a bird together, I would have heard a great sea story with powder kegs, cutlasses and galleons, and how, and how we rule the waves.'

'And it's because we rule the waves,' said Gramp, 'that your Daddy, and thousands more like him as well, won't be home this Christmas. You see it's like when you were catching a bird just now. When you are fast asleep at night, our sailors and soldiers, and even airmen these days, are keeping watch while we're asleep, working or enjoying ourselves, or even doing nothing. They keep watch and guard our shores and Empire every minute of the day. Why, even now, this Christmas Eve, in some parts of the world, our ships will be sailing through beautiful sunshine and calm seas, while in other parts they will be sailing through darkness and maybe rough seas, with the sea coming over the funnels. Because of men like your Daddy, and other little boys' Daddies, we rule the waves, and the sun never sets on the good old Union Jack.'

I was about to ask Gramp about the sun and the Union Jack when Gramp started to cough as he bent forwards taking deep breaths. I jumped from the couch knowing that Gramp had 'got too excited', as Granny called it, so I patted him on the back harder and harder, just in case, in his excitement, smoke had gone down the wrong way!

Suddenly the door opened, and Granny came in with the front room oil lamp, giving a sniff of disgust at the cigarette smoke.

'I can't understand why you have to pollute the air with those things Father, my Godfathers I can't. And they can't do you any good,' said Granny.

'That's where you're wrong Mother,' said Gramp. 'They're good for the tubes!'

---

72 'Striking his colours' means the lowering of the Spanish flag to be replaced by the British flag indicating surrender.

'Tubes or no tubes Father, I can't think enough of you. They will be here in just over an hour. I have to make the beds up for Len and Morris in here, not to mention the other beds. A fine pair you are at Christmas I must say,' said Granny.

'No place for us wicked ones,' replied Gramp, squeezing my hand. 'Here! Let's go upstairs and look at Portsmouth. We might see the steamer moving out.'

Everything was different with Christmas as we climbed the stairs. There was a little oil lamp on the hall table casting holly shadows against the wall. Reaching the upstairs landing, I could see the flickering warm firelight coming from each open bedroom door. At last we were along the corridor into the front bedroom. With Gramp sitting me on his shoulders, we looked out towards the glittering fairy lights of mainland Portsmouth.

'I think I can see the steamer[73] moving,' said Gramp.

I pressed my nose against the cold window pane and wondered how Gramp could see all that way.

'I can't see anything but the flickering lights Gramp,' I said.

'You might if I black out the firelight,' replied Gramp, drawing the curtains around us like a tent.

'Oh yes! I can see even better now,' continued Gramp. 'Why there's Uncle Harry walking along the deck, and there he goes, he's just gone down the stairs to get a drink at the bar!'

'You can't, you didn't really see him Gramp, did you?' I cried, flattening my nose against the cold window with renewed effort, trying to catch the slightest movement within the twinkling lights across the sea.

'Yes! And there's the name. I do believe it's the *Solent* steamer,'[74] said Gramp, giving my ribs a playful tickle.

---

73 This would be the Portsmouth-Ryde ferry.

74 This could have been the *PS Solent* II acquired in 1923 and disposed of in 1948. However, as it sailed between Lymington and Yarmouth this may have been incorrectly identified (Paddle Steamers, 2019).

'Come on you two,' said Mummy, interrupting. 'It's teatime. It will be nice to get ours over soon. Then we can give all our time to them when they arrive. Depend on it, they'll be cold after their journey.'

In the dining room it was suggested I should have a lightly boiled egg.

'This would do him most good,' Mummy said, 'because he's so excited.' And in Granny's ear I heard her say, 'It's the easiest and quickest thing to do.'

'That's it,' replied Granny. 'Let us all have lightly boiled eggs. That will be nice!'

'But I don't want a lightly boiled egg,' I said, and added 'I'm not excited.'

'Objection overruled,' said Gramp, which made me smile with Gramp, as I knew he was thinking of the last Ashey races when first Gramp's horse won and he was very pleased, and then the red flag was up and he was miserable. And then Gramp jumped high in the air when, as he put it, 'the objection was overruled' with the green flag, and he had won after all.

'Are you going to have a lightly boiled egg too, Gramp?' I asked.

'Yes of course!' said Gramp.

'Then I'll have one to make things easy,' I said.

With this, I saw Mummy look at Granny, and Granny look at Gramp. Though Gramp didn't say anything, I knew he was very pleased as he gave my cheek a little pinch. In a moment the eggs were brought in by Granny. Gramp turned the wick of the oil lamp up in order for us to see what we were eating. I had been told more than once that watching people eat was very rude. However, I found it both interesting and funny. Granny had a very fixed expression about her face as if eating her egg was the most important thing in the world, whereas Mummy ate her egg with little dips of her spoon as if she was afraid of it. Gramp, however, ate his as if it was a real treat, quickly starting on his second egg because he had mentioned that he thought he could manage two. Every now and then he smiled in my direction between mouthfuls of bread 'doorsteps'—no lady slices for Gramp! I now joined in with great enjoyment, eating my way through a crust which Gramp said reminded him of half a loaf. Placing my second crust on my side plate, I continued the eating-watching game. Granny had a piece of yellow egg on her chin. Would it fall? It moved up and down, up and down, until I thought

I would burst. At last it fell with a little splash right into Granny's teacup. I giggled so much I thought I would never stop. Everyone wanted to know the joke.

Gramp said, 'Whisper in my ear,' but every time I tried to whisper, one of Gramp's long white hairs from his ear tickled me on the nose. This made me laugh more and more, until at last Gramp said, 'Tell you what, tell me later,' so at last I stopped giggling and spread treacle in little rivers on the rest of my crust. Tea over, Gramp lit another medicated cigarette, and Granny said from the head of the table, 'Let's sit a little before we clear away, as we won't have much time later.'

While eating my treacled crust, I started thinking, and then placing my crust on the plate I even forgot to carry on eating. I could feel my cheeks burning hot from the fire and this made my thoughts wander even further. It felt as if, somewhere within myself, my eyes were looking at the pages of some giant fairy tale picture book as I turned page after page. Granny was wearing her best woollen dress, making her have, what Gramp called, a 'full figure,' which he liked. This made me giggle inside. To me, Granny's figure looked like an upside down five. From Granny I looked sideways at Gramp who was now and again puffing at his cigarette, his eyes smiling with little side creases. He was wearing his best dark blue suit with a white shirt and his 'Forester'[75] tie, which made me very proud as it was very secret. His silver watch chain, with attached silver compass, glittered in the oil light. Every now and then he would take his watch from his waistcoat pocket, snap back

---

75    He must have been a member of the Ancient Order of Foresters Friendly Society, Court 1821 (Island Foresters). The society was founded in 1834. Members recognised that 'they had a duty to assist their fellow men and women who sometimes needed help 'as they walked through the forests of life.' This need arose principally when a breadwinner fell ill, could not work and received no wages […].Back then, Members recognised that by paying a few pence a week into a common fund, they would be able to offer sick pay and funeral grants when needed' (Foresters Friendly Society, 2019). The Wootton Bridge Lodge of Foresters used to hold their Forest Day annual event at the Sloop where they sat down to 'a good substantial dinner' and in fine weather they paraded with their regalia behind the Brass Band around the village (Gosden, 2002, pp 3-5). Edmund Morris, Granny Harriette's father, belonged to a similar society, the Earl Yarborough Lodge of Oddfellows, now known as the Vecta Branch, Newport. Such societies provided financial support and security before the introduction of the NHS, Social Security and the State Pension.

the silver cover and look at the time. He didn't really want to know the time, as Granny often told me, but he looked at it because he loved his watch and this was his way of showing it. Gramp's white moustache and his silver hair sparkled like silver chocolate paper. The front and the top of his head had no hair because it was too tired to grow anymore. As Granny often said, the top of his head was 'like a pinky bladder of lard.' In Gramp's boots I could see the mantelpiece looking back at me. I looked at Mummy playing with her wedding ring, dressed in her Handley's costume, so named because it was bought at Handley's[76]. It was all purple and bright.

Gramp coughed with his smoke, taking quick breaths. It was only the other day I'd overheard Mummy saying to Granny, 'I don't think Father's too well, do you?'

Granny had looked very sad, and then said, 'No! He hasn't been well for some time, though he never complains and won't see the doctor. That's the trouble, none of us can live forever.'

'None of us can live forever,' I thought.

Taking a deep breath I pushed my plate with half-eaten treacled crust away. I knew Gramp wouldn't mind going to Mount Joy, and of course he would play a silver whistle-pipe. He would love that, but I wished Gramp could live forever—Mummy, Granny, Daddy and me as well.

'What's the matter with you Peter,' Mummy asked, feeling my cheeks with both hands. 'You are flushed, and your cheeks *are* burning. And you've stopped eating. Do you think he's sickening for something?' she asked, turning to Granny.

Gramp finished his cigarette throwing the end in the fire.

'Pon my puff, Ethel,' he said to Mummy, 'how many times do you sit and just think?' adding, 'and no penny for his thoughts this time!'

'Here, Peter,' Gramp said, almost as if he knew, 'come and sit on my knee.'

---

76   Handley's was a fashionable emporium founded in 1869 by George Handley in Palmerston Road, Southsea. After his death in 1926 the business was continued by his sons Douglas, George and Trevor. The store was destroyed by a German bombing raid during the Second World War and was rebuilt becoming part of the Debenhams chain (The News, 2019).

I climbed onto Gramp's knee, playing with his watch chain, as Mummy and Granny cleared the table. The old bracket-clock struck six o'clock quickly, like it had a train to catch.

Gramp looked at his watch and said, 'Yes! It's keeping perfect time since I adjusted the pendulum. It's right by my watch, and that means it's right by the Newport Town Hall clock. My puff, your Uncle Harry will soon be here!'

I smiled, closing my eyes, as Gramp stroked my hair like he was stroking the cat. I felt drowsy and happy, wriggling my toes with contentment within my buttoned slippers. I awoke with Gramp digging me in the ribs saying, 'You've had a little nap. Let's go outside and see if we can hear their train.'

Outside it was cold and very dark as we stood at the back door. There was no light to be seen anywhere until suddenly footsteps and a flickering oil light appeared coming up the path showing red one side and green on the other. My big brother Morris turned the wick of his cycle oil lamp out as he joined us.

'You'll get it!' I said, imitating Morris. 'You're late, and I've eaten all the treacle, and you won't have any tea 'cause they've just cleared the table.'

'You greedy kid,' said Morris, 'You haven't,' he said.

'I have,' I said.

'You haven't!' he said.

I hadn't, of course, and Morris knew I hadn't, but all our greetings were always, as Gramp put it, 'sensational,' like an early morning newspaper.

'They arrived yet?' Morris shouted, as he entered the house.

'See next week!' I shouted back, giving the most unsatisfactory reply I could think of, like the ending of each part of the serial in my weekly comic.

'They won't be long now,' Gramp said, cupping his ear. 'Listen.'

I listened, and there it was, the puff, puff of the Ryde to Cowes train.

'It must have just left Havenstreet Station,' continued Gramp, 'and allowing ten minutes for the walk from the station, and the time for Havenstreet to Wootton, they should be here in a quarter of an hour.'

'My puff, it's cold,' added Gramp, sniffing the air, 'and by the sound of the train it wouldn't surprise me if it snowed.'

'Might it snow?' I shouted, jumping up and down. 'It will snow won't it Gramp? Say it will snow.'

'I'll bet ten to one on it does,' replied Gramp, much to my delight, for I knew ten to one on would be a very good horse.

'It'll snow before midnight,' said Gramp turning to Granny. 'Bet you kisses after midnight there will be snow before midnight.'

Granny looked up from her biscuit making, catching Gramp's wink meant for me. 'My Godfathers, there'll be no after-midnight kisses for you, you old rascal, snow or no snow. After midnight, indeed, at your age!'

I noticed with pleasure that Granny did however enjoy the bet and I had a feeling that win or lose, snow or no snow, Gramp would have his after-midnight kisses. After midnight of course, because Granny would be much too busy with Christmas until then.

'Too cold for us mortals,' said Gramp. 'Let's go in and have a warm, and then you can help me put the glasses on the tray, and get the drinks ready. That's a man's job.'

I went into the warmth of the kitchen with the kitchen range bars all hot to help Gramp carry a 'selection,' as he called it, of beer bottles to put on the dining room sideboard. This was so that Uncle Harry could 'back his fancy' and take his pick if he wanted beer, or 'How's your Father' if he wanted whisky, with port or sherry for the ladies. For the 'boys,' as we were called, were bottles of lemonade, though I would have preferred Guinness. Some of the bottles were coloured and flavoured strawberry, lime and orange. What I liked most about them was not the contents but the marbles in their throats, as Gramp called them, which I used to collect.[77] Gramp used to break the necks of the bottles carefully, and let me have the marbles. He explained that this made them very dear as you didn't get your deposit back on the bottles.

Between mouthfuls of treacled bread and butter, Morris helped Gramp polish the cut glass wine glasses and tumblers, arranging them on the tray.

---

[77] In 1872 Hiram Codd of Suffolk developed a bottle that used the effervescent pressure of the mineral water to force a marble against a rubber washer in the upper ring of the neck of the bottle making a very efficient and durable seal. Codd's invention was so effective in England that it was implemented by nearly all the English fizzy drink manufacturers of the time (Ruger, 2018).

*Uncle Harry & Auntie Flo's Wedding 11 June 1910 © C M Lansley*

I was not allowed to polish them in case, Gramp explained, I should break the glass, as cut glass was very valuable, and besides I might cut myself. Then there would be trouble.

'Cut glass from Waterford,' said Granny, which seemed just right to me, as glass and water went together and being so thin, it would break and cut your hand if you didn't watch out.

'Cut glass' and 'Waterford' was sensible but 'tumbler' was silly. As Mummy always said, 'Mind you don't tumble down the stairs.' A tumbler would break if it did! I was just about to ask Gramp why a tumbler was called a 'tumbler,' when, just like the unmistakable sound of Great Uncle Albert's[78] pigeons,

---

78   Albert Edward Stark (1863-1952), was William Stark's brother. He ran a grocer's shop in Cowes and helped Harriette set up her stock at her own grocer's shop at 2 Cyprus Terrace, Adelaide Grove, East Cowes. Albert died seven weeks after his wife Emily, and the money from the sale of his house was willed to the Carisbrooke Pigeon Fanciers Club and provided for a Stark Memorial Trophy.

I heard voices and the sound of feet on the gravel path which could only mean one thing. Suddenly there were Uncle Harry, Auntie Flo, big cousin Len and small cousin Barrie with everyone talking, hugging and kissing at once. They had come with Mickey the dog as he couldn't be left behind. Our old cat Tiddles was spitting and swearing at Mickey and had to be saved by Uncle Harry with Gramp opening the living room window for Tiddles to be pushed out, still spitting and swearing as he disappeared into the cold night.

At last with everyone's outside coats off and everything stowed away and 'shipshape,' as Uncle Harry put it, I sat proudly on Uncle Harry's knee sliding my fingers along the gold braid of his navy uniform. Gramp meanwhile served sherry to Auntie Flo because he knew she liked sherry, and port to Mummy. He then asked Uncle Harry, 'What do you fancy Harry?'

'A drop of short Father, because I already had a couple of whiskys in the bar coming over, and I'd better keep to it.'

'There you are Peter,' said Gramp, turning to me. 'Didn't I say I could see Uncle Harry from the window upstairs walking along the deck going down to the bar?' Before I could reply, with Uncle Harry smiling all over his face, Gramp asked, 'And it was the *Solent* you came over in wasn't it?'

'Yes it was, yes it was,' shouted Barrie jumping up and down, his red hair joining his freckles.

'That kid,' Morris shouted, pointing at me, 'will believe everything.'

I was about to shout back in defence when Granny slipped a tumbler half-filled with Guinness into my hand as a special Christmas Eve treat, as we all raised our glasses to a 'Merry Christmas.' As soon as I could I asked, 'Uncle Harry, how is it Gramp can see so far when he can't read without his glasses, as I couldn't see the boat from upstairs?' Everyone laughed for some reason, and then Uncle Harry said, 'Why, when you reach your Gramp's age you can even see round corners!'

'And don't you start,' said Uncle Harry quickly to Morris. Whatever Morris was going to say he didn't.

So that was it. Now I knew Gramp's secret. No wonder he knew what I was up to in the garden when I was out of sight! I'd certainly have to be careful in future. But if he could see round corners and all the way across to

Portsmouth in the dark, I didn't see how it would be any use being careful anyway!

I was just a little envious when Granny also treated Barrie to Guinness, and Morris and Len were allowed more than just a taste which was more than I got. However, unlike Barrie, I very often had a sip of Granny's Guinness and so I wasn't envious anymore.

I listened to Uncle Harry and Gramp talking about their luck on the horses.

'On the QT,'[79] I heard Gramp say, 'I had a good treble up a couple of weeks ago and I won,' and here his voice dropped, and try as I could, I couldn't hear what Gramp said.

'Auntie,' I said to Auntie Flo, as soon as there was quiet between Granny, Mummy and Auntie Flo, 'what does "on the QT" mean?'

'It means you want to keep something secret,' said Auntie Flo quickly.

Gramp pinched my cheek suddenly looking all fixed. I then understood and he laughed. He was very pleased when I tried to give him a wink, which I could never seem to do as both my eyes always blinked at once! But he went on smiling and gave me a wink so he understood!

'Father,' Granny said to Gramp, 'just climb up on a chair and see to that curtain ring. That's what comes of not drawing them properly with the walking stick.'

I noticed the curtain eye had slipped out of one of the large wooden curtain rings and as Gramp saw to it he said, 'Pon my puff! I've backed a winner. It's snowing heavens hard!'

There was a mad rush from the living room. Len won the race and threw open the back door revealing the white night treasured in all its fairy beauty. Thousands of silver starry-crosses chased and followed each other until they became part of the white, cushioned world. It gleamed in the kitchen lamp-

79  'On the QT' means 'secretly' or 'in confidence'. QT is short for quiet. 'On the QT' gained popularity when it appeared in an 1891 minstrel show number called 'Ta-ra-ra-boom-de-ay' (Phrase Finder, 2019).

light, until dying away at the old pear tree on the lawn, it joined a darker white reaching old Joliffe's[80] hedge on the edge of a white, white forest.

Breathless and speechless in the different-tasting air, I didn't join my brother and cousins in their footprints of ever increasing circles, but remained waiting for a trapper to appear with his huskies. Perhaps soon I would hear the call of a wolf. But instead of my wolf, I heard Gramp's voice close to my ear saying, 'Hold out your sleeve Peter and catch the flowers of the night, and then if we're quick enough I'll show you something wonderful.' Gramp took my blue-pullovered arm and held it under the falling snowflakes. He then pulled me into the kitchen and said, 'Look! Each snowy flower has six petals, all with different shapes, but all of them have six petals.'

'Yes!' I said excitedly, 'They have, they have,' but as I spoke they disappeared into little drops of water. Gramp explained that the warm air was jealous of the cold air and that this always happened when they met. But he said that the flakes hitting the cold of the ground would stay until the warmer weather came and that this would not be until after Christmas. This made me very, very happy and Gramp was happy too.

---

80   One of the neighbours.

# 12

# THE CAROL SINGERS

Back in the living room our glasses were refilled, but this time I had to be content in having lemonade with Morris, Len and Barrie. This pleased me as it would mean I would get four extra marbles from the bottle-throats. Auntie Flo said she was sure I would get the 'wind' and a fizzy nose drinking my lemonade so fast. Granny said she hoped I wouldn't 'retch'[81] after all the mixtures I had had, though what it was I would 'reach' for I couldn't understand. Suddenly feeling about to burst, I let out a sound which Auntie Flo said was inhuman. Gramp said he thought it was more human than inhuman and everyone laughed until Mummy, looking very serious, said, 'Though I know Peter didn't mean to do it, it's wrong for us to make fun of it because he might forget and do it when we are having something out.'

For some reason Uncle Harry found this so funny he nearly choked, saying between coughs, 'How I'd love to be there when he does!' Gramp, taking his brassy whistle-pipe from the sideboard, played a little tune with Uncle Harry singing over and over again, 'How I'd love to be there when he does,' making Auntie Flo look even more serious. Granny then chimed in saying, 'Laugh and grow fat,[82] that's what I say. My Godfathers, no wonder you are so lean, you don't laugh enough!'

At once everyone stopped talking and laughing hearing another sound. Gramp was listening intently with his head on one side, just like the Rhode Island Red Cockerel would do when it was listening out for feeding time. From the direction of the kitchen back door came the singing of *Away in*

---

81  'Retch' can also be pronounced in the same way as 'reach' thus Peter's misunderstanding here (see Oxford Concise Dictionary).

82  'Laugh and grow fat' is an encouragement to be cheerful rather than solemn as laughter can relieve stress. Not long ago, unlike today, being fat was a sign of good health.

*a Manger,* along with other carols I'd never heard before. Everyone looked fixed with thinking. Mickey tried to bark, but Uncle Harry held his jaws.

'Let them sing for a bit,' said Gramp, 'and then we will ask them in.'

We tiptoed with Gramp into the kitchen. When they had finished *Away in a Manger*, Gramp opened the door.

Three boys were there. With their legs red with cold, they looked like three small snowmen. Only the tallest one with a piano around his neck wore a cap. This, together with his redder-than-red face and black hatpin-eyes, made him look like the top of an iced cake.

'A Merry Christmas,' the three boys said together, with the 'iced cake's' voice coming from underneath the other voices like a grown-up man with a cold.

'A Merry Christmas,' we all answered. Gramp stood to one side, saying, 'Come in.' Little pools of water collected on the stone kitchen floor as Mummy took the melted 'ice-cake's' cap and dripping snow-water coats to hang behind the brown 'Odds and Sods' cupboard door.

'Goodness, what a night to be out,' exclaimed Mummy, which made me think, 'what a wonderful night to be out.' The best chairs from the living room now mixed with the kitchen chairs. We all sat around the kitchen range with its shining bars and red hot coals. The three boy carol singers were each handed a wine glass of fine old port, as Gramp named it. To my joy I was given a whole wine glass full of Granny's Guinness. This made me feel very important compared to Barrie's lemonade, though he didn't seem to notice, which made me sorry.

To Gramp's 'A very Merry Christmas to you all,' we all stood up. With Uncle Harry's, 'And many of them,' we all took big sips, repeating, 'Many of them' as we sat down.

The three boys had walked, they said, from 'Fishhouse.' Mummy quickly corrected this to 'Fishbourne,' adding, 'And fancy on such a night.' Gramp said it was a good two miles at least and that he had walked it many a time, there and back, when he went to the Fishbourne Arms[83] on a Sunday to give him an appetite for Sunday dinner.

No one talked for a little bit. You could tell everyone was thinking hard about the walk on such a night. For a moment the kitchen was quiet, as if it were all alone, apart from the sound of the oil lamp which you could always hear if you listened hard. This was accompanied by the warming sound of the hot coals moving behind the bars of the kitchen range making me yawn with happiness. I kept saying to myself, 'I must be careful not to yawn again in case Mummy said it was my sleepy time.' Gramp also knew what Mummy was about to say to me, but before she could say it, and with a quick wink at me, he gave a big yawn followed by another, saying it must be the hot room.

'Time we had a singsong,' said Gramp, taking his brassy whistle-pipe from his inside pocket to the admiring glances of the carol singers as he ran over the scales. The big boy stood up, piano around his neck, running his fingers over the white keys, making the scales float through the air like greased lightning, as Uncle Harry described it later. He told me that the piano was an accordion. This sounded much more like music to me than a piano so I made up my mind to buy and play an accordion as soon as I was grown-up. I thought it would be great fun, especially on Christmas Eve, to play the accordion and be treated to wine in people's houses. With a nod from Gramp, both whistle-pipe and accordion joined together in, *Come All Ye Faithful*. All of us joined in the singing at the top of our voices.

Carol after carol was played, with in between drinks and biscuits, and more drinks until at last the carol Gramp said he loved the best, *Silent Night*, was played and sung. It finished with everyone clapping their hands and Uncle Harry handing round his Navy cap for a collection, which he started with half a crown.

'And now,' Mummy said, looking at me, 'I think we had better call it a day.'

But I was careful not to yawn and was very pleased when Gramp said, 'Not yet, I would like to have two of my favourite hymns for this special

---

83   Now known as The Fishbourne.

occasion, *There Is A Green Hill Far Away*, and author Midlane's, *There Is A Friend For Little Children.*'

I then heard Uncle Harry say to Auntie Flo that author Midlane[84] had been a member of the family with Auntie Flo replying that she had heard this forty thousand times before. This made me laugh, for who could have ever told this to Auntie forty thousand times, and now Uncle Harry had told her again! I giggled and giggled. Before Auntie Flo leaves, I thought, I would tell her again just to see if she remembered to add it on to the forty thousand.

'And what's biting you?' Gramp asked me, but I giggled and giggled so much I couldn't tell him, and then he said, 'You would laugh to see a pudding crawl',[85] tickling me under the chin. With this I saw one of Granny's Christmas puddings crawling along the table which seemed to me to be the funniest thing of all and in the end we were all laughing our heads off. Uncle Harry said, 'When the wine's in, the wit's out,' whatever that meant, which started the grown-ups into renewed laughter. I joined in as hard as I could, though I couldn't understand why.

Gramp wiped the tears of laughter from his red cheeks with his snowy-white breast pocket handkerchief, starting to play, *There's a Green Hill Far Away Without a City Wall* on his brassy whistle-pipe making everyone look fixed with thinking. Then the verses were sung followed by the tune again with the accordion and Gramp's whistle-pipe finishing with *There is a Friend for Little Children.* The three carol singers sang this all by themselves at Gramp's request. The accordion and whistle-pipe finished softly, as if not wanting to end, with everyone looking different now, taking deep breaths, like people do

---

84  This was Albert Midlane (1825-1909) born in Carisbrooke and buried at Carisbrooke Cemetery (Mount Joy). He was a British poet who wrote several hundred hymns. His most famous hymn was *There Is A Friend For Little Children*. His first hymn which brought him eventual fame was *God Bless our Sunday Schools*. This was written on 24 May 1844 and used the National Anthem as its tune (Ennever, 2019). He also wrote *The Vecta Garland, and Isle of Wight Souvenir; Consisting of Original Poems on the Scenery and Beauty of the Isle of Wight* published in 1860 by Richard Griffin and Co. He had an Ironmonger's shop at 29, Upper St. James' Street, Newport. Albert's brother, Egbert Midlane (1823-1883), married Eliza Stark (1820-1863) who was William Stark's aunt, the sister of William Stark's father, Peter Stark (1827-1893).

85  'To laugh to see a pudding crawl' means someone is easily amused and will laugh at anything.

on a railway station platform when seeing people off to the mainland for the Ryde to Portsmouth boat.

Uncle Harry stood up and said, 'Ladies and Gentlemen, The King.'

I stood very proudly beside Uncle Harry, with my feet together, my chest out, and my arms by my sides, not blinking even an eyelid until *God Save the King* was finished. But I didn't cease to wonder, within my mind, what our King had ever done to need God to save him so often. He must be a very great man to be always in such great danger, I thought, making me continue to ponder over the fact that he was my King.

With much handshaking, and many Merry Christmases, the three boys walked out into the snow-lit night. The flakes were still falling, much to my delight. Uncle Harry said their feet sounded like 'muffled oars'[86] as they walked down the garden path. At the garden gate both the accordion and their voices were carried to us with *We wish you a Merry Christmas, a Merry Christmas and a Happy New Year*. Back in the warm living room, the chairs had now been returned. Barrie was so tired he had fallen asleep with his head on the table and had to be carried to his little bed in the middle bedroom. While he was still asleep, Gramp undressed him, with me watching and dozing between his shoes being removed and his nightshirt being put on. Gramp tucked him in saying he was more dead than alive.

In the bathroom, Gramp gave me a lick with Granny's scented face flannel, leaving my ears and teeth because it was Christmas Eve. But with his eyes creasing at the corners, Gramp explained we would more than make up for it the next day even though it would be Christmas. Gramp tucked me in within my little bed beside Mummy's big brass bedstead. It always gave such wonderful reflections of the firelight from its brass knobs. You could unscrew them at terrific speed when no one was looking. Smiling with contentment I noticed my pillowcase was all ready for Father Christmas. It was hanging

---

86  Oars are muffled by putting some matting or canvas round the loom when rowing to prevent it making a noise against the tholes or in the rowlocks. This was done in war time if rowing near enemy ships or batteries (Definitions, 2020). As a Naval Officer this would be an action Uncle Harry would be familiar with.

from the rail of my little bed, like a flag on a windless day. I felt sure it would soon be filled with exciting-looking boxes of fascinating shapes.

Gramp clasped my hands together, and after my prayers he said he had never heard so many God Blesses in all his puff! Then I thought of Mickey just in time. I hoped God would see to it somehow that both Tiddles and Mickey would have a Merry Christmas and that they would not meet to spoil it, though I was rather sorry for Tiddles as it was, after all, Tiddles' home.

'Are you sure now you haven't forgotten anyone?' Gramp asked as he was about to leave. 'Just in case,' he continued, 'let us say God Bless everyone everywhere, and all the animals and all the birds.'

So we said God Bless all the animals and all the birds everywhere together. Gramp gave me a final tuck in leaving the door ajar with a piece of firewood.

Gramp had no sooner left the room when I remembered something very important, which we had both forgotten. 'Gramp,' I called. 'Something very important.'

'My puff,' said Gramp. 'What's that?'

'Why, we have a fire in every grate in the house. How will Father Christmas manage? Last Christmas you said it was quite alright as Father Christmas would have no trouble. We didn't have a fire in the bedroom then. We only had the oil stove which made those beautiful rings on the ceiling.'

'Did I say that about not having a fire?' asked Gramp.

'Yes Gramp, you did!'

For a moment there was silence from outside the bedroom door, though I could hear Gramp taking long breaths.

'There's no need for any of us to worry,' said Gramp at last.

'But what will Father Christmas do?' I asked excitedly.

'It's a very simple thing,' said Gramp, 'for I should have remembered to have told you before. You see, Father Christmas carries a little magic gold key on a gold chain around his neck, and it can open any door in the whole wide world. Of course, it's far easier in the normal way to come down the chimney when he comes over the rooftops. But if there's a fire in the grate he just tethers his reindeer to the chimney pot, unlocks the back door with his magic key, comes quickly upstairs, fills the stockings and pillows and is on his rounds again almost as quickly as he would have been if he'd gone down the chimney. And being Father Christmas, he understands these things because it's all a part of his job. You can rest assured our house is not the only house in the village tonight with a fire in every room. I'll leave a plate of ham sandwiches and a bottle of Granny's Guinness on the table for him. That will please him.'

'Thanks Gramp,' I said, already half-asleep, wriggling my toes with contentment, hearing just briefly the sound of laughter from the living room below as I gave an extra 'God Bless' for Gramp.

# 13

# CHRISTMAS MORNING

It was all dark when I awoke, apart from the slight glow of the fire from the grate which just showed the mantel shelf and that part of the ceiling above. I raised myself on my elbow, looking towards my pillowcase hanging in darkness at the end of my bed.

There was not a sound from the house, from within or without. I hoped it was still snowing. With anticipated happiness I wondered if Father Christmas had called, though I was sure in my mind he had, for it must have been a very long time ago Gramp had left me judging by the loneliness of the fire.

I listened very hard for any movement, cupping both my ears as Gramp did, trying to catch the most silent step, but all I could hear this time was the reassuring sound of Mummy breathing from the big bed. I was just thinking of creeping out of bed to my pillowcase, when suddenly a piece of half-burnt-through wood became stranded on the firebricks at the back of the grate and slipped down with a shower of sparks onto the coals below. It burst into flames, lighting the whole bedroom with its magic light. I looked towards my pillowcase, thrilled with excitement, noticing how it bulged in all places with different-shaped packages and boxes.

One shape near the top of my pillowcase must be my asked-for Hornby train engine, and the two shapes further down I suspected were the two Pullman railway carriages[87] I had wanted to add to my 'rolling stock,' as it was called. But there was something most strange making the pillow stick out into a kind of point on the other side. What could it be, I wondered? Perhaps it was something Gramp had especially asked for, for me!

---

87    Pullman carriages were first-class coaches with a steward service provided by the British Pullman Car Company (PCC) from 1874 until 1962, and then by British Rail from 1962 until 1972.

As I wondered, the fire flickered and died leaving but a large black shape for my pillowcase. I nestled down into my bed again, thinking and thinking so hard about this shape and what it was, that without knowing I was soon fast asleep.

When I awoke next, it was still quite dark with no glow at all from the fire, but there seemed to be a whiteness coming from the sides of the window curtains and from downstairs I could hear sounds of movement. I gave a little cough, followed by another cough and then a very big cough which brought the desired result from Mummy's bed of, 'Merry Christmas, nice little bird to taste.' Whenever Mummy called me a 'nice little bird to taste,' it meant I could do almost as I liked. So with a quick, 'Merry Christmas Mummy' and an even quicker, 'Can I light my candle and look at my presents?' I groped around until I found the matchbox with its one match sticking out from under its lid so you wouldn't have to fumble with matches in the dark. Very carefully I lit my candle which was all straight and new and held fast in its newly-cleaned Christmas candlestick. In a moment the candle had settled down, lighting the room.

I jumped out of bed to get to my pillowcase and quickly opened the top, revealing all the fascinating boxes and, most of all, the big peculiar present all wrapped up in paper with the long thing sticking out of it. Without bothering to open them, I put all the boxes onto my bed. I knew they contained my Hornby engine and carriages and this made way for lifting out this strangely-shaped present. It seemed to have a handle at the top and a handle at the side. At last it was out onto my bed. I tugged away at the string. Why oh why did presents have to be so closely wrapped, I thought, when all you wanted to do was to see what it was as quickly as you could. I couldn't stand trying to undo the string any longer and with one pull I ripped the paper revealing a bright shiny object. Another rip and there it was. I jumped up and down with delight. 'Gramp, I mean Father Christmas, I mean Gramp' I shouted to Mummy, 'has given me my own new galvanized iron watering can!' 'All my very, very own,' I added.

'Which just proves,' Mummy said, 'how Father Christmas listened to Gramp.'

The watering can itself was filled with oranges, sweets and all sorts of nice things, including apples and pears from our own store of 'keepers,' which I had helped gather near the end of summer. But a watering can of my very own! That was *something*.

'I think I can hear Gramp moving about downstairs,' Mummy said, 'and if you dress quickly and put on all your warmest clothes, I think he has something else for you which was impossible for Father Christmas to put in your pillowcase.'

I dressed quickly and silently so as not to disturb the others who were still fast asleep. Besides, I wanted Gramp all to myself.

My heart jumped an extra jump, or so it seemed, as I pulled on my thick outdoor woollen pullover. Whatever it was, it must mean the present was something in the garden. Not forgetting my shiny new watering can, and without so much as a glance at the bathroom, I tiptoed downstairs to find everything already lit up by the hall oil lamp. I found Gramp in the living room just finishing his bacon.

'Merry Christmas Peter,' Gramp said, 'and thank you for the Sherbet Fountain. It's just what I wanted, and I'll have it later today after my Christmas nap.'

Gramp pushed his plate to one side giving me a hug.

'And thank you Gramp for the wonderful watering can Father Christmas brought me,' adding quickly, 'it's just what I wanted!'

'Yes, I knew you would like it,' Gramp said, 'but really the can is a part of your other present. It's light enough now. Let's go into the garden.'

With my hand in Gramp's, we entered the garden with the white world of soft, soft snow helping the light of slow-coming day. We had only gone a few crunchy steps when Gramp stopped at the new hen house he had made. This time I noticed the covered-in run was occupied by the four hens who I usually fed in the run, up the garden.

'And there you are Peter,' Gramp was saying. 'There's your present, just from me. The four hens are now all yours along with the henhouse and you can have a special place in the food shed for their food.'

'You really do mean it Gramp? Are they really mine?' I asked, jumping up and down, causing the hens to answer back and say, 'What's a matter, what's a matter!' amongst themselves.

'Yes,' Gramp replied, 'they're yours now for keeps, not that they were not really yours before as you've done most of the looking after.'

I put my hands right round Gramp's legs, and gave him a big, big hug. Then together, we walked to the run door. I reached up, opening it, taking out the wooden peg from the clasp, and we entered the run. At once one of the hens, whom I called Emily because she reminded me of Aunt Emily[88] when she was alive, crouched down on her legs, arching her wings, head on one side, to be stroked. As I stroked her soft, feathered neck she closed her eyelids with delight. At once Auntie Aggie[89], named after Granny's other sister, came over all talking, giving Emily a quick peck, arching and spreading her wings for her turn. I then stroked each one, saying 'Merry Christmas' with each stroke, until Gramp said he thought we had better return to the house for my Christmas breakfast.

The bracket-clock struck the hour as we entered the house and Gramp busied himself cooking my favourite breakfast, giving me an extra slice of bacon with another tomato because it was a special day. Meanwhile, I was allowed to warm some milk on the kitchen range for Tiddles who entered the kitchen as if, Gramp said, she had something on her mind. With every few laps of her milk, she would look expectantly around the kitchen. It was then I remembered Mickey who had been forgotten with the other happenings. Gramp explained he had been kept safely away from Tiddles as he had had a bad dream in the night and had woken up barking. Uncle Harry thought this might have been because of Tiddles so he had taken Mickey upstairs to their bedroom to sleep to make sure he was out of harm's way. 'You see,' Gramp said, 'I expect being in a strange house made Mickey restless. Animals are just like us really, when it comes down to it, only they have four feet.

---

88   This is the Aunt Emily who came to lunch in an earlier chapter.

89   This is Agnes Ellen Morris (1863-1936). She was married to Walter William Moore (1862-1936). He was an engineer at J.S. White's Shipbuilding Yard, Cowes.

I had just finished my last piece of fried bread and a second cup of tea in the living room when everything became all laughter, barks and voices. Gramp winked at me and said, 'I think I'll go and feed the birds.' With this signal, I slipped out with Gramp almost unnoticed by the others into the garden. 'Christmas or not, the birds need their breakfast just as we do,' Gramp reminded me.

We did the watering first. How proud I was of my watering can, all shiny and new, with steam rising from its top as it met the cold of day. We had taken the chill off the water by putting a little hot water from the kitchen range tap into our cans. There was ice on my birds' drinking water which I quickly removed replacing it with the new warm water, each bird saying 'many thanks' as they drank. Steam curved upwards from their beaks, as they held their heads back to swallow the water.

It didn't take us long to water and feed all the birds. We broadcast the corn in the scratching sheds, where the birds happily scratched and fed.

'You can always tell a contented house by the conversation,' Gramp said, taking a seat on the end of a perch and lighting a medicated cigarette as we finished. 'When the birds are all talking quietly as if they have secrets, you know they're healthy and happy. It's then their food will do them most good, and they will give their best.'

I made myself comfortable on the perch beside Gramp. I felt happy and contented too, and, looking down at my new watering can, I felt that this Christmas was the most wonderful Christmas of all.

Suddenly all the birds stopped scratching for food. With their heads raised, they were talking anxiously. Tiddles was busy making her way across the snow. Now and again she stopped to shake the snow from her front paws. As she stopped, she looked in our direction, at the birds. I called her over and over again, but she didn't seem to hear.

'Poor Tiddles. I'm sorry for her,' said Gramp, as Tiddles picked her away over the snow as if it was something hot, without so much as another glance towards us.

'Why didn't she come when I called?' I asked. Usually Tiddles would run towards me, tail high in the air with pleasure, head rubbing against my legs, purring with contentment.

'There are two reasons,' said Gramp. 'Firstly all cats hate the touch of snow on their paws, which are all pinky and sensitive just like our hands. The other reason is that we have hurt her feelings, and she's fed up with us humans. Of course,' Gramp continued, 'the trouble is Mickey. You can be sure we won't see much of Tiddles this week. She won't be too friendly to any of us either, which reminds me you must be very careful, Peter. Don't pick Tiddles up, or she might even scratch and bite the way she feels at the moment.'

I couldn't think of my Tiddles ever wanting to scratch and bite me and I said so. 'Tiddles wouldn't really want to hurt you,' Gramp said, 'but she feels all mixed up, excited and worried through Mickey.'

'I don't think I like Mickey very much,' I interrupted.

'You mustn't say that,' replied Gramp, thinking very hard. 'Now how can I put it,' he said, thinking very hard again.

'But why should Tiddles want to bite and scratch me because Mickey's here?' I insisted.

For a moment Gramp didn't say anything, but then he asked, 'Do you remember the other day when Granny was annoyed with me because I arrived home late for dinner from the Sloop?'

'Yes, I do,' I replied.

'Well, because I was late, the baked potatoes were baked hard. That made your Granny even more annoyed. Just at that moment the butcher arrived and asked if we had any orders. Although he hadn't done anything, Granny was very annoyed with him too and said "no" with not even so much as a thank you, pushing the door to before the butcher could say a word. That's how it is with Tiddles. Animals and people are very much the same. They sometimes hurt each other when they don't really mean to, all because they're worried and excited at the time by something else, just like Granny was with the butcher. So you will be careful with Tiddles, won't you?'

'I'll be careful Gramp,' I said.

All at once there was a terrific banging coming from the direction of the back door. I could see Granny hitting a metal tray with a scrubbing brush.

'Time we were not here, I'll be bound,' said Gramp, and with this we left the scratching shed, complete with our two watering cans and walked down the garden.

'You're a fine pair on Christmas morning I must say,' said Granny, 'staying out there with all there is to do. Apart from being rude to our guests, I should have thought you would have known better!'

Gramp just smiled as if he hadn't heard, and started to clean the vegetables as if he'd never stopped. Granny gave me a big kiss which meant she didn't mean anything. I could tell she had been eating chocolates, and from her apron pocket she slipped one into my mouth, with another, 'Happy Christmas.'

'The others are all in the front room, and Victoria's waiting too. She has a new farmyard,' Granny said, giving me a friendly push towards the passage door.

Victoria was having a pillow fight with Barrie when I entered, but immediately took a terrific swipe at me. I hit back with another pillow, taking sides with Barrie to her screams of 'not fair!' Breathless we stopped. Len slipped out of the room for something and Barrie pushed the rail-back of one of the old dining chairs under the door handle to keep him out at the same time sitting on the edge of the chair.

In a moment Len was hammering on the door. He then pushed against it to our shouts of 'stop,' as the mahogany rail-back of the chair splintered at the top.

'I wouldn't be in your shoes,' said Len to Barrie. 'You've broken the chair.'

'Not me. Was you,' yelled Barrie.

At this moment Granny and Gramp entered. Gramp looked very serious.

'Well, worse things happen at sea,' said Gramp, but I could see he was very upset from his eyes. But then smiling once more he said, 'After all, it is Christmas morning.'

'You might have known Father,' said Granny, 'that something would happen with all of them in together, but I expect we can have it repaired. Now scatter all of you!'

I thought Victoria might cry any minute so I took her hand, with Barrie's in the other. Together we climbed the stairs to see my presents, which I confessed, much to their surprise, I hadn't really seen yet because of my watering can.

'This is just like Father Christmas all over again,' said Victoria, seeing my presents in my pillowcase and on my bed, still in their Christmas wrappings. At once Victoria became very busy unwrapping my presents.

'What a lovely engine!' exclaimed Victoria, lifting my Hornby engine from its spotted cardboard box and smelling of lovely machine oil.

'And now you have two engines,' added Victoria, clapping her hands with delight.

Meanwhile Barrie had discovered some rails which he had fixed together. He was most impressed with my two Pullman carriages and another L.N.E.R.[90] coal truck which he said should have been an L.M.S.[91] like my engine. Coupling them together he gave them a push. They ran off the end of the rails to disappear under the bed with a smack against the chamber pot, causing Victoria to rock on her heels with laughter saying, 'Fancy an engine crashing into a funny old po.'[92] With this she dived under the bed to reappear with the po which she sat on with great pleasure.

Barrie's face went quite red, as he said, 'I think you are very rude.'

'I'm not rude,' said Victoria.

'You are,' said Barrie.

'There's nothing rude about sitting on a silly old po.'

'There is,' said Barrie, giving Victoria a push.

---

90 L.N.E.R. stands for the historic London and North Eastern Railway which operated between 1923 and 1948. It is not to be confused with the present day L.N.E.R. London North Eastern Railway owned by the Department for Transport (DfT).

91 L.M.S. stands for The London, Midland and Scottish Railway which ran from 1923 until it was nationalised in 1948. It was the largest of the big four railway companies in its day.

92 Chamber pot.

Victoria fell off the po and with the po on its side her head was almost inside it.

Barrie forgot about all he had said about being rude as he stood astride Victoria holding his knees, bending over with laughter. With this Victoria jumped to her feet and bowled Barrie over. Before any of us knew what was going to happen, she took hold of the po with both hands and put it over Barrie's head to our yells of laughter and Barrie's muffled grunts from within.

Seeing Barrie's neck disappearing into the po, making his head all po with his hands on the rim, was, I thought, the funniest thing I had ever seen. I just laughed and laughed into hiccups. Victoria continued to shriek with laughter, pointing to Barrie as he moved around in helpless circles, until suddenly the bedroom door opened and there was Gramp.

'My puff, my puff, never in all my life,' said Gramp with laughter all over his face. 'This is a fine to do,' but added, 'but what goes on must come off,' and carefully moved the po round, then lifted it slightly until at last Barrie's face reappeared all flushed and hot with Barrie taking great gulps of air.

'You dirty thing,' he shouted recovering, aiming a blow at Victoria, which cat-like she avoided.

Gramp caught Barrie and Victoria under his arms, seating them on the bed. At last he managed to explain between my laughs and hiccups the dangers of putting a po over someone's head to our solemn promises that we would never put pos or anything else over each other's heads again. Gramp then made sure that we went to the bathroom to receive a wash fit for a king, which in Barrie's case included his hair, ears and face under the ice cold tap to Victoria's obvious pleasure. Gramp became quite breathless as he rubbed Barrie's hair in the huge bath towel. He rubbed it until it shone and shone, reminding him of a Harvest Moon[93] on pay day.

'What lovely coloured hair,' said Victoria. I was just thinking that Victoria had never said anything so nice about me, when Uncle Harry's voice boomed

---

93  A Harvest Moon refers to the full, bright Moon that occurs closest to the start of autumn. The name goes back to the time before electricity when farmers needed the Moon's light to harvest their crops late into the night. For Gramp this was probably the moonlight required to light his way back from the pub on payday rather than any involvement in the harvest!

up the stairs. 'Come to the cookhouse door boys, come to the cookhouse door,' mingled with the delightful smell of Christmas turkey.

Downstairs, Gramp unbolted the front door which was seldom used. He explained to Victoria that if she went this way it wouldn't upset Granny by going through the kitchen. He said it was always wise to give Granny and the kitchen a wide berth, especially at serving time on Christmas day.

Gramp left us by the half-open door looking out onto the ice-cake snow outside. Victoria didn't race out onto the snow path as I had expected, but waited and then said, 'You haven't thanked me for my Christmas card, but I thought yours was nice.'

I felt a little uncomfortable and said, 'I haven't looked at my cards yet. I wonder where they are.'

'I know where they are,' Victoria replied. 'Yours are on the little table in the corner. I looked when you were out in the garden and saw several of them. I could tell one was mine by the writing in capitals.'

'Oh!' I said.

Victoria went into the front room and I followed. She carefully selected the envelope from the others and handed it to me.

'It's a nice card isn't it!' exclaimed Victoria.

'Yes, it's a lovely card,' I said, looking at it closely. It showed a man and a lady in a big bed on Christmas Eve with their stockings hung over the bedrail. The man was about to put the candle out and there were some words written underneath the picture.

'Can you read what the man is saying?' asked Victoria.

'Not really,' I confessed.

'Well, you see the lady? That's me, and you see I have all the bedclothes.'

'Yes,' I said.

'And that's you about to put the candle out,' Victoria explained. 'And you're saying to me, so Mummy says because I've learnt what it says …,' Victoria paused.

'Yes, go on,' I said, at last interested.

'You're saying to me,' recited Victoria:

'Good night, sweet repose,

121

Half the bed and all the clothes'.

And with this Victoria skipped to the front door out into the snow.

'I think your card's lovely,' I shouted. Victoria stopped, and ran back.

'You must come round and play with my new farmyard as soon as you can. Promise?'

'I promise,' I said.

Suddenly Victoria put both her arms around my neck and gave me two big kisses.

'I like you best of all,' she said, slamming the front door before, rather bewildered and with a red face, I could answer. I looked at the card again. Though I was going to be in for a rather cold night with Victoria having all the bedclothes, I decided I would keep the card forever.

Gramp came up the passage into the hall where I stood and he said,

'My puff, that's a nice card.'

'It's from Victoria,' I explained.

'That's Victoria and me in bed just going to sleep on Christmas Eve.'

Gramp read the words smiling, ending with a good chuckle. 'How old's Victoria now?' Gramp asked.

'She must be getting on for four,' I replied seriously.

'What a wonderful age to be,' said Gramp, when from the living room door Granny appeared waving a carving knife.

'Come on Father. Come and do the honours! It will be cold if you don't come now. We're as hungry as hunters. Fancy expecting me to do it all!'

Gramp put my card into his inside pocket. 'I'll take care of it for now,' he said. Then taking my hand we walked from the hall down the passage into the living room.

The living room dining table was the longest I had ever known it, with all the leaves in use. Gramp sat at the end of the table in the mahogany carver. It had arm rests for one's elbows when you became tired of carving, or tired through eating. The plates had been put out and served with steaming vegetables and lovely-looking crunchy potatoes waiting to be completed with the turkey. I noticed Granny at the other end of the table looking very unsettled as she watched Gramp at work on the bird.

'My Godfathers,' Granny said to Gramp, suddenly. 'You do take a time. I'd better take all the plates back to the range. They'll be as cold as charity before you've finished. This is the one day out of the three hundred and sixty five that I'm not going to do your job.'

The plates rapidly disappeared from the table to reappear again a few minutes later. Gramp served the turkey portions with stuffing, starting with Auntie Flo first and me last of all. During this time I had to look at my plate with my tummy rumbling as I wanted to start on my crunchy roast potatoes. At last everyone had been served, and Uncle Harry said we could all 'cast off,' and we did!

A moment later, Gramp, with his mouth full of turkey, said, 'My puff. Pon my puff! This turkey's a good bird. As I said before, it must have led a good life. Here's to the butcher!'

'Yes, I'll drink to that,' said Uncle Harry, raising his beer glass. 'Not only did the bird lead a good life, but it came to a good end!'

We all raised our glasses, but I wished my lemonade was Guinness. I could see Granny was reading my thoughts over the top of her Guinness, but I didn't say anything for I knew the real toasts to come were never drunk in lemonade!

There was silence for a moment but for the noise of knives and forks and people swallowing until Gramp said, 'And here's to the cook.' He drained his glass and smiled at Granny who quickly wiped her mouth and blew Gramp a kiss across the table, to our cries of 'Here's to the cook!'

'What a lovely parson's nose this is,' said Auntie Flo suddenly.

I looked across at Auntie Flo's plate expecting to see the nose of the parson as he spoke in church. But whatever it was on Auntie Flo's plate, it didn't look very much like the parson's nose to me and I said so. This made everyone yell with laughter with cousin Len saying, 'You stupid rating, the parson's nose is the bird's back side!'

With this I drew in my breath, almost choking with laughter, requiring everyone to hit me on my back as I thought of the parson at morning service. When I had recovered I asked between giggles, 'But how is it possible for the turkey's backside to be called the parson's nose?'

'Now let me see,' said Gramp about to explain but being interrupted by Auntie Flo saying, 'Barrie has the wish bone.'

He *would*, I thought, saying, 'Let me pull it with you,' hoping I'd win, but Barrie, with a slippery twist of the bone, won, shouting, 'I wished for…'

'You mustn't tell us you kid,' said Len, 'or you won't get it. Anyway I bet you wished for a million!'

'I haven't wished for a million,' said Barrie. 'I've wished for…'

'No, it's true, you mustn't tell us,' said Gramp quickly, 'or you'll break the spell.'

'But there's no fun in making a wish if you can't share it,' retorted Barrie.

Morris, looking very wise, replied, 'Out of the mouths of babes and sucklings come forth truth,'[94] with Mummy looking very proud.

'Well, all you philosophers, I've finished,' said Uncle Harry.

'And there's not much left for a starving man on your plate. Pon my puff,' said Gramp.

Sure enough, Uncle Harry's turkey leg was scraped clean, like a new pin. Looking around the table I could see everyone had finished. I was quite sorry for Mickey and Tiddles for I could see they would get more of a taste than a bite!

'Come on you boys, help me clear away the plates for the Christmas pudding,' said Granny.

Pudding was the best part of Christmas dinner, I decided; that and the toasts, especially if you were lucky enough to find the silver threepenny bits.

With the plates having been cleared away, Granny came in proudly holding up the Christmas pudding for all to see, to our cheers and claps until it was placed in the centre of the table for Uncle Harry to light the brandy as Gramp called it. When it had been lit, it gave out a wavering light and

---

94   This phrase originates from the King James Bible, Psalms 8:2: 'Out of the mouth of babes and sucklings hast thou ordained strength because of thine enemies, that thou mightiest still the enemy and the avenger.' Matthew 21:16: 'And said unto him, Hearest thou what these say? And Jesus saith unto them, Yea; have ye never read, Out of the mouth of babes and sucklings thou hast perfected praise?' The modern use refers to the truthful comments of children who are honest and innocent (Wiktionary, 2019). It's ironic here that Morris not only knew his Bible but, as a 'babe,' was also giving an example of this truth.

then, when Granny blew it out, it made a little plopping sound as the light disappeared. The pudding was then all shared out with hot steaming custard.

'Please can I have the skin?' I asked quickly.

'I like the skin too,' said Barrie.

'Afraid Barrie's the guest of honour,' said Gramp, so Barrie had the custard skin.

'Then I'll clean out the saucepan,' I said.

'If you help clear away,' said Mummy.

Custard saucepans were always good so I readily agreed.

'I've found one. I've found one,' shouted Barrie.

He would, I thought, picking my pudding over bit by bit.

'And another, and another,' yelled Barrie.

'It's not fair, not fair,' I shouted.

Then more quietly I added, 'Not only have you got the skin but three threepenny bits as well. It's not fair.'

'But you have the saucepan,' Barrie reminded me.

'Now then, enough of that you kids,' said Uncle Harry, looking very stern. Remembering that Uncle Harry was a naval officer, I gave my pudding and custard all my attention.

At last we had all finished. Much to my delight, Gramp said that I could have his silver threepenny bits for taking my bad luck so well of being the only unlucky one not to find any. 'Just this year of course,' he added.

'Now,' commanded Granny, bowing her head, hands clasped. And with all our heads bowed and hands clasped, she said:

'Thank God for all our Christmas dinner, remembering too those who have not been so blessed like us this Christmas. Let us never forget our blessings at any time, and for all we have received this Christmas day.'

'Amen,' said Uncle Harry.

'Amen,' we all said, raising our heads quickly. Now for the toasts I thought! But we still had to wait, for Uncle Harry said:

'Let's be silent for a minute remembering all our friends everywhere, especially those who died in the Great War, particularly brother Will,[95] and those killed with him on the Drake.'

We were all silent. Granny looked very, very sad as she looked at Uncle Will's photo in its gold frame hanging over the sideboard, with him dressed in his full naval uniform with cocked hat and sword. How I wished I could have known him so I could have been allowed to handle his sword. But I knew I would never be able to handle it or see it for it went down with Uncle Will in the Drake somewhere in the Irish Sea. How proud I was sitting there with the silence, thinking of Uncle Will going down with his ship. Not every boy could say that after all. I knew Uncle Will would have been very proud too, if he could have only seen us all remembering him.

As the remembrance was now over, Uncle Harry filled all our glasses with port, although I was still thinking about Will's sword. Barrie's and my glasses were only half-filled because, as Gramp reminded us, that port was strong stuff and Christmas day had a long way to go.

'Years ago,' said Uncle Harry, 'when I was a kid, I sang in the choir at Whippingham Church, and when the Queen[96] was at Osborne House we used to have to sing before her on Sundays. Afterwards we were all given a glass of port to drink her health, being told to drink it, not sip it, when we drank the toast.'

'You must always drink the health of your sovereign in one go, remember that,' added Uncle Harry looking across at me, making me feel excited at the prospect, and proud to have an Uncle who had sung before the Queen!

'Ladies and Gentlemen,' said Uncle Harry, as we all stood up with our port glasses raised, 'The King!'[97]

---

95 This is Adolphus Edward William Stark (1880-1917), Peter's mother Edith's and Uncle Harry's brother who died at sea when his ship *HMS Drake* was torpedoed at sea off the coast of Northern Ireland on 2 October 1917. The ship is now a war grave.

96 Queen Victoria (1819-1901).

97 King George V (1865-1936).

'The King,' we all repeated, and in one go I swallowed my port, beating all the others with such speed that I was quite sure the King would have been pleased if he'd seen me!

The glasses were refilled as we regained our seats and our breath. This time only a little port was put into my glass.

Gramp proposed the toast this time.

'Ladies and Gentlemen, I propose a toast to the Royal Navy,' with a look at Uncle Harry, and I thought of Daddy[98] at Gibraltar.

'The Royal Navy,' we all said.

Next we drank to the Merchant Navy and the fishing fleets and all those in peril on the sea. Then the toast was, 'To the Army.'

'And now,' said Uncle Harry, 'to our newest fighting force that makes us mightier still. Ladies and Gentlemen, the Royal Air Force.'

'The Royal Air Force,' we all said.

Sitting down, I remembered how wonderful it was the other day when Gramp had called me into the garden, and for the first time in my life I had seen an aeroplane, with Gramp telling me that he was quite certain one day I would fly in one.

One day when I was grown-up, I thought, I would. That would be a wonderful thing to do.

'It's nearly two o'clock,' said Uncle Harry, looking at the bracket-clock.

'I don't think those boys should have any more port,' Mummy said, looking at me. Whenever Mummy said we were not to do something, or were not to have anything more, she always looked at me. I wished Mummy would only look at Len, Barrie or Morris for a change, and not always at me, I thought.

'Stand up Peter, and tell me how your sea legs are,' asked Uncle Harry.

I stood up, to be at once reassured by Uncle Harry before I could say anything, which made me very pleased.

'Nothing wrong with his sea legs I can see,' exclaimed Uncle Harry. 'After all he hasn't had anywhere near a wine glass of port. Another little taste won't hurt him. It's only the grape, and it's Christmas day.'

---

98   Peter's Father, Percy Lansley, was also serving in the Royal Navy.

*Adolphus E W Stark in naval uniform with sword © C M Lansley*

Gramp saw to each glass in turn, with the right amount of port, and we waited for the bracket-clock to strike two o'clock.

With the clock striking the hour, and with everyone looking very serious, Gramp said, 'A toast to absent friends everywhere,' and this time we all touched glasses before drinking.

I was glad to sit down. Mummy said to me, with Granny giving her a long look because she didn't agree, 'Your face is flushed. I wonder…,' to be interrupted by Gramp who said with a laugh, 'You should just look at yourself,' and for once Mummy didn't reply.

A little later I helped clear the table, enjoying the custard saucepan. Uncle Harry smoked a long fat cigar and Gramp smoked one of his own Dr Blosser's[99] cigarettes. Through the grown-up wisps of curling tobacco smoke, Uncle Harry said, 'It's good to bring the boys up to be proud of their country and family.'

'Yes,' said Gramp, 'it's the source of England's greatness. Family life and the love of one's home makes one's country. I don't think we have much to fear. Our youngsters today will be as good as or better than us if ever they are needed for another war. Please God it won't come to that again.'

If ever I was needed for war, I thought, I would go down with my ship like Uncle Will did. But then giving it more thought, I decided I would much rather be at home on Christmas day doing the remembering, and saying the toasts!

---

99 Smoking medicated cigarettes, such as Dr Blosser's, retained a central position in the treatment of asthma during the early twentieth century and was advocated by many prominent physicians (Jackson, 2010).

# 14

## 'A WIGWAM FOR A GOOSE'S BRIDAL'

I was quite pleased when Gramp suggested he would see to all the birds that Christmas afternoon. He said that, if we liked, Barrie and I could play with the trains and put the railway lines down from the front room to the kitchen. We wouldn't be annoyed by Morris or Len either, explained Gramp, for they had gone out to walk off their Christmas dinner and find out what the rest of the village was like under the snow.

We had just enough rails with 'curves' and 'straights' for the two rooms to reach each other. At first Barrie wouldn't agree to the stations being called Newport and Ryde because he wanted his to be Portsmouth Harbour. But when I pointed out that trains from the Isle of Wight couldn't run directly to Portsmouth and that this would be silly, he asked if his could be Ryde because he wanted to be near the sea. Because it was Christmas I agreed so the front room was Ryde and my station by the kitchen range was Newport.

All the trains ran backwards and forwards, sometimes with carriages, which made me think of my friend the engine driver, and sometimes with coal trucks. As the day started to become darker, Granny lit the little hall oil lamp before going upstairs for her Christmas nap, 'to sleep it off,' she explained, like the other grown-ups.

I'd just sent a coal train through to Ryde and was waiting and waiting for the 'up' train to return to my station, but it didn't come. As far as I could make out there was no noise from the front room, so eventually I thought I would go and look. I could see Barrie fast asleep with his mouth wide open and his head on a cushion by his platform of books on the front room floor. I didn't wake him. Just looking at Barrie made me sleepy, so I took the other cushion from the couch and put it under my head. In the flickering firelight within, and the greying daylight from without, I too was soon fast asleep.

When I awoke Barrie was still asleep, but someone had drawn the front room curtains. The fire had been made up and was casting flickering fireguard-shadows onto the ceiling. The front room door had also been pulled to as much as possible without disturbing the railway tunnel and track by the door.

Getting up from my cushion, I stretched myself thinking I would go and find out if anything was happening anywhere, though it was all very quiet. There was a red glow from the kitchen range, and a light was shining from the living room door, which was ajar. Peeping through I could see Granny seated at the end of the dining table, which was laid for tea with the Christmas cake in the centre. A bright and gleaming Christmas cracker had been placed next to each plate. Granny was reading. Every now and again she gave a little chuckle of delight.

I entered the room. Granny said, 'Just wait until I have finished this chapter, then I'll call the others for tea.'

'What are you reading Granny?' I asked knowledgeably.

'*Tom Brown's School Days*,[100] which I have read more times than I can remember, but I just want to finish the bit about the paper chase.[101] There's a good boy.'

So I sat down. Granny, with obvious enjoyment, read on until, closing the book, she rang the little school bell, calling, 'Tea, tea,' at the top of her voice.

Soon everyone appeared, including Morris and Len who were damp and cold from the outside snow. Much to my envy, and Mummy's look of concern, they said that they had been sliding on the village Mill Pond which was frozen over.

---

100   *Tom Brown's School Days*, a novel written by Thomas Hughes, was published in 1857. It was about life at Rugby School in the 1830s.

101   The Paper Chase is a cross-country running competition in which one person is the 'hare' and everyone else are the 'hounds.' The 'hare' runs ahead leaving a trail of paper which represents the scent of the hare. The hounds follow the scent and attempt to catch the hare before they reach the end of the race. In Tom Brown's School Days two 'hares' out of forty or fifty boys carried the bags of paper across the fields and laid the trail (see Robinson, 2012, pp. 1-13, for the history of the paper chase).

'I don't know about all of you,' Granny said when we were all sitting at the table, 'but I don't feel the least bit hungry. A small piece of cake and a cup of tea will do me.'

'It looks so pretty it seems a pity to cut it,' Mummy said.

'Cut it I will,' replied Granny picking up the knife, 'but cakes are almost human,' she continued, 'for they often turn out worse than you *hever* expect at times. And sometimes they turn out better than you *hever* expected. And you never know until you get beneath the surface. But soon we shall see.'

I hoped and hoped Granny's cake would be better than she had ever expected. I thought there was a chance it might be as I could tell she was very excited by the use of her aitches.

Granny started to cut the cake, easing out a slice, and then suddenly saying, 'My Godfathers!'

Oh dear, I thought and I could see everybody else was thinking the same thing. Something terrible must have happened. But then everything seemed to be alright as a smile appeared all over Granny's face and she said, 'Well if it eats as good as it looks I think it will be the best cake I've *hever* made!'

We all agreed it was the best cake in the world. Though everyone had said they weren't hungry, I could see Granny was very pleased when we all asked for another slice. Icing and sugar and tea went beautifully together and I asked for another cup, my third.

'I don't know what it is,' Granny said, 'but I wonder why at Christmas everyone seems to drink so much tea. Here, fill the teapot again Father.'

Gramp took the copper kettle off the hob of the living room grate and filled the large funny-shaped teapot. I waited for what I knew was going to happen next, and began to giggle. Granny knew too, because she looked at me with a toss of her head and a glint in her eye.

Gramp placed the teapot back on its stand. Then he tried to put the lid back on the teapot. He turned it first one way and then the other, getting redder in the face as he peeped at Granny with his eyes without moving his face.

'My Godfathers!' Granny said. 'After all these years you can't fit the lid back on that pot. You're about as useful as a mousetrap with no cheese!'

'Pon my puff, it's you that's the trouble,' replied Gramp. 'You make me nervous. Here, you do it,' and with this he pushed the lid towards Granny.

In one movement Granny had the lid back on the teapot and started to refill the cups.

'Don't know what I'd do without you Mother,' Gramp said.

'And I don't know…,' Granny began.

'Stop it you two kids,' Uncle Harry interrupted. 'You're forgetting the other kids are waiting to pull the crackers, and I've been waiting long enough wondering what's inside as well.'

This was true because we had been squeezing our crackers and holding them like telescopes towards the oil lamp to try and guess what was inside. I hoped for a whistle and looking at Barrie I knew he hoped for a whistle too. I had a feeling that if there was a whistle in any of the crackers he would get it. 'Lucky little brat,' I thought, thinking my brother's expression.

I pulled my cracker with Auntie Flo closing my eyes hard. I waited for a whiz-bang but no bang came, although the cracker split down the centre.

'Here's the banger piece,' said Uncle Harry, holding a long strip of cardboard-like paper towards me. One end was bent and it had a line of black stuff down its middle.

'Is, is it safe to pull it?' I asked, feeling very frightened but wanting to be brave.

'Of course,' said Uncle Harry, 'but you can close your eyes if you like.'

I closed my eyes harder than ever while I pulled the bent piece. I then opened my eyes again as if they'd never been shut.

'You had your eyes closed,' shouted Barrie. 'You were afraid. I saw!'

'I didn't!' I shouted.

'You did!' shouted Barrie.

'Shut up you little brats!' shouted Morris and Len both together.

I picked up the contents of my cracker to throw at Barrie, but thinking it might, after all, be a whistle, I withheld my throw and unrolled the coloured paper hat to find out what it was hiding. Whatever it was, it was very small and my hopes of a whistle faded. At last I had it in my hand, but what was it supposed to be? Surely there must be some mistake.

'But what is it?' I asked, holding it in the palm of my hand.

'It's a wigwam for a goose's bridal!' said Len, looking very wise.

'A wigwam for a goose's bridal?'[102] I repeated, and then to roars of laughter I asked if it had something to do with Nokomis by Gitche Gumee in my *Hiawatha*.[103]

Meanwhile Granny was looking at the cracker box.

'My Godfathers,' she suddenly said, louder than I'd ever known Granny say before.

'You wait till I get hold of that grocer! He's sold me all lucky charms. I'll charm him! I asked especially for novelties which included whistles.'

'Another thing,' Gramp said. 'These crackers are old stock. You can tell that because the hats are discoloured. That grocer saw you coming and that's a fact!'

'Saw me coming indeed!' repeated Granny. 'Well I can tell you this. He'll see me coming just once more after Christmas to give him a piece of my mind and that's the last he'll see of my money *hever*!'

And with this, Granny threw her cracker into the fire, making the best bang of all, sending sparks all over the grate.

---

102   This was originally 'a whimwham for a goose's bridle' and dates back to the fifteenth century. A whimwham was an ornament or decoration, possibly relating to a whim, but it is now obsolete. It has been replaced with a word that has a similar sound but not meaning. The phrase is meant to be nonsensical as no one would put a bridle on a goose and decorate it. It is used to deflect a question or comment that we do not wish to answer (Macquarie (2014).

103   This is *The Song of Hiawatha*, an 1855 epic poem by Henry Wadsworth Longfellow. The story follows the young Objibway warrior Hiawatha into the unspoilt wilderness where he learns the ways of nature from his Grandmother Nokomis, experiences the tragic death of his Dacotah wife Minnehaha, and becomes a leader and defender of his people. The poem was inspired by *The Myth of Hiawatha* by Jane and Henry Schoolcraft and the epic Finnish poem *Kalevala*. Events in the story occur on the south shore of Lake Superior in Canada known as Gitche Gumee (Schmoop, 2020). The 'wigwam' Peter refers to can be found in the lines: 'By the shores of Gitche Gumee, by the shining Big-Sea-Water, / Stood the wigwam of Nokomis, daughter of the Moon, Nokomi' (Longfellow, 2020, p.1, line 3). Longfellow visited the Isle of Wight in July 1868 and stayed at the Crab Inn in Old Shanklin. He was asked to write an inscription which is displayed on the fountain outside on a shield with the Union Jack and the Stars and Stripes. It reads: 'O traveller, stay thy weary feet; / Drink of this fountain pure and sweet; / It flows for rich and for poor the same. / Then go thy way remembering still / The wayside well beneath the hill, / The cup of water in His name' (Townsend, 2019).

'Mother, you shouldn't have done that,' said Mummy quietly, looking very serious.

'Here, let me smooth your feathers,' said Gramp, placing a paper hat on Granny's head and putting an arm around her waist. Granny smiled, giving Gramp's hand a little kiss, saying, 'Come on, it's time we cleared away. We can then go into the front room for a singsong.'

After clearing the table, Gramp made up the front room fire and lit the piano candles. He said we could leave the railway track where it was as we would no doubt need it the next day.

Soon we were all in the front room with the blazing logs on the grate. We all gathered around the piano as Mummy played Christmas carols with everyone singing at the tops of their voices. Every now and again we would stop for breath and take a sip of our lemonade with the grown-ups having a drink of what they fancied. After the Christmas carols we sang some sea shanties. The one I liked best was about the Bay of Biscay[104] and we ended with *Rule Britannia* which made me very proud. Gramp played *Daisy Daisy*[105] on his whistle-pipe followed by *Dolly Gray*[106] which made me remember Mrs Jones. This was followed by the *Home Sweet Home* of the music box and reminded me of the little old lady who showed us around our new house before I had even thought of school. This seemed a very long time ago now. I felt happy, so happy, but at the same time sorry again for Tiddles because Mickey was stretched out in front of the living room fire.

My head fell forward onto my chest. I heard Gramp say, 'I'll take care of this little one,' and Uncle Harry say, 'And I'll take care of this one.' Gramp carried me under his arm and Uncle Harry carried Barrie under his. At the top of the stairs I said, 'Good night Barrie,' but he was already away, as Gramp

---

104    This is '*The Bay of Biscay, Oh*' (Bay of Biscay, 2020).

105    Also known as *Daisy Bell* or *Bicycle Built for Two* composed by Harry Dacre in 1892 (Daisy Daisy, 2020).

106    This is *Goodbye Dolly Gray*. It was a music hall song with lyrics by American Will D. Cobb and music by American Paul Barnes. It was first published in 1897 and was used as a Boer War anthem and was sung during the U.S.-Spanish War of 1898. It became popular again with the onset of the First World War in 1914 (Dolly Gray, 2020).

put it. We didn't stop at the bathroom. I asked Gramp if it would matter very much if I left my prayers for that night.

'Tell you what,' Gramp said. 'I'll say your prayers for you tonight, that is if you'll do the same for me one day. Promise.'

'I promise,' I said. Gramp tucked me in.

'You'll soon be with the fairies,' he said, giving me a little kiss.

I was just going to ask Gramp to explain what 'a wigwam for a goose's bridal' was, but before I could I had slipped away into fairyland.

# 15

# WHAT IT'S LIKE TO BE SOMETHING ELSE

All of us, except Gramp, who had watered and fed the birds, slept late into Boxing Day morning. It was not until the bracket-clock had struck ten times that Barrie walked with me into the crunchy snow-covered garden to see the birds. Much to my surprise, Barrie didn't seem to be very interested in the birds. However, he was fascinated by the rat holes in the earth floor of the old shed, although he was ready to run at any minute if a rat appeared. I explained that this would never happen if anyone was around. This time Mickey was with us and I was very careful to keep him away from the birds as he was not bird-trained and he would have frightened them out of their wits.

Mickey barked at each rat hole, then jumped back ready to spring. All at once there was another sound, the sound of spitting and swearing. Looking up we could see Tiddles on top of the old fruit cupboard, digging her claws into the wood in anger. Remembering how Gramp had explained that cats usually jump onto their victim's back, I persuaded Barrie to leave the rat holes to the rats and the shed to poor old Tiddles while we took Mickey for an outing up the road. After we had gone a little way we took Mickey off the lead and threw him some snowballs. He chased them running around in circles and barked with both anger and delight when the snowballs burst into a thousand pieces becoming part of the ground again. We laughed tears when Mickey jumped high into the air to try and catch one. We ended up having a snowball fight ourselves, with Mickey barking himself hoarse until, breathless, we leant against the snowy hedge.

'My hands are cold,' Barrie said.

'So are mine,' I replied.

We both blew into our hands.

'Do you think Mickey's feet are cold?' Barrie asked.

'They must be,' I said. 'Our feet would be cold too if we had been running around all this time without our shoes and socks on.'

Barrie took Mickey by his collar and I blew as hard as I could onto his front paws. To answering barks of thanks, Barrie blew onto his back paws and then we did the same again.

'He's smiling now you see,' Barrie explained. 'You've made a friend for life.' As if he knew, Mickey suddenly licked my nose making my whole body tickle until I rolled over and over in the snow with laughter trying to make Mickey stop. In the end, to Mickey's barks of protest, I succeeded and we walked back down the road to the house. Though I was still sorry for Tiddles, I was glad that Mickey was enjoying his Christmas. After all, Mickey would soon be returning to Portsmouth and then I would have Tiddles again every day. Poor Mickey lived in a town with lots of houses and that must make him feel very unhappy too. I was happy for Mickey to be with us and on entering the house I gave him a big hug.

After a huge meal of cold turkey, ham and pickles, Christmas pudding and custard, in which to my delight I was lucky this time to find a silver threepenny bit, we played trains for a time. Gramp then suggested we could put some bread down on the snow-covered lawn to watch the wild birds. We placed some broken pieces of bread on a breadboard in the centre of the lawn returning to the living room to watch through the window. Birds appeared from every direction. There were starlings, blackbirds, sparrows, blue tits, robins, thrushes and a couple of wood pigeons, all trying to outdo each other for a piece of bread. Two starlings fought very hard over an extra big piece of brown bread. They became so intent on their struggle, with their beaks pecking at each other and their wings flapping, that they didn't notice a blackbird, with a white speck on its head, nip in and fly away with the bread.

'There's a lesson to be learned there,' Gramp explained. 'Those who fight for gain seldom win.'

Soon the bread was all gone. When we put out some more, the birds didn't fly far away but perched on the tree branches, sending down little snow storms. The starlings and the two wood pigeons watched from the top of old

Jolliffe's[107] roof. After we had returned to the warmth of the living room, they swooped down again. But before we left the garden, a large mistle thrush suddenly flew down and fell forwards when it landed.

'Something's wrong with its leg. I wonder what's happened?' said Gramp, concerned.

The thrush was keeping its left leg held up into its feathers.

'There's only one thing to do. Let's catch the thrush to see if we can give him some treatment,' Gramp said.

'But how can we catch him, Gramp?' I asked, becoming excited. 'He'll fly away.'

'Yes!' Barrie exclaimed. 'He'll fly away before we can catch him. We're not cats!'

'Well, if we're patient, providing we can be patient long enough,' Gramp replied, 'we will be able to catch him.'

'Go into the "odds and sods" cupboard,' Gramp said turning to me, 'and bring me the large ball of string, a clothes peg and the garden sieve.'

We both rushed out into the kitchen to return with the string, the peg and the sieve, though how Gramp was going to catch the thrush with these three things we couldn't decide.

In the garden, Gramp tied one end of the string halfway up the peg and gave me the ball of string at the other end to hold through the slightly-opened kitchen window. He then asked Barrie to go with him into the garden. From outside the window Gramp walked with Barrie, helping him unwind the string on the peg, until they got near to the breadboard. Gramp then pushed the peg into the snowy lawn and balanced one edge of the sieve upon it. Gramp then put some bread under the sieve, leaving just a few crumbs on the breadboard.

'Now,' he said, on returning to the house with a very important-looking Barrie, 'when the lame bird goes under the sieve, and we may have to wait some time, all you have to do is to give the string a quick pull. The sieve

107 According to the 1921 census, the following Jolliffe family members lived in Station Road and these are likely to have been Peter's neighbours: Laura Jolliffe, Narvel George Jolliffe and Vernon Jolliffe (Wootton Bridge Historical, 2015: 'Genealogy: 1921 Census report').

will then fall onto the ground and the bird will be inside it, unharmed, but captured.'

'Let me hold the string!' said Barrie.

'No!' I said, 'I'll hold it!'

'I asked first!' shouted Barrie.

'There's an easy way out,' said Gramp looking serious, slipping the string round both our hands. 'Now, when I say pull, you both pull, but not until I give you the word.'

One or two birds approached the sieve. A starling almost went in. Then a sparrow went in and swallowed a piece of bread so fast you could see him with his beak half-open, gasping for breath. It then came out and flew to the old pear tree.

'They sense there's something not quite right,' said Gramp.

'There's a blackbird about to spy out the land,' said Uncle Harry who had joined us.

Sure enough, the blackbird, with the white speck on its head, had stretched its neck into the sieve and then went inside. The lame thrush meanwhile had been hopping closer on its one good leg. It must have made up its mind too because suddenly it also went in.

'Now,' ordered Gramp. 'Pull!'

We gave a terrific pull making the clothes peg fly across the lawn.

'We've caught them! We've caught them!' we shouted.

'Let's go and see,' said Gramp, 'but let's make no noise for we don't want to frighten them more than we can help.'

We followed Gramp across the snow. Gramp lifted the side of the sieve just enough to slide the tips of his fingers underneath. The blackbird buried its yellow beak into Gramp's hand several times until at last Gramp got hold of the thrush. We then lifted the sieve, releasing the blackbird, enabling it to fly high in the air towards Brodie's Copse[108] and out of sight calling, 'I'm free, I'm free!'

---

108   This was probably a name they gave to the woods in the grounds of Fernhill House owned by the Brodies, as a copse by the name of 'Brodie's Copse' cannot be located.

'Pon my puff, poor, poor thrush,' said Gramp, stroking its head with his other hand. I wanted to cry. I am sure I would have cried if Barrie hadn't been there, for its leg had been badly cut. Gramp thought that it looked as though it had happened quite a long time ago.

'I think it must have caught its leg on a piece of wire,' confirmed Gramp. 'Perhaps it was a wire snare, but we must set up a bird hospital at once and see what we can do.'

Clean newspaper from the 'odds and sods' cupboard was placed on the kitchen table. Gramp carefully bathed the leg in an old dish filled with warm water and potash crystals to kill the germs. He talked to the thrush all the time telling it what a marvellous bird he was. He wiped the leg with a piece of red lint every now and again saying with each wipe that its leg would soon be as good as new. The bird made contented little chirps with half closed eyes, nodding its head.

'The thrush understands we are trying to cure him. That's the best medicine,' said Gramp. 'Pon my puff, you'll soon be stronger and more beautiful than ever you were,' continued Gramp, stroking the thrush under its beak.

With Uncle Harry holding the thrush, Gramp carefully dried its leg, first laying a piece of lint over the cut and then tying on a bandage. From the high-up cupboard Gramp found some aspirin. He crushed one of the tablets in a saucer and opened the bird's beak. He managed to get a little of the powdered aspirin inside. Then with Gramp holding its beak between his finger and thumb, the bird swallowed the aspirin because it couldn't do anything else!

'He'll be better for that and should get a little sleep,' said Gramp.

We found an old shoebox. After making breathing holes and lining it with a piece of old towelling, Gramp placed the thrush carefully inside, securing the lid with a large piece of elastic. Visiting hours wouldn't be until tomorrow, informed Gramp, as he placed the little hospital in a corner of the front room where it was neither too hot nor too cold.

By this time the day had darkened but was lighter than it would have been because of the snow carpet. Outside there was now a cruel wind tearing at the tree branches, blowing the snow, first this way and then that. Gramp remarked that it was an ill wind which was no good for man nor beast. I was glad that the thrush in his little hospital was with us in the warmth of the room. Every so often we would kneel down by the box to listen by the air holes for any sign of movement, but there was none.

'The aspirin's done the trick,' Barrie said, 'and I expect he'll sleep through to the morning.'

'Have you ever had aspirin?' Barrie asked.

'Yes, when I've had a cold, I've had half a one crushed up in my milk,' I answered. 'They can be dangerous things,' Barrie reflected. 'If you take more than you should, you might not ever wake up again. I mean,' Barrie continued, 'you wouldn't wake up in this world. And when you did wake up after you'd died, you might find yourself turned into a dog, a cat, or a snail. That's why we must be kind to everything.'

I laughed and laughed. 'You're silly,' I answered. 'Do you mean Mickey might once have been a grown-up before he was a dog and know all about us?'

'For all you know, he might have been Charles the First, or even Queen Victoria,' giggled Barrie.

The prospect of Mickey being the King or Queen of England was too funny for me, and I just laughed and laughed picturing, in my mind, Mickey with a crown on his head!

'But why, if Mickey had ever been a king or a queen, should he suddenly become a dog?' I asked, thinking of the difference between eating what was left of a scraped chicken's leg from someone's plate put in a dog bowl, and eating a wonderful Christmas dinner in a palace.

'It's just because everyone's got to know what it's like to be something else so that when enough people know what it's like to be everything else then everyone in the world will be good to one another and kind to animals, and,' added Barrie, looking at the little hospital, 'birds and things.'[109]

---

109   This is akin to Darwin's concept of sympathy: 'Sympathy is an essential part of Darwin's own thought processes in feeling that all creatures share a common consciousness. This not only enables Darwin to feel a common empathy with animals but enables him to get into their "minds"' (Lansley, 2018, p.10).

I didn't speak for a moment, thinking about what he'd just said and then asked, 'Did you make it up?'

'No! I was in the front room at Pompy[110] playing with my bricks and a nice old lady called collecting money for sick animals. She had lots and lots of cups of tea with Mum and told us all about it. I knew Mum believed it 'cause when the lady left Mum took Mickey's lead from a hook by the fireplace and said, 'Come on Charles the First, I'm late for the shops. All because of you!'

It was then I told Barrie about Gramp and Mount Joy and that he would play a silver whistle-pipe after he had died. I was rather worried in case Gramp was wrong considering what Barrie had just told me. I liked Mickey but I thought Gramp would be very disappointed to wake up when he was dead and find himself a dog. Then he wouldn't be able to play a whistle-pipe either, which would make him very, very unhappy I knew.

'Let me think,' said Barrie, thinking very hard after I'd finished, running his hand through his hair.

At last he said, 'Gramp's so kind he must have been everything by now; dogs, cats and all sorts of things, so when he dies he's bound to become an angel immediately. He wouldn't have told you about the silver whistle-pipes if it hadn't been true!'

'Of course!' I said and I took a deep breath of happiness for Gramp.

---

110   Portsmouth.

# 16

# LEARNING TO LOSE

It was now quite dark. The only light came from the flickering fire as Granny came in to draw the curtains and put the front room oil lamp, with its pinkie glass, on top of the piano.

'I don't know what you two have been talking about, I'm sure,' said Granny, 'but for the last hour all I've heard are your voices nonstop!'

'It was something very important,' we both said, Barrie's voice following mine.

'Anyway it's teatime once again,' replied Granny, 'and after we've cleared away it will be Banker time.'

'Banker time!' we both shouted, rushing into the living room.

The talk during teatime was all Banker. It was decided Uncle Harry would start off with the Bank at one pound. Grown-ups would be allowed to stake one shilling on any one game. Barrie and myself could stake one penny, and Morris and Len could stake threepence, because they were older and had more to lose, Uncle Harry explained with a knowing wink at Gramp. The Bank could be sold at any time to the highest bidder provided the bank could restart with a pound.

'Ace high, with no Joker,' said Gramp.

'No Joker, Ace high,' agreed Uncle Harry.

Soon it was time to clear away the tea things, and, as there was no lack of helpers, we had everything washed up, stowed away and shipshape in double quick time.

Uncle Harry sat at the end of the living room table with the oil lamp on the sideboard among the oranges and nuts, its wick turned up as high as it could safely go. Granny exchanged all her farthings from the button box for silver and pennies to be exchanged back at the end of the game.

Looking at Uncle Harry's Bank made up of farthings, pennies, silver threepenny bits and even half-crowns, together with little piles of money opposite each player, reminded me of an Aladdin's cave. If only I could win all the money, I thought, how happy and rich I would be! Barrie interrupted my thoughts.

'Don't plunge[111] and lose your money all at once,' Barrie said.

'You know what will happen if you do,' he added. 'We'll be packed off to bed too early, and we'll miss all the fun!'

Gramp shuffled the cards, cut them and then cut the pack again into nine groups[112] which he laid face down on the table.

'Right Ladies and Gentlemen!' Uncle Harry said. 'Back your fancy. Ace high!'

'And don't forget,' Mummy said, as if we would, I thought, 'it's Ace high,' looking at me.

Bearing in mind Barrie's good advice, I started with only one farthing, which I placed on the group of cards farthest from me. Gramp put a sixpence on the same group. Len, just to be in the swim, so he said, put threepence on it as well.

'Finished?' Uncle Harry asked.

'Yes!' we all answered.

'There are three groups not covered,' Uncle Harry indicated. 'Remember the last group the Bank turns up belongs to the Bank. The Bank takes all the money on the lower cards, paying out on even cards. If you win, you double your money.'

'Understood,' Gramp retorted.

'Yes, I understand too,' I said quickly, looking at Mummy.

This was the great moment. Uncle Harry turned up Mummy's card first.

'Good Queen,' he said. Auntie Flo only had the five of spades which made Uncle Harry chuckle with pleasure. Gramp gave me a wink of encouragement when Uncle Harry came to our cards. Barrie gripped the edge of the

---

111 Plunge means to gamble heavily or to run into debt.

112 This means the whole family were playing: Gramp, Granny, Mummy, Uncle Harry, Auntie Flo, Peter, Len, Barrie and Morris.

table and held his breath. 'A good Jack,' Uncle Harry said, making Barrie laugh with delight. I felt certain that at least I was going to double my money in the first game which was a good start to the evening. Morris had a four and Len had a six, so things looked pretty black for them I thought, feeling not in the least bit sorry for them in their moment of fear.

Only the three card groups no one had forced now remained. I tingled with excitement. The first two groups were low cards. Uncle Harry gave a big smile, reaching across to the last group, expecting to scoop most of the money for the Bank. With a flick of his wrist, Uncle Harry turned the last group of cards. It was the two of Clubs! We all cheered and cheered. We had all doubled our money, all except poor Uncle Harry who now paid us our winnings as if he loved losing. He said he had never lost before when playing the Banker.

The bracket-clock had struck seven when we had started. At eight I found I had won a whole sixpence. Then suddenly I started to lose. Until then I had been backing in single farthings. I now started to back four farthings at a time and lost six times in succession. I now had only one farthing left. I was desperate. I felt very unhappy, so unhappy I couldn't look at anyone. Yet only a short time ago, when I was winning, I was joining in the fun and laughing at everything. I knew I was going to cry. I felt a tear run down my cheek but I managed to hide it, or at least I thought I did.

Uncle Harry still had the Bank which had grown to have a large pile of money. It was definitely not for sale, Uncle Harry said. At the beginning of every game he would say, 'Roll up, roll up, back your fancy you lucky people!'

Time after time he would turn up a high card, taking most of our money.

'Just one more game before supper,' Gramp said. The cards were shuffled and the groups were dealt. For the first time ever I put my farthing on the card nearest to me.

'I am not going to bet on your card,' Barrie taunted. 'Your luck's right out!' giving me a dig with his elbow.

'Agreed,' Morris said, with Len's encouragement. 'I wouldn't touch your card with a barge pole!'

I swallowed several times. I knew I couldn't win, yet I had to try. I even said a little prayer within my mind.

'I've just thought of something,' Barrie whispered fiercely. 'If you lose this time, both of us will be packed off to bed after supper and I'm on a winning streak! I told you not to plunge.'

I couldn't speak.

'I'll put you out of your misery, Peter,' Uncle Harry said, turning up my group first of all. I didn't know what to say, or where to look. I just looked straight ahead, somehow holding back my tears, for it was the six of Clubs. When Uncle Harry came to turn up his card I didn't look at it either, for I knew I had lost my farthing. I hung my head, looking straight down at my knees. Then Gramp came to my rescue.

'Come, Peter,' he called across to me. 'Come into the kitchen, quick as you can. Help me with the plates.'

In the kitchen, Gramp closed the door quickly, giving my eyes a quick dab with the roller towel.

'I'll lend you four farthings,' Gramp said. Then almost thinking aloud he added, 'It would be wrong to give them to you. But you have learned a lesson tonight. We all have to learn some day, and that is, we can't always win!'

'Yes, Gramp,' I murmured.

'And there's only one thing to do, Peter, when you lose, and that's to smile. If you don't smile then your face will crack!'

'Yes,' I whispered.

'And if your face cracks you'll cry!'

'I know,' I answered tearfully.

Gramp slipped four farthings into my hand, saying, 'Put them into your pocket and say nothing. Be like Brer Rabbit.'[113]

---

113 Brer Rabbit means 'Brother Rabbit.' It refers to stories and tales of a rabbit surviving by tricking his foes and adversaries. The stories were written by Joel Chandler Harris (1845 - 1908). They show that the strongest do not necessarily win. Harris portrayed the narrator, Uncle Remus, as a kindly former slave telling folktales to children with the main character Brer Rabbit often in conflict with Brer Fox or Brer Wolf. Some believe the tales represented the enslaved Africans who used their wits to overcome their adversary and that this symbolised hope and inspiration to the slaves of the time. Peter made a mistake when he said Brer Rabbit said nothing. It was in fact the Tar-Baby, in a story of the same name. One day after

This made me laugh for I loved Brer Rabbit and he always said nothing!

'I think I can hear someone coming,' Gramp said, adding quickly, 'but when we start playing again, don't play in every game. Unless your luck changes, you will be packed off to bed too soon!'

Granny entered the kitchen. 'My Godfathers, you two have been a time. And you haven't started on the plates yet.' Then she smiled, giving Gramp one of her 'I know all about it' looks, and I was happy.

After supper, I lost on the first game and smiled happily but felt unhappy inside. Barrie stared at me with a funny look and said, 'I thought you had lost your last farthing.'

I received a wink of pleasure from Gramp when I said, 'I think I'll miss this game out.'

'You lucky thing,' Barrie said to me when Uncle Harry won again, once more scooping the pool. 'You must have guessed.'

'You little brat,' Morris said, glaring at me. It was then I noticed with almost a feeling of satisfaction that Morris' money had dwindled to a few farthings. I then joined in the next game and my luck changed. I started to win, with my farthings gradually building up in front of me. I found it easy to smile again because I didn't have to try. Winning certainly made you happy. With the clock striking ten I decided to risk four farthings once more, having a 'can't lose' feeling. I won and the next game too. I was beginning to think I would end up very rich. But then I knew I wouldn't because Mummy glanced at everyone before looking at me, saying, 'I think it's about time Peter and Barrie called it a day.'

'Yes,' Gramp agreed. 'You and Barrie must make this the last game'.

Shaking with excitement, Barrie asked if he could plunge with eight farthings as it was the last game.

'If you don't mind losing,' Uncle Harry agreed while Gramp cut the cards. I could see from Barrie's face that he dreaded the thought. Meanwhile, feel-

---

Brer Rabbit had fooled Brer Fox, he made a doll of turpentine and tar to get his revenge. He sat her in the middle of the road and hid in the bushes. Brer Rabbit asked the Tar-Baby various questions and when it didn't answer he hit it. The more he hit it, the more stuck he became (Rabbitmatters, 2020; Abelard, 2008).

ing very wise, I staked one farthing. Barrie wriggled in his seat like a worm coming up from the earth as Uncle Harry started to turn up the cards. Barrie smiled with pleasure when his card was the Jack of Hearts but closed his eyes with his hands while waiting for Uncle Harry to turn up the Bank's card.

'You can look now,' I shouted suddenly, giving Barrie a push. 'Uncle's card's a ten.'

Barrie uncovered his eyes, and jumping in his seat he banged both his knees against the table. Wincing with both pleasure and pain, he yelled, 'I've won! I've won!'

I had lost but looking at my pile of farthings I knew I needn't worry as I felt that, even when I had repaid Gramp, I would be about right. I started to count.

'I've won three ha'pence,'[114] Barrie said, 'thanks to that last plunge.'

'And I've only lost one farthing,' I exclaimed.

'You can't grumble at that,' Gramp said, giving my cheek a little pinch. ''Pon my puff you can't. You've had all the fun of the fair for a farthing.'

Granny stood up at her end of the table for us to join hands for Auld Lang Syne.[115] I didn't know the words but I followed the tune with my voice, jerking my arms up and down until they nearly left their sockets. With many good nights, sweet dreams, hugs and kisses, Granny volunteered to take Barrie and myself up the wooden hill.[116] I had just put my foot on the first stair when I suddenly remembered the farthings. I ran back into the living room and pressed four farthings into Gramp's hand and rushed out again before he could say anything. Breathlessly rejoining Granny, I climbed the hill to dreamland.

---

114   Three half pennies.

115   Auld Lang Syne was written by Robert Burns in 1788.

116   The wooden staircase.

# 17

# THANK YOU IN A SONG

The next day our first concern was for the wild thrush. Barrie was already up, listening at the air holes of the bird hospital when I entered the front room.

'I can hear him moving about,' Barrie said. Sure enough there was movement within the hospital. I rushed to find Gramp who had just returned from feeding the birds.

'The thrush is awake, Gramp,' I said.

'I thought somehow he would be,' smiled Gramp, warming his hands before the kitchen range fire bars. 'But he'll be alright until we've had breakfast and cleared away. Then we can borrow the kitchen table again to see what he's like in eye and feather.'

With breakfast over we prepared the kitchen table for the bird hospital as before. Gramp carefully placed the hospital in the centre of the table as we waited anxiously for the lid of the box to be removed. In silence we waited breathlessly and in fear as Gramp slowly lifted the lid.

'He's standing on both feet,' whispered Barrie excitedly. And he was. The thrush straightened his neck looking enquiringly over the side of the box giving a flap of his wings in pleasure.

'He'll do,' Gramp observed. 'His leg will soon be well and he'll be a brand new bird. Won't you my beauty?' added Gramp, stroking the side of the thrush's neck with its eyes half closed in contentment and our wonderment. With hushed breath we waited. Gramp tenderly removed the bandage from its leg.

'See,' said Gramp. 'It's just as I expected. The cut is no longer like an angry fire but is clean and quiet like a storm that has blown itself out.'

In answer the thrush hopped to the side of the box and flew around the kitchen. It then perched high up by the tea caddy on the kitchen range mantelpiece.

'The patient is ready to leave,' said Gramp opening the kitchen window as wide as he could, bringing in the cold day which touched our hands and faces like a cold wet flannel. I was happy for the thrush in his beautiful coat of downy-soft feather-bed warmth. The thrush pecked happily at the mantelpiece top, sharpening its beak for what Gramp called 'better things.'

From his vest pocket, Gramp produced his brassy whistle-pipe and started to play *There Is A Green Hill Far Away*.[117] But when he started it was so silent you could only just hear the tune. Then gradually, like a band coming nearer, Gramp's playing became louder until it was just right. As Gramp finished, the thrush straightened his head from listening and then sang a most beautiful song.

'He's all happy now,' said Gramp, 'and in a moment he will go to the woods. If only everyone could say thank you in a song.'

Once more the thrush flapped his wings. Then with a muffled chirp, chirp, he flew around the kitchen before flying through the open window to the leaning apple tree on the snow-covered lawn. The thrush made one of the branches sway, bringing down a few stranded snow crystals. Now standing on yesterday's bad leg, he scratched his beak with his right leg at terrific speed. Then with a wild cry of delight he flew across the lawn over old Jolliffe's hedge and out of sight. He's gone, I thought. Although he was now out of sight in the wild, in my mind I knew I could always see him anytime and hear *There is A Green Hill Far Away* and be back in the kitchen even if I lived to be older than old. I would always remember, too, Gramp's words of the thrush, saying 'thank you in a song.'

---

117   The hymn was written by Cecil Frances Alexander (1818-95): 'There is a green hill far away, outside a city wall, / Where our dear Lord was crucified / who died to save us all' (first verse).

In it she answers the question why Jesus died. She talks about God's forgiveness and says that man can reclaim his original close relationship with God through the giving of love. It is generally believed to have been written at the bedside of a sick young person (Albert, 2020). Perhaps Gramp chose to play this tune as the bird had been sick and through this expression of love for the bird was also able to reclaim his relationship with God.

# 18

# NEW YEAR'S EVE FAREWELLS

The last few days of Barrie's visit melted away with the snow. These had been happy days with trips to Victoria's house, train games, snow fights and Banker in the evenings in which I had won and lost, lost and won again with the happy outcome that I had neither won nor lost. Now it was the last day with only a few hours remaining before that fateful hour of everyone's departure. There was no excitement now. No longer could we plan tomorrow or look forward to the evening's Banker. The grown-ups didn't talk much either. As Barrie helped Gramp and myself with the morning feeding and watering of the birds, we hardly spoke.

When we had finished the birds, we entered the house to find the luggage all packed and strapped up by the front door. I sat on the edge of the big brown portmanteau[118] nestling between the smaller cases. Uncle called it a portmanteau, I thought, because it must have something to do with the sea, being always in and out of port and being so important and large it had to have a big name too. I took a deep breath and looked at Barrie as he sat with his elbows on his knees and his head in his hands on one of the smaller cases.

'The portmanteau has just said it wants to go back upstairs,' Barrie said without looking up.

'Yes, I know,' I replied, 'and the smaller cases want to go too. Do you hear them now?'

Barrie placed his head on one side listening very hard. The morning's winter sun shone through the coloured glass of the front door making Barrie's red hair shine redder than the Rhode Island Red cockerel's neck as he

---

118    A portmanteau is a large trunk or suitcase that opens into two equal halves with one half enabling clothes to be hung. It comes from the French 'porter' meaning 'to carry' and 'manteau' meaning 'coat' (Merriam-Webster, 2020). This was no doubt a very useful piece of luggage for Uncle Harry as a naval officer but its name had nothing to do with the sea or ports as young Peter assumed.

listened surrounded by thousands of dust specks. Sunshine and dust specks always made me very sad. Perhaps it was because I nearly always seemed to see them when I was already sad. I took another deep breath.

'You are right,' Barrie said at last. 'The little blue case wants to be carried upstairs to hide under the big bed. It's asking the portmanteau to hurry up. They all want to go.'

'It's no use,' I said after a moment. 'If they did hide, they would all be found and brought downstairs again.'

'Yes,' Barrie paused, and then his case gave a little creak as he straightened up. With a tear in his voice he said, 'I think my case is going to cry.'

We didn't look at each other. I noticed the sun specks were becoming all misty. If only the cases could hide. If only today was yesterday, I thought, as a tear rolled from my cheek falling onto the brown portmanteau.

'You mustn't cry portmanteau,' I said suddenly. 'It's silly to cry, but it's nice to know you want to stay.'

'We will all come again next year and the next and the next,' said Barrie, his voice getting stronger.

'Yes! Yes!' I added, patting the portmanteau's side. 'So don't cry. Don't cry.'

'They've stopped crying,' exclaimed Barrie, 'for they know now they're coming again next year. That's something too, for we shall be a year older next year which means we shall be able to stay up later.'

*Stay up later, stay up later!* With this, the thought of parting vanished and all I could think of was the next visit and being one wonderful year older.

Granny then appeared interrupting our happy thoughts. 'Why don't you two go out into the garden and have a last romp around while there's still time.'

'Yes,' we both answered, having to be brave all over again. We entered the garden.

The wintry sun filled the garden with the music of melting snow. Little rivers flowed down the garden path with lumps of snow now and again falling from the roof, reminding us of that wonderful Christmas Eve. It seemed years ago now. It felt so long ago that it could all have happened before I was born. Then just as now everyone had arrived to visit us. Then just as now everyone was about to leave and the snow had melted because there was no need for snow anymore.

We visited each chicken house starting at the top of the garden. We then went to the summerhouse and last of all the old shed with its rat holes. Nothing seemed the same anymore. Even Mickey, who had barked at the rat holes before, just sniffed and Tiddles was nowhere to be seen. We didn't speak. From the shed we wandered down the garden path across the road into Hendy's[119] field, which was now showing green islands of grass with, here and there, deep snowdrifts by the copse edge.

'Let's pretend I've just arrived,' said Barrie.

Mickey knew our change of mood. For a time we were back in yesterday. We were all barks and laughs until suddenly we were again today running as fast as our legs could carry us so as not to be late for lunch. Lunchtime was different too. On other days it had been all talk and laughter. Today there was only the noise of eating, yet no one seemed to be eating much.

Then Granny said, 'My Godfathers, can't you do better than that! You've hardly touched your plates.'

'I can never seem to eat much before a journey,' replied Uncle Harry and this time Granny said nothing.

With lunch over, the port and glasses appeared to be filled to the brim by Gramp. Barrie gave me a glance of almost happiness with our luck.

'It's the last day of the old year,' said Gramp as he stood at the end of the table.

'Stand up all of you and here's to a Happy New Year.'

'A Happy New Year,' we all said, touching our glasses.

The wine seemed to fill my whole being. I knew my face was flushed a bright red, but even Mummy was too busy talking with the others about train and boat times to notice.

---

119   James Andrew Hendy was one of the proprietors of Hendy's Library, High Street and had a successful newsagents business. He passed away at his home at 129 High Street Wootton in 1942 aged 74 (Wootton Bridge Historical, 2015: 'James Andrew Hendy – 1942'). This was likely to have been his or a member of his family's field.

Barrie stood, leaning against his chair, in his buttoned overcoat looking almost happy with a slight smile which increased into a wide grin every time he looked at me. Meanwhile, Morris and Len were quietly planning next Christmas and Uncle Harry insisted we mustn't go any farther than the gate to see them off.

'Besides,' Uncle Harry said, 'Now that the sun has gone, it will be slippery too and we shall have to hurry or we'll miss the train.'

I looked at the brown portmanteau. Barrie didn't say anything this time either. Port was certainly good when you felt sad, I thought.

There were many port-wine kisses and hugs by the old red gate of swinging-memory. We shouted over and over again 'Many Happy New Years' until they vanished with the curve of the road. I could still hear Mickey giving several farewell barks as I walked hand in hand with Gramp back up the garden path.

In the dining room the glasses remained with Uncle Harry's cigar smoke showing a greyish-blue between the table and the ceiling. Mickey's ball, forgotten in the rush to leave, was still in the corner where it had rolled that morning. I hurried from the smoke-filled room, the glasses and all that was Christmas, and walked to the top of the garden. There I heard the sound of a train which must have been their train as it puffed out of Wootton Station for Ryde and the boat. Then something brushed against my leg. I heard a purring sound and there was Tiddles, my Tiddles, just as Gramp had said she would be. I picked her up in my arms, burying my head into her fur. It was all wonderful. We were so happy. That night I had to catch up on my beauty sleep and slipped through the old year into the New Year dreaming of Christmas.

# 19

# THE HIGHWAY ROBBERY

Before my father had sailed away to the deep blue sea, or the Mediterranean as he called it, to join the Mediterranean Fleet, we had some wonderful times. He was a great one for telling stories which he used to make up as he went along. It was great fun because neither of us knew what was going to happen next until it happened.

Many of these stories were sea stories, of course, when the decks of the ships used to run with blood, but one of my favourites was a story of a highway robbery. It was about a highwayman on a black horse who would hold-up people and shout, 'Your money or your life!' People always used to part with their money, I discovered, but never with their lives. The men travellers used to place all their valuables in the highwayman's large black hat followed by the ladies' necklaces and rings. With a flash of his sword in the sunlight, my highwayman would ride off into the undergrowth greatly enriched. So it was with this in mind, sometime after that wonderful Christmas, that I decided to become a highwayman.

I spent a long time shaping a piece of wood for a blade in the old shed. It had a large handle and Gramp gave me some silver paint for the blade. When it was finished it was quite a horrifying sword. Gramp splashed some red paint on the end which he wouldn't allow to be too pointed. I was now ready for my first hold-up. Gramp completed my guise making a mask out of a piece of old leather. I practiced strutting around the house shouting, 'Your money or your life!' and everyone obliged by placing things in my black hat. It was great fun and now at last I decided I was ready for my first hold-up. I considered jumping out on the coalman but it wouldn't be real I decided. Besides, the coalman might not like being held-up! Once, when Granny said she had only counted four sacks, he had become very, very angry.

Yes, that's it, of course! I would hold-up someone on the way home from the village school. As my school was mornings only, it would be easy to carry out my plan. I would wait down the lane in the bushes just like the real highwayman. I would await my chance as he did, carefully selecting my victim. I tingled with excitement. As the quarter past three milking cows lurched down the road, I left the house, complete with my huge sword and my mask ready to slip on. I knew that shortly after the cows went down in the afternoon children, about my own age, would be approaching Packsfield Lane for their long walk home.

I hid in the bushes by the side of the lane and waited. I then heard some children's voices. I slipped on my mask and I waited. I heard several voices. There were too many, I thought. Why must they all walk home together? The last group of voices had died away and I was about to give up when I heard some faint footsteps. With my black hat, mask and sword at the ready, I held my breath. There was someone alone. Through the bushes I could just see the top of a little head. I pounced, 'Your money or your life!' I shouted. And then I saw my victim. She was a little older than me and obviously quite frightened. She didn't seem to know what to say or do, so waving my bloodstained sword I shouted again, 'Your money or your life!'

'I think,' she whispered falteringly, 'I, I think I'd rather give you my money if you don't mind.'

'Thanks Ma'am,' I said in my best highwayman fashion. 'I see you're being sensible. In my hat please.' She obliged by dropping a halfpenny into my hat.

'Now Ma'am, any trinkets, necklaces or brooches.'

'My mummy ha, had a beau, beautiful brooch once but she, she lost it on the beach. If I ha, had it I would gi, give it to you.'

'I see you're telling the truth Ma'am,' I said. 'You may go.'

She turned and walked away down the lane, increasing her steps.

It was then, and only then, that I realized I had really robbed her of her money.

'Stop! Stop!' I shouted. 'It's only a game. Stop!'

She started to run and I ran after her. My mask fell off and she looked around. I was gaining and then my sword caught between my legs and I fell head long into the grassy bank. My legs were bruised and my sword was broken but I had the spoils of a highway robbery in my black hat.

The awful truth of my deed and its consequences filled me with terror. If caught, my father had explained, highwaymen were always hung by the neck. But surely they wouldn't hang me for a halfpenny. Then I remembered my father telling me about two unlucky highwaymen who had been hung for attempted robbery. And that was only for attempted robbery. They hadn't even succeeded and their bodies had swayed in the moonlight at that very spot where my hero highwayman had appeared and held up a coachman shouting, 'Your money or your life.' Oh, what could I do? What should I do, I thought, and if I didn't hurry back I would be late for my teatime too.

'You have broken your sword,' said Gramp, as I entered.

'And you're late for teatime,' said Mummy, 'and you know how I worry.'

If only they knew, I thought, dry mouthed.

'You can make another sword from the other piece of wood that's left tomorrow,' said Gramp.

'No thank you, I, I don't think I want another sword.'

'You don't want another sword!' exclaimed Gramp with surprise.

'Father,' Granny said, 'let Peter have his tea. I want to clear away.'

But I couldn't eat.

'I think he must be sickening for something,' Granny said.

'See how he is tomorrow,' replied Mummy, and with this Gramp piggy-backed me to bed.

# 20

# A REMORSEFUL HIGHWAYMAN

I always enjoyed bacon and eggs for breakfast but the next morning I hardly touched them. When would they come for me, I wondered? If only my mask hadn't fallen off.

'I think I must call the doctor,' Mummy said.

'I should give it until this evening,' replied Gramp.

The butcher arrived mid-morning and over his cup of tea with Granny I heard them discussing someone who had been in trouble with the police. They had been talking about it last week but then I hadn't been interested, but now I was. I listened through the half-open kitchen door.

'Of course,' said the butcher, 'if he'd made a clean breast of it, it would've been taken into consideration. He might even have got off!'

My heart quickened.

'That's just what I say,' said Granny. 'If you ever find yourself in trouble, make a clean breast of it. The truth will out.'

'A clean breast of it. That's it. He ought to have gone to the police before they came to him and made a clean breast of it,' the butcher went on. 'He would have got off then, I bet,' he added.

'He would have, I'm sure,' replied Granny.

A clean breast of it, I thought. But what was a clean breast? I remembered Mrs Jones who was very big in the breasts. But how could a clean breast have anything to do with anyone being in trouble with the police? If only I knew how a clean breast could help me, I thought, as I heard the butcher say, 'Well, goodbye Mother, see you next week.'

'Goodbye butcher,' said Granny.

The butcher was hardly down the garden path when I asked with a trembling voice, 'Please Granny, what did the butcher mean when he said the man was going to the police to make a clean breast of it?'

'You mustn't worry your little head about such things,' said Granny, wondering what I had heard.

'But why should the man go to the police to make a clean breast. How …'

I was just going to mention Mrs Jones when Granny interrupted with a laugh.

'It's just a saying. If you make a clean breast of anything you just tell the truth about everything and that's it.' Granny then added, 'If the man had made a clean breast of it to PC Luckett in the first place I'm sure he'd have got off.'

I quickly decided I would go down the hill to the police house and make a clean breast of it to PC Luckett.[120] It was my only chance.

I took a long last look at our house as I left for the police house. When I got there, PC Luckett was standing by his front gate with his bicycle. I think he was the largest man I had ever seen in my life. I was sure, I thought, he had grown since I first saw him at the village show. I crossed the road and said, 'Please sir, I've come to make a clean, a clean breast of it!' And then as he bent double to hear what I was saying, I just ran and ran without looking back.

At lunch Mummy said, 'If you don't eat your lunch today I shall have to call the doctor. Whatever's the matter with you?'

'Can't think what can be worrying him,' said Granny looking all thinking.

I ate my food now, though without tasting it, for suddenly I had another plan. Of course I would wait at the same place again for the little girl only this time without a silly old sword, a hat or a mask. And I would give her money back. I would increase it to a penny from my money box as well.

That afternoon I waited at the same place and at the same time just after the cows went down the road. But she didn't arrive. Again the next day I waited but still she didn't appear. I was frantic. I couldn't eat a thing. At last

---

120   PC Lucket was the local police constable. There are a number of local references referring to him during this period. He gave a lecture on 'The Dangers of the Road' to the pupils at Whippingham Wootton Council School sometime between 1924-26 (Gosden, 1999, p.23). On 16 June 1928 it was reported in the Isle of Wight County Press that PC Luckett had assisted with the artificial respiration of William Gordon Grimes, an errand-boy, who got into difficulty at Woodside while bathing. Unfortunately he could not be saved. At the inquest PC Lucket had said that it was a very popular place for bathing and that sometimes there were as many as 200 children on the shore.

they sent for the doctor. From my bed at any moment I expected to hear PC Luckett's deep voice. I prayed each night with all my might that the doctor would let me get dressed so that I could slip out to try and find my victim again on her way home from school. I prayed very hard too for forgiveness and promised God I would never play highwaymen again if I was not hung. The doctor looking all fixed in the face said he was undecided what was wrong with me. When he turned to leave he said to Mummy, 'I think he's caught the bug that's going round. There's a lot of it about you know.'

So I've caught a bug, I thought, whatever that was. As ill as I felt, I couldn't help thinking that I knew why I couldn't eat and the doctor didn't. If only they knew, I thought, and pulled the bedclothes over my head.

Well PC Luckett didn't call and after several days the doctor said I could get up and get dressed.

'Thank God my prayers have been answered,' Mummy said, kissing and hugging me. But if only God had listened to me at the very beginning I thought, I would have been saved by now. Perhaps he was answering my prayers after all as I was now up again. I would find out later. I would slip out as soon as I could. I felt funny about the legs but I would get there somehow.

Mummy and Granny were resting upstairs. I was supposed to be asleep on the front room couch at the time the cows came down the road. I knew Gramp had gone to Newport. So I slipped out of the back door with a penny in my hand and disappeared down the lane to the bushes of my robbery. After a short time I heard some children's voices just as I had on the day of my crime. I watched the children go by. Two more went by followed by three more. Would she never come? I leant against the bushes. My legs felt so weak. Then I heard a faint step. Could this be her? Yes, I saw the same little head through the bushes that I'd seen last time. I jumped out but this time with no sword, no hat and no mask. I completely blocked her path.

'I didn't mean to rob you,' I said. 'Please believe me. I was not a real highwayman.' I pressed the penny into her hand. She looked at it.

'But you have given me a whole penny,' she said, 'and, and you only took a halfpenny'. She turned to hand it back.

'Please take it,' I said.

She had a bag of sweets in her hand. 'Then have a sweet,' she replied. 'A real sherbet one,' she added.

'You are kind,' I said.

'I like you too,' she said, 'and tomorrow with this penny I can buy millions and millions of sherbets. Now I must hurry.'

She skipped down the lane waving to me excitedly as she turned the corner out of sight. I hurried home as fast as I could, my legs getting stronger all the time, or so it seemed.

At the gate stood a tear-stained Mummy and a worried Granny and Gramp but before they could say anything I shouted, 'I'm so hungry. Please can I have bacon and eggs.'

'Two eggs,' said Gramp, 'and three slices of bacon,' smiled Granny.

'Oh thank God he's home and on the mend,' said Mummy between hugs. 'Nature knows what's best. His outing has done him some good after all!'

That night, after my candle had been taken from my bedside table, a very grateful ex-highwayman renewed his thanks and vows in his prayers.

# 21

# EXPLORING WITH VICTORIA

One Saturday after midday dinner, Victoria called for me to go out to play. It was a beautiful hot day in mid-May. For a time we played at being fairies. Victoria pulled the largest leaves from the summerhouse horse chestnut tree, tucking them in our sleeves for fairies' wings, arranging the beautiful white blossoms in our hair in the way of the fairies that lived in the garden. We danced and danced in the fairy circle on the mound of the greenest grass you have ever seen, shaded by the giant William pear tree in its cloak of white. Tiring of dancing, as even the fairies must, we wandered round to Victoria's garden to play hide and seek in and out of the huge laurel hedge which bordered their lawn. Breathless after many games, we lay down on the grass in the hot summer sun, discussing what we should play next.

'Let's play explorers,' I said. 'When I'm grown-up I want to explore places in Darkest Africa[121] where lions and tigers jump out on you in the dark and you shoot them and …'

'How can lions and tigers jump out on you if they can't see you, you silly,' laughed Victoria.

'There's always the Moon with huge stars. At least I think so, but it must be very, very dark sometimes or it wouldn't be called Darkest Africa. And I'm not silly because if animals can't see you they can sniff you out,' I replied, feeling very proud.

Victoria, in her little white dress with her dark tomboy cut-away hair, moved her nose up and down, wondering very hard.

'What is an explorer?' she asked.

'He's a very great man,' I said, 'and he goes out into the world finding things out that no man has found before. He may even come back with some

---

121   Henry Morton Stanley's Expedition, *In Darkest Africa*, 1890.

funny animal with six or seven legs. He tells stories that nobody believes because they haven't seen it and he sets foot where nobody but the animals have …'

'Oh, I do want to be an explorer,' interrupted Victoria, before I could finish. 'Let's start now.'

Hand in hand we left the garden and went into the road.

'Let's explore Wootton Creek,' said Victoria.

We walked down the hill until we came to the turning by the Mill Pond. For a time we forgot about exploring. We played at dropping sticks into a little stream which bubbled into the creek to see whose stick would sail out the farthest until Victoria said, 'Let's go right up to the end of the creek and explore the big trees.'

'Is it safe?' I asked, beginning to wonder and then I asked, 'Could we get lost?'

'I thought you wanted to find an animal with six or seven legs,' insisted Victoria, looking pleased. 'But if you're afraid of getting lost you'll never find anything like you said.'

'I don't want to find an animal now with six or seven legs. I want to find it when I'm grown-up,' I replied.

'You're afraid,' said Victoria.

'I'm not afraid.'

'You are, and I'm not, and I'm only a girl,' answered Victoria.

I was now very afraid and wondered if we would find an animal with six or seven legs. Say a dragon lived in the forest at the end of the creek—or a giant! I would have turned back and run all the way but for Victoria being so brave. If only she hadn't said anything about being only a girl. We reached the tall grass that was taller than us, with water and mud coming over our summer shoes. We were now among reeds with furry tops and I suddenly wondered if there might be any crocodiles there.

'Let's turn back Victoria. Please let's turn back,' I pleaded. 'I don't want to be an explorer when I grow up after all.'

'I'm going on to the big trees. If you go back I won't play with you again, ever again,' replied Victoria.

It was no use, so I followed Victoria until at last we reached the end of the furry reeds. But between us and the big trees was an inlet of the creek which we would have to cross. Victoria removed her shoes and socks, tucking her dress into her little white pants. Copying Victoria, I also removed my shoes and socks and hung them around my neck. Victoria rolled up the ends of my shorts as high as she could. She had taken charge now suggesting we should start to paddle across. The water was very warm to my feet as the mud tickled my toes and squelched between them.

We hadn't gone very far when the water started touching the tops of my rolled up shorts. I was about to suggest again that we should go back when Victoria screamed and slipped with the water going up to the top of her arms.

'Help! Help!' she cried.

Frightened and shaking with fear, I tried to catch hold of her dress with the water rushing over my shorts and reaching my shirt pocket. Victoria was crying now and her face was all twisted and wet with tears.

'I'll pull you out!' I shouted but I was sinking further into the water. I closed my eyes and for a moment I imagined myself back home in the galvanized bath in the living room. I was downstairs because the upstairs bathroom was too far away from the copper[122] and Gramp was bathing me. I then opened my eyes again and said my prayers just as I knew all brave men did. As I prayed it seemed that the undisturbed mud to the right of us was only just under the water. I quickly found Victoria's hand. Then with all my might I tried to pull myself out of the mud and drag my feet towards the undisturbed mound but my feet wouldn't move. We were both crying now. I thought of Granny, Gramp and Mummy. If only they knew; they would save us.

Holding Victoria's hand, I pulled and tugged, and tugged and pulled us towards the mud mound, again and again. Suddenly I fell forwards with a splash, almost going under. I recovered to find that the water was now only just above my knees and that Victoria's hand was still in mine. I gave one

---

122   In Victorian and Edwardian England, 'the copper was like a deep cauldron with a lid, built into the corner of the room with a space underneath for the fire' (Allette, 2020). It was used to heat large amounts of water for washing or for having baths.

*Wootton Creek © Francis Frith Collection. Permission to reproduce the image kindly granted by Francis Frith.*

*Wootton Bridge 1900. Unknown original copyright. Assumed in the Public Domain.*

more huge pull and we were both on the upper slope of the mud which consisted of a firm mixture of stones enabling our feet to get a good grip.

We waded along the rising slope towards the high grass to where the water ended and a little farther on to where the forest began. At last we were out of the water.

Only then did Victoria speak. 'You are brave,' she said. 'You saved my life. I always want you to be my friend.'

'One day,' I answered, 'I'll be a great explorer.'

Her eyes looked very large through her mud-splashed face. Her tears began to carry the mud from her eyes to her cheeks and then from her cheeks to her chin.

'Whatever are we going to do now?' faltered Victoria as creek water dripped from our clothes.

The high grass suddenly ended and there we stood in a little clearing surrounded by grass. Wondering what to do, Victoria said, 'Let's take our clothes off to dry them in the sun.' She didn't wait for me to say 'yes' or 'no' for in a moment she had pulled her clothes off over her head and laid out her dress, pants, shoes and socks in the sun to dry.

It was the first time anything like this had ever happened to me. Wondering what to do for a moment I then removed my shirt and shorts which I spread in the sun with Victoria's clothes. We lay safe within this magic circle warming our bodies in the sun. I watched the long grass waving in the blue-eyed day. The little sailboat clouds raced to win, just like the boats I had seen at the Cowes Regatta with Gramp, with the bang of the Royal Yacht Squadron gun for the leading cloud crossing the line and winning the race.

My eyes closed of their own accord without meaning to close. What would everyone say if they could see us now? 'My Godfathers,' Granny would say. With a 'Pon my puff, look at those two,' from Gramp. 'Make haste and get dressed,' from Mummy, and 'You'll catch your death of cold, that you will,' from Mrs Jones. Oh, but the sun was so beautiful like a warm kiss! I listened to Victoria's breathing mixed with the grassy voices of varied birdsong and insect sounds, one moment loud, then quiet and unheard like the still mouse who just watched. My body felt all sleepy as if it were being sprinkled with fairy sleep-dust. It felt almost real. Upon opening my eyes, I could see Victoria sprinkling mud-dust with little stones onto my tummy. Laughing, she sprinkled more and more making little roads with her finger on my skin.

'You are brave,' she said again. 'When we are grown-up, let's go millions of miles away together and explore.'

I sat up looking at her smiling face. Taking a fist full of mud-dust, I let it run through my spread-out fingers onto her body.

'You haven't got a tail,' I exclaimed.

'No,' said Victoria. 'I know but my brother has! Girls never have them!'

'Wouldn't you like one?' I asked.

'No! I wouldn't,' exclaimed Victoria, creasing her face. 'Not after what happened to my brother. Tails are silly things. They get in the way.'

'What happened?' I asked.

'Well, you know the laurel hedge where we played hide and seek? Well, my brother climbed up inside the hedge and then slipped. Do you know what happened?'

'No,' I said.

'Well, there's a barbed wire fence belonging to next door. They removed it afterwards but my brother slipped and fell onto the wire. It tore his trousers right through. It caught his tail and it bled and bled.'

'We ran indoors and Mummy put a clean handkerchief around it till the doctor came. The doctor was very busy with my brother's tail stitching it up or something. My he did cry. Then my Dad came in. The doctor looked very pleased and said, "That will be a half sovereign."[123] Mummy said, "That's what comes of having a tail!"'

'What do you think the doctor said then?' Victoria asked. 'Well he said something very funny. He said, "It's tails that make the world spin round." Who ever heard of the world spinning round on a funny old tail!' Victoria added, giving me a friendly push.

---

123   Gold Sovereigns were minted until 1926 although they were minted as commemorative coins thereafter. At that time a half sovereign had a face value of about half a pound. In 2017 its value was about £130.

We laughed and laughed about funny old tails with the world spinning around on them. It was so funny I laughed till it hurt. At last I said, 'I wouldn't like my tail caught on barbed wire, but I'm glad I have it because without it I couldn't go to sea in the Navy 'cause I wouldn't be a man.' [124]

'I thought you only wanted to be an explorer,' Victoria contemplated.

'I want to be a man and do millions of things men do when I'm grown-up,' I replied.

We busied ourselves rubbing our bodies with our hands and removing the dried mud. We did the same with our still-damp clothes. Then we got dressed and cleaned our shoes as well as we could with grass. We walked back along the winding bank of the creek to the bottom of the hill for our return journey. Breathless, we hurried faster and faster up the hill. Each grown-up we saw on the way said that our mothers were looking for us all over the village and one said to me, 'Ye Grandfather along top road is asking about ye!'

'Oh dear,' said Victoria. 'Whatever shall we say?'

'I shall tell the truth,' I explained. 'Once when I was a highwayman, I should have made a clean breast of it at once to PC Luckett. But I didn't and I could have been hung! If you make a clean breast of anything it means you've told the truth,' I went on. 'And then when you've told the truth about everything, well everything's alright.'

But Victoria was not listening. Tears were spilling from her eyes again. I placed my arm around her damp dress.

'I shall tell them everything,' I said.

Nearing the corner of Wootton Lodge at the turning into our road, there appeared Victoria's mother and father with my Granny and Gramp. My Mummy ran towards us.

'Wherever have you two been? Goodness your clothes are all wet. Just look at those shoes!'

Meanwhile everyone was talking, laughing and hugging each other with loud kisses. I felt sure we wouldn't get into trouble. I was just going to make a clean breast of it when Victoria answered.

---

124  Women first went to sea in the Royal Navy in 1990.

'We were playing explorers by the creek. I slipped into the mud. Peter pulled me out and we both fell into the water. Peter rescued me. He was very, very brave but we both got very wet.' She pressed my hand.

'You mustn't go there ever again,' Mummy said.

'Not for a long, long time,' said Gramp.

'Here's a silver shilling for being a brave boy,' said Victoria's father.

We reached Victoria's gate with many 'goodbyes' and 'see you tomorrows.'

Suddenly Victoria put her arms around me, giving me a big kiss.

'You're my best friend,' she said.

I thought a lot about Victoria when I was having my hot bath. It would be wonderful to explore Darkest Africa with Victoria when we were grown-up.

# 22

# PREPARING FOR ASHEY RACES[125]

'Pon my puff! Next week's Whitsun. That means Bank Holiday Monday and Ashey races,' Gramp announced, looking all smiles at Auntie Millie's Christmas calendar.

'Ashey races Gramp, Ashey races,' I repeated, leaving my bricks to join Gramp by the mantelpiece.

'You will take me won't you?'

'Why of course,' Gramp replied, 'as if we would leave anyone behind on race day.'

'Fancy,' said Granny, 'it's Whitsun again. It only seems like last week we were at Ashey, but it's a whole year ago.'

'It was a beautiful Whitsun week then and a wonderful Bank Holiday Monday. I hope it won't rain this time,' Gramp replied.

The thought of rain and Whitsun Bank Holiday with Uncle Harry holding the Bank at Banker made me make the top of my tower of bricks fall with a crash.

'If it's Whitsun how can it rain with the sun shining? And if it's a Banker holiday won't that mean that there will be Banker with Uncle Harry as well as Ashey?' I asked all in one breath.

'My puff, my puff, that's quite a mouthful and no mistake,' replied Gramp looking at his watch for words. Then finding them he said, 'Whitsun's just the name of a holiday. A Bank Holiday has nothing to do with Banker or Uncle

---

125   The original racecourse opened in Ashey in 1884 but its grandstand burned down in 1929 and was never rebuilt. Amateur racing was revived at the end of the 1990s at its original location at West Ashey Farm but no betting is allowed (Isle of Wight County Press, 2019). In the past, the Ashey races 'had a reputation for being the most corrupt racecourse in the UK [...]. Rumour has it that when the horses went round behind the wood, people would come out on a different horse on the other side.' (Almroth-Wright, 2014).

Harry. Banks, where shops and people get their money, have a holiday, so it's called Bank Holiday because banks close.'

'Then how can it rain if it's called Whitsun?'

'It can always rain in England whatever it's called and that's a fact,' Gramp said quickly.

'But why is it called Whitsun, Gramp?' I asked.

'Oh dear,' Gramp said, 'let me think. That's what comes of mentioning Ashey races!'

Gramp thought and thought. When he had thought enough he said, 'I'm stumped right out of my crease and no mistake!'

I didn't say anything. I just waited. I knew Gramp would find out if he thought long enough. At last, after walking around the table three times, Gramp sat down, as I knew he would, and began, 'You remember how I told you one day I would go to Mount Joy?'

'And you will play a silver whistle-pipe when you are with the angels,' I interrupted.

'Yes, and you really believed what I told you, didn't you Peter?'

'Of course, Gramp,' I answered climbing onto his knee.

'Yes, I knew you really did believe me,' Gramp continued, 'but you see Jesus' Disciples found it difficult to believe that Jesus was not dead. They couldn't quite believe that Jesus was already born again like we do when we die because their faith was not strong like yours was when I told you about Mount Joy. To put their minds at rest, Jesus descended among them so all his Disciples could see Him in the room. Then they believed in Him and were not sad anymore. This happened fifty days after Easter. Now you know why we have a holiday just like we do at Easter to remember Him, only this one is called Whitsun.'

'Thanks Gramp,' I said, 'and now I know it can't rain on Ashey race day because it's to do with Jesus.'

'That's wonderful weather news too,' smiled Gramp and we were happy.

For the rest of the week everything was about Ashey races. Would Uncle Harry manage to slip over from Pompy? What train should we catch to Ashey? Did it matter if we missed the first race? What sandwiches would we take? I knew they would be mainly egg and chicken because of the birds.[126] And there would be no flask of tea, beer or powdered lemonade because there would be a refreshment tent, which I knew was very exciting.

Form, Gramp explained, was a most important thing. Sometimes horses wouldn't run to form because the horse didn't feel like running just as sometimes I would do badly at my lessons because my mind was on something else. This would mean I was off form and would receive a low mark. Horses were just the same as us. Some were always a little better than others unless they were off form. So I learned the meaning of form until the butcher asked Granny to witness his signature on a form which was something very different. The butcher said with a laugh and a wink that he always found Granny's form very pleasing which made Granny very pleased though she pretended to be cross. Race form and lesson form I could understand but Gramp explained it would be wise not to worry about all the other forms just yet as there was time enough for that when I was grown-up. But what really mattered was when Morris announced he'd made a duck at cricket for I knew then he must be off form, which was very, very important.

Gramp now studied form at every opportunity. Several times I discovered him sitting on the perch in the Rhode Island Red chicken house making notes in his form book from a pink newspaper[127] which he carried everywhere. Often too, Gramp would be at the front gate on my return from morning school, pink paper flashing in the sun, deep in conversation with Mrs Freeman. I heard Gramp say, 'On form there's nothing to beat it,' and Mrs Freeman said, 'That's the one for me every time. I mean to say, with that breeding and that form he's already past the post.'

All this was much to Granny's annoyance who thought form coupled with Mrs Freeman were great time-wasters, unlike Granny's way of picking winners by throwing a few kidney beans over the racecard to back the name the bean fell on. This didn't take any time at all, especially considering, as

---

126   That is, the hens.

127   Sports newspapers were commonly pink and known as 'The Pink'.

Granny explained, at the end of a race day, she would often have won more times than Gramp.

From Gramp's front gate conversations I discovered he was going to act as Mrs Freeman's 'runner' at the races because she was helping at a wedding breakfast which seemed funny because the wedding was in the afternoon.

I walked up the garden path wondering about Gramp running for Mrs Freeman particularly because Gramp was often very short of breath when walking. I didn't see how he could run for Mrs Freeman. The very thought of Mrs Freeman trying to run gave me the giggles. Often when I spoke to her coming along the road she would puff and blow like a traction engine and say, 'Jus, just ye, ye wait till I gets me breath, me dear!' I would ask Granny and see what she thought.

'Granny?' I asked, entering the kitchen.

'Do you think Mrs Freeman is very fast?'

'My Godfathers Peter', Granny said. 'What *hever* do you mean?'

'Well, I've just heard Gramp say he'll be Mrs Freeman's "runner" at the races because she has to go to a wedding and …'

'My Godfathers, Heaven preserve us, the old rascal', Granny interrupted. 'You just wait till I see him. Running for Mrs Freeman indeed!'

I drew a deep breath wondering how big a secret I'd told Granny. Then I noticed she was smiling with her eyes so I waited.

'But it has nothing to do with running', Granny continued. 'You see it means Gramp will back Mrs Freeman's fancy for her, only I hope he knows what he's doing. Once I put a whole crown[128] on for a friend years ago. The horse lost. I didn't get my crown back either. Never place a bet for anyone unless you get the money first, that's my motto. People can have short memories if they lose!'

'Gramp?' I asked later as we sat on the perch in the top-of-the-garden chicken house. 'Mrs Freeman will let you have the money first before you back her fancy at Ashey in case she has a short memory, won't she?'

---

128    A crown was five shillings or twenty five pence in decimal currency. In 1924 this would have been equivalent to about £36.00 in today's money (see http://www.concertina.com/calculator/).

'Well that beats cockfighting! My puff it does!' said Gramp, adding, 'Whatever made you think of that?' with a tickle under my chin.

'Granny,' I said.

'What! Have you been discussing points and things then?' Gramp asked, looking all-knowing.

'I just wanted to know what a "runner" was,' I explained, 'and Granny told me.'

'I'll wager you two to one on Granny mentioned the crown', Gramp said looking all-knowing again.

'Yes Gramp,' I said. 'She did.'

'And not a day under forty years ago and she still remembers,' Gramp replied, looking all thinking. 'There's no need to worry about Mrs Freeman though. She's as safe as the Rock of Gibraltar! Anyhow I know she will give me the money first. She always does!' continued Gramp.

Now I knew the Rock of Gibraltar was the safest place in the world, so I must tell Granny not to worry, I thought.

'It must be getting on for teatime,' said Gramp, taking my hand as we left the chicken house. 'Always remember,' Gramp explained, as we walked down the garden, 'that if you lend money or anything it may be the last time you see it. If you can't bear the thought of losing it, then don't lend it! Some people have short memories because they never intended to pay it back in any case. Others really do forget. Whichever way it is, it can make bad friends or make you very disappointed like your Granny all these forty years. You can't help being disappointed Peter, but never let it make bad friends for life's too short for that. Besides, every quarrel makes it shorter. Promise me you won't ever make bad friends, Peter.'

'Promise?' Gramp repeated, giving my hand a squeeze as we entered the house.

'Of course I promise, Gramp,' I said, saying over and over again within my mind, I wouldn't ever make bad friends for Gramp's sake.

On the Sunday evening before Ashey race day we had Heaven's Artillery [129] with lightning. Granny called from the upstairs back bedroom, saying she had seen a ball of fire fall from the sky. Gramp said this was only Old Nick[130] cleaning his kitchen range of ashes. But this made the heavens angry so they swept black clouds across the sky bringing rain to oust Old Nick's fire. This meant there would be a clear dry day tomorrow.

And now tomorrow was today. Ashey Whit Monday was here at last with a blue sky, a golden sun shining through Brody's Copse with soaring rooks calling and the sweet, sweet fresh smell of after-rain. I was up early helping Gramp with the birds. We finished in double quick time having an earlier than usual breakfast for the great day. No sooner had we finished breakfast than there was a loud knock, knock at the back door followed by the familiar voice of Mrs Jones arriving to 'hold the fort' as Mummy called it during our race going. Mrs Jones greeted me with two carbolic kisses and the smell of bloater[131] which didn't improve the aftertaste of my bacon and tomato breakfast.

'Love 'is little 'art', said Mrs Jones. 'He's grown like Jack and the Bean Stalk since I saw 'im last, that 'e 'as! 'Ere take this copper fer luck,' she added, pressing a bright new penny into my hand.

'Thank you Mrs Jones,' I said, and remembering Gramp's words whenever he met a lady, which always made the lady very, very happy, I added, 'You seem to get younger every day.'

This so pleased Mrs Jones that, before I could even think Jack Robinson, she smacked more kisses and carbolic bloater on each cheek, and holding me right above her head the front of her blue blouse went up and down like the fireplace bellows. At last, Mrs Jones sat down with me on her lap, gasping, 'I've overdone it sure enough I 'ave. It's one of me 'ot flushes I'm 'aving,' her face going redder and redder until it was all red. Granny looked at Mrs Jones,

---

129   From Jack London's short story The White Silence (1899)

130   Another name for the devil.

131   The carbolic would be the smell from carbolic soap which has a mild disinfectant property and has a sweet smell. The bloater smell would be from a type of whole cold-smoked herring.

all-knowing. Gramp looked out of the window not noticing, though he had of course, like Mummy who said, 'It's the price of being a woman.' This was something new to me and made me feel all the more sorry for poor Mrs Jones who must have been a woman without much money. Poor, poor Mrs Jones, I thought, her hot lap warming through my summer shorts. The hot spreading flush was due, I concluded, to the May thundery weather, which also caused the milk to go sour, the butter to go off and Granny's quick temper to flare up when Gramp was in trouble. I was just going to console Mrs Jones by saying that the thundery weather must be causing her hot flush, when the living room door opened and there stood Uncle Harry in his summer white trousers, white coat and brown-strapped field glasses from last year's Ashey races.

As I jumped down from Mrs Jones' hot lap, everyone started talking at once with Mrs Jones' hot flush being forgotten for many a day.

'I managed to change my duties at the last minute,' Uncle Harry said, when everyone had stopped for breath. 'We will be in nice time for the first race if we catch the 12.30 train.'

'What would you like to drink, Harry, before we leave?' Granny asked, making my mouth water in anticipation.

'I've had my usual on the boat, Mother,' Uncle Harry said, 'so if you don't mind, knowing race days, I'll have a nice cold glass of milk to give a lining to my stomach.'

The cool glass of milk made me see my vision of a sip of beer fade making me very disappointed. But there must be something in a cool glass of milk if Uncle Harry wanted one and a lining to a stomach sounded very exciting so I said, 'Please may I have a cool glass of milk,' being careful to add, 'to give a lining to my stomach.'

Everyone rocked with laughter and with, 'Bless 'is little 'art,' Mrs Jones left the room returning with two beautiful glasses of golden milk filled to the brim.

Mummy looked towards me concerned. I knew there was something important coming so I started to drink my milk quickly, finishing it all in one go without stopping.

'I was going to say,' Mummy said, 'do you think he should have all that milk? It takes time to go through and…'

'Bless 'im,' said Mrs Jones, 'there's one of them canvas tents 'e can go be'ind when 'e wants to go.'

Grandpa began to laugh, slapping his knee, with everybody laughing. I remembered now what had happened last year. We had arrived early, long before the first race, to find a nice place by the rails near the winning post. For some time I had wanted to go before anyone noticed. Then Granny said, 'I think he wants to go!' Gramp took me by the hand leading me towards a tent place when suddenly he stopped to talk to a very old friend he hadn't seen, so I overheard, for a month of Sundays. Wriggling myself free from Gramp's hand, I rushed into the tent. I had nearly finished going when a big man entered and sat down at a table to look at a lot of papers. Suddenly he saw me. He let out a roar, as if, Gramp explained afterwards, the place was on fire. This frightened me so much I wet my shoes.

'Out of here. Out, you, you …,' he shouted. Then Gramp appeared, wonderful Gramp, to save me. The big man said a lot of things to Gramp I didn't understand, his face going shepherd's delight[132] with his blue nose going bluer. Gramp just stood there by the table without saying a word until suddenly he lent across the table and whispered something in the big man's ear. The big man opened and closed his mouth without a sound coming from it.

'Come on Peter,' Gramp said to me, 'time we were not here,' taking my hand and leading me to the place next door, which was like a tent but with no roof and was all sky.

Now I didn't want to go anymore, which made Gramp chuckle and chuckle. All at once, who should enter our sky-tent but the big man himself! Gramp and the big man looked at each other, their eyes all sparkling, saying nothing. Suddenly they began to laugh, the big man stooping to pat Gramp on the back and Gramp reaching up to pat the big man's back. They shook

---

132  'The concept of "Red sky at night, shepherd's delight. Red sky in the morning, shepherd's warning" first appears in the Bible in the book of Matthew. It is an old weather saying often used at sunrise and sunset to signify the changing sky and was originally known to help the shepherds prepare for the next day's weather' (Met Office, 2020). Here it is used to describe the big man's face going red.

hands, up and down, up and down like my tree trunk seesaw. When they had finished the big man patted my head saying I was a real Anglo-Saxon if ever there was one, making Gramp's face all pleased. I received a silver sixpence for luck which made me feel very, very happy. Gramp told me the big man was really one of the best when you got to know him, which he really was.

I was glad to remember the big man. A year ago seemed such a long time. If I wanted to go today I would find the sky-tent. Perhaps I would meet the big man again. That would be nice. He might even give me another silver sixpence. That would be lucky too.

'Ready to leave?' Gramp asked, fixing his favourite flower, a Coxcomb Red Carnation, in his best blue, serge lapel, giving his bowler hat a friendly pat, with Uncle Harry sitting his straw hat well back on his head. Mummy and Granny were all fairy-dressed and garden-hatted. Granny's hat had hot-house grapes all ready to pick from the rim. They now dusted their faces with powder. Granny was worrying about her shiny nose while I was wanting to leave for the train and Ashey. Mummy was wondering why, on this of all days, she had to suffer a gnat bite, giving her a red eyelid, with Mrs Jones saying, 'That's life, goodbye, good luck, go now or you'll lose your train'. We moved down the garden path to Uncle Harry's 'under way at last.'

Gramp hummed *Land of Hope and Glory*,[133] marching out in front carrying the round deep blind-made[134] apple and egg basket full of all sorts, as if, Uncle Harry explained, we were going to be under siege instead of just going down the line to Ashey.

On our way along Station Road, we passed all sorts of people in our hurry, some in twos, some in threes, and even more. Others also passed us being too fast for Gramp. Everyone knew Gramp and they all wished him and all the

---

133   Sir Edward Elgar's (1857-1934) famous tune is performed at important events around the world and represents British patriotism. It was written before the First World War as a celebration of the glory of war and Britain's international power. However, the song is now used in different ways. The first verse is: Land of Hope and Glory, Mother of the Free, / How shall we extol thee, who are born of thee? / Wider still and wider shall thy bounds be set; / God, who made thee mighty, make thee mightier yet, / God, who made thee mighty, make thee mightier yet. (London, 2018).

134   Basketmaking workshops were set up after the First World War to provide employment for disabled ex-servicemen (Chandler, 2017).

family luck for the day's sport. Gramp said if horses were wishes we couldn't lose, making my heart jump for I'd already decided to buy a new Hornby engine out of my winnings. One man, passing on a bicycle, called out to Gramp, 'I bet you've guessed all the winners, Mr Stark.'

'I have that,' answered Gramp with a laugh. Knowing the meaning of 'guess' I was surprised at Gramp. He certainly hadn't guessed winners with all the hard work of pink paper form-book talks with Mrs Freeman during the week.

Arriving at Wootton Station, the one small platform was so crowded with people you could hardly move. They were from one end to the other, even underneath part of the road tunnel at the Ryde platform end. PC Luckett was there too looking even taller. Each time I saw him he seemed to grow. I felt better when he gave me a smile and to find he was such friends with Gramp, but I felt sorry for him in his high-necked black tunic which was mentioned many times in his talk to Gramp. Sweat was running down his face in little wavy lines to his chin, neck and the edge of his tunic, which Mummy said was cruel on such a hot day. PC Luckett said regulations were regulations. Gramp repeated many times that that was what comes of being a part of the Force. PC Luckett looked pleased when Gramp mentioned the Force and told Gramp not to forget to do Warner King in the 3.45—as if he would, I thought!

The train appeared around the curve from Whippingham. PC Luckett at once became PC Luckett, looking very stern, not wanting to have a friend in the world, shouting, 'Stand back there, stand back, can't you see the train?' which was funny to me as the train was so long around the curve, making loud whistles of enjoyment, that everybody would see it in any case. The engine had now reached the platform and was going slower than Gramp could walk when he was out of breath and my great friend the engine driver was leaning right out of his cab. I was the happiest and proudest person on the platform too when he waved at me, not noticing any of the other people. PC Luckett looked at me unbelievingly that I should have such an important friend, especially when the engine driver called out to Gramp, 'Warner King for the 3.45 Mr Starks.'[135] PC Luckett then forgot that he was a policeman saying, 'I told you so,' to Gramp and then, suddenly remembering again he was part of the Force, he spread his arms out like wings, shouting, 'Keep back there. Keep back there, plenty of room for everybody!' making me wonder if there was.

In the train, I sat on the knee of a man I didn't know. His breath was all hot with the smell of onions which crept round from the back of my neck. A tall man standing by the window opened it wider, saying, 'Who's been eating onions for God's sake?' though why he ate them for God's sake I couldn't imagine. My knee-man laughing out onion-smells told the carriage it was from Saturday night's Isle of Wight Rifles[136] reunion at which raw onions were his favourite. The tall man by the window complained there should be a law against it, which I knew would please PC Luckett!

For the rest of the journey the talk was all about horses, riders, owners, trainers and the all-important form, but my main concern was the difficulty of holding my breath when my knee-man breathed out, because I had to make quick in and out breaths when he breathed in. This continued until the swaying, jerky, rattling of passing over the points told me we had arrived at Ashey Station.

---

135   Stark and Starks were used interchangeably.

136   The 8th Battalion, The Hampshire Regiment, Princess Beatrice's Isle of Wight Rifles, known as the 'Isle of Wight Rifles' was formed to defend the Isle of Wight. They served as infantry during World War I and as coastal defence artillery during World War II (Isle of Wight Rifles, 2020).

# 23

# AT ASHEY RACES

From the carriage we were rushed along by the crowd. I couldn't see Granny, Mummy or Uncle Harry though I could hear their voices. Gramp was also out of sight but I held onto his hand tighter than ever. His hand dangled like a rope between a large woman and a small man who were arguing about whether the man had remembered to put water down for the dog, let the cat out or had bolted the door.

At last we were out of the station and free from the crowd on to the beautiful Ashey racecourse of Ashey Down. One man, who was all dressed up in a funny top hat, knew all the horses that would win. For just one shilling he would let anybody into the secret of last minute news straight from the stable. This was very confidential which Uncle Harry said meant it was top secret.

'Roll up, roll up! Be a millionaire by the last race all for a shilling,' he shouted over and over again. Gramp, much to my surprise, didn't believe this jolly man, though many did judging by the tinkle of shillings thrown into another upside down top hat for pieces of paper containing the secrets. I was very, very sorry Gramp wouldn't let me become a millionaire just for a shilling.

It was a wonderful day with sips of Uncle Harry's beer in the refreshment tent between races. We ate our sandwiches sitting on our coats with an old worn out sheet for a tablecloth laid on the soft grass. I looked at horses and things through Uncle Harry's field glasses which you wouldn't have guessed what they were without them. They had another funny name I couldn't say which is why I called them field glasses which was easier. The smiles on Uncle Harry's and Gramp's faces showed that the horses were running true to form which meant Granny's beans had landed on the wrong names, though she was doing her best to look pleased. Mummy wouldn't have a bet because she knew she would lose anyway. I couldn't understand why she could know if she didn't try. Mummy must be very, very clever, I thought, to know she couldn't win. Gramp explained that it made her very lucky because she couldn't lose.

For each race, I looked for a horse with a name I liked with yellow colours. On the 3.45 racecard I found a horse which Gramp called Master of Arts. I knew that to be a Master was really something, especially if you were a School Master, a Master of the Hunt, a Ship's Master or a Master Butcher. So when Gramp told me a Master of Arts was Master of everything you could ever think of, and when I found the jockey had a gold cap and a yellow shirt and sash, I knew this was the horse for me.

'Peter,' Gramp said, looking all sorry, 'you will lose your shilling. You are up against Warner King!'

Oh dear, I thought, Warner King! The engine driver, PC Luckett and everybody said it was bound to win. Mrs Freeman had said it was already past the post. Even all the papers, Gramp explained, said it was the best thing ever!

'Mind you,' Uncle Harry said, looking all wise, 'I'm going to miss this race out. I can't afford to put ten pounds on with the chance to win one. There's no such thing as a racing certainty. If there was there would be no bookmakers.'

'Quite right,' Gramp said, being pleased at Uncle Harry's knowledge. 'I think I'll take a leaf out of your book. I'll miss this race out too!'

'Gramp, please, please let me do Master of Arts,' I said.

'Go on Father!' Granny exclaimed, 'Put it on for him, sixpence each way.'

'That's just it,' Gramp replied. 'He'll have to have it on to win, because there are not enough runners for place money, so Peter is bound to lose his shilling.'

Everybody looked most unhappy over my shilling but I had made up my mind, so I pleaded again.

'Victoria's father gave it to me for being brave,' I remarked. 'If I lose it, it only means I mightn't have been brave!'

'You win!' Uncle Harry laughed. 'Fortune favours the brave. Give me your shilling. I'll put it on for you.'

My heart seemed to go all funny as Uncle Harry walked away with my shilling, and it went all funny again when he returned, handing me a shiny card with a number on it, for Uncle Harry to collect my winnings if a miracle happened. If it won I would have sixteen whole shillings and my shilling back. I would be able to buy one more new Hornby engine for twelve shillings and sixpence and I would have enough left over for one more coal truck as well. I would persuade Mummy to take me into Morgan's toy shop[137] in Newport tomorrow.

Gramp took me to the Paddock to see my horse. He was beautiful, all conker-brown with a yellow jockey on his back.

Gramp looked at Uncle Harry. 'Mind you,' said Gramp, 'if it wasn't for Warner King, I could fancy him.'

'But just look at Warner King,' said Uncle Harry.

Warner King was all black, reminding me of *Black Beauty*[138], even more beautiful than my horse. Oh dear, I thought. I've lost my shilling. What could I do? So I said a little prayer under my breath for Master of Arts. The horses then left the Paddock for the post. Gramp said one thing was certain and that was that my horse would jump over the sticks all right, never fear.

Just before the race started, we found a farm wagon with several men standing on it all ready for the off. They made room for us, Uncle Harry holding me like a piggyback upstairs with my arms around his neck. All the men on the wagon had backed Warner King. Proudly I said, 'Well, I've got a shilling on Master of Arts to win!'

'Have you indeed,' said one of the men, removing his cigar. 'Well! I'm afraid sonny you've lost your shilling. Mind you if it had rained for a week like it did last evening you might have had a chance. Warner King hates soft going.' He gave the back of my leg a friendly pat with Gramp saying, 'There you are Peter. Promise you won't be too disappointed.'

'Sorry,' I said to the cigar man, 'but I think Master of Arts will win', though by now I didn't!

---

137   In 1924 its proper name was Morgan's Toy Fair located at 112 Pyle St, Newport, next door to the Corn Exchange (Isle of Wight County Press Archive, 1924).

138   *Black Beauty* is an 1877 novel by English author Anna Sewell. It is an autobiographical memoir told by the horse named Black Beauty. The story is an earnest attempt to appeal to all horse owners to treat their animals in a more humane manner (British Library, 2020).

*Asbey Races. Unknown original copyright. Assumed in the Public Domain.*

'In that case,' the cigar man cut in, 'my Landlady won't see me for dust and small stones,' with all the other men looking all-knowing and enjoying the fun.

'They're off,' everybody shouted at once. For the first two jumps my horse was in front. Gradually Warner King gained, passing my horse, going faster and faster. Now he was three jumps clear of Master of Arts, the other horses being even farther behind. They passed the winning post the first time round and I knew my shilling was gone forever, the cigar-smoking man having the biggest smile I'd ever seen.

'One thing sonny,' the cigar man said, turning to me, 'your horse is a wonderful jumper.'

Warner King was now four jumps in front of mine with only three before the winning post. I began to understand what it meant to go against form. Suddenly there was a terrific shout. 'The favourite's down, the favourite's down!' In the excitement, one of the men pushed forwards, not believing his eyes, making the two men and the cigar man fall from the wagon into the mud. With much laughter the men clambered back onto the wagon, the cigar man wiping mud from his face with his clean white show-handkerchief, smiling and saying to me, 'You've won sonny,' squeezing my hand, 'like you said you would. You're a punter after my own heart who picks his horse and sticks to it through thick and thin.'

Had I really won? There were still two jumps left, now one. To cheers, Master of Arts was up and over, running on to pass the winning post and my jockey patting his neck with pleasure.

'What a jumper,' the cigar man said again, shaking my hand, with Uncle Harry lowering me to the ground. I was just going to ask him what he meant by his Landlady not seeing him for dust and small stones but he'd disappeared into the crowd, tearing up his race ticket before I could ask him. The green flag was up showing there were no objections. Uncle Harry took my card to collect my winnings, returning with seventeen separate silver shillings to give me. With the thrill of counting them I was hardly able to believe my eyes, seeing my new engine and coal truck at the same time.

I had already had several visits with Uncle Harry and Gramp to the canvas sky-tent but now I'd told Gramp I really wanted to go. Mummy said it must be all the excitement of my big win, Granny nodding her head with an 'of course I know' look.

On our way I asked Gramp if he could take me to see the big man of last year's tent memory to tell him how lucky I was with Master of Arts. Gramp put his arm around my shoulder saying he had just heard that the big man had gone to Mount Joy but that he would be very happy, adding that he would have plenty of races to arrange and horses to love. I looked up at Gramp. His eyes were all loving, joining mine. If only the big man could have waited until after today to leave for Mount Joy. I was glad to hear how happy he was but I was disappointed I couldn't tell him of my luck. He would have laughed I knew. One day when I went to Mount Joy I must remember to tell him about Master of Arts. He would like that.

If I could, I would have left at once, after my win, to put my money safely in my money box, but, of course, I had to wait until the last race, with Granny still hoping her last race-bean would win all her money back. The last race was over. Granny was disappointed, Uncle Harry and Gramp both saying they couldn't grumble, which I knew meant they were not really happy. Mummy said she'd enjoyed every minute of it—but what a story I had to tell everybody! They would hardly believe it. I could just see the butcher's face. That would be fun. It was like something from my storybook; to go to Ashey races with one shilling and come back with seventeen. I said this over and over again to myself, carried along by the crowd all hurrying to catch the first of the extra race trains leaving Ashey.

Uncle Harry's train arrived first, taking him back to Pompy. He waved his straw hat, waving until he was out of sight. There must have been hundreds of people on the platform. Gramp observed that it was black with people. It was the one time in the year Ashey paid for its keep twice over. On other days it was left to the quietness of the Down, day old chicks and eggs from Pike and Bennett's farm, with perhaps three passengers a day, the trains hardly stopping with just the blow of a whistle most times. All the people seemed to be very happy, yet some must have lost, I considered. When I asked Gramp about this he said, 'Remember Banker. The older you get the easier it becomes to lose because you expect it more. But of course it's far better to win every time,' which I knew was so very true much to my delight.

Waiting on the platform we heard the sound of music, then singing and music together. This was something Gramp could never resist. ' Let's go and investigate,' Gramp said following the sound. All at once, struggling through the crowd, we came upon three jolly policemen. One was playing a mouth organ, which Gramp called a harmonica, and the other two were singing *When the Red, Red Robin comes Bob, Bob Bobbin' Along, Along*.[139]

'Now, all together everybody,' said one all-smiling policeman. Soon everyone seemed to be singing. I put in a lot of 'sweet songs', and 'alongs', with the 'red, red robin', which the policeman said was a great help. Gramp produced his brassy whistle-pipe from his inside pocket, joining in with the harmonica to every one's cry of 'more, more' for the 'red, red robin' again. This was then followed by *Bye Bye Blackbird*[140] and *Keep the Home Fires Burning*.[141] By this time everyone from the Newport and Ryde sides of the platform were joining in. They were not smiling now. Their faces looked all fixed like the singing in a church. I noticed one lady had tears going down her cheeks. Granny said it must be something to do with the war. Though Granny tried to hide it, I could see she felt the same. I knew she was thinking of Uncle Will of the

---

139   *When the Red, Red Robin (Comes Bob, Bob, Bobbin' Along)* was written by Harry MacGregor Woods (1896-1970). He was born in North Chelmsford, Massachusetts. The song was written in 1926, which means that Peter was at least seven or eight years old when he went on this visit to Ashey Races (Songhall, 2020). The lyrics start: 'When the Red Red Robin Comes Bob-Bob Bob·bin' Along / When the red red robin comes bob bob bob·bin' along along / There'll be no more sob·bin' when he starts throb·bin' his old sweet song / Wake up wake up you sleepy head / Get up get out of your bed / Cheer up cheer up the sun is red / Live love laugh and be hap·py / What if I were blue now I'm walk·ing through walk·ing through the fields of flow·ers' (Lyrics, 2020).

140   *Bye Bye Blackbird* was written by Jerome Hosmer Remick (1867-1931) who was a Detroit music publisher. It was written in 1926. The lyrics start: 'No one here can love or un·der·stand me / Oh what hard luck sto·ries they all hand me / Pack up all my cares and woe, here I go wing·ing low / Bye bye black·bird' (Lyrics, 2020).

141   *Keep the Home Fires Burning* was written by the Welsh composer Ivor Novello (1893-1951) in 1914, originally published as *Till the Boys Come Home*. The lyrics start: 'They were sum·moned from the hill·side / They were called in from the glen/ And the coun·try found them ready / At the stir·ring call for men' (Lyrics, 2020).

*HMS Drake*. I didn't say anything but I joined in the words, 'Until the boys come home,' as hard as I could.

The sound of the *Home Fires* died away under the puff, puff, puff of the Newport train. This was the longest train I had ever seen with an engine at each end. It reminded me again of my tomorrow's new Hornby engine from the winnings of my never-to-be-forgotten-day of Master of Arts at wonderful Ashey. I fell asleep on Gramp's knee during the short journey home waking up with a start when the train stopped at Wootton. Gramp said it was a wonder I didn't find myself in the middle of the following week. And I was glad I didn't because I would never have known what I might have missed, I thought.

Gramp piggybacked me most of the way from the Methodist Church up the hill past Shedden's Copse[142] and White's one petrol pump. Though there were many offers to help, Gramp did all the piggybacking with many stops and puffs along the way to our gate. Gramp explained that it made the end of a perfect day, Ashey being a long way before it did the rounds again.

'Home is the sailor, home from the sea,'[143] Gramp said, putting me down like a sack of feathers at Mrs Jones' feet, with all the news from Granny.

Mrs Jones said, 'Bless 'is little 'art, who would have thought 'e would 'ave come 'ome with all them shillings.' She produced a fresh brown egg for me to eat but I was too tired. Mrs Jones said, with her sniff, that money always upset the works, whatever that was. My head fell forward, tired, tired, too tired to keep my eyes open. Upstairs on the bed, Gramp pulled my little white special Ashey boots off, then my socks followed by my shirt and shorts. I could then feel the cool silky touch of the blue bedspread once I was all undressed. I felt so cool and so drowsy like an end of summer's wasp, with my

---

142   This must be the copse in the grounds of Miss Mary Constance Shedden (1862-1938).

143   This is a quote from Robert Louis Stevenson's (1850-1894) poem the *Requiem*. It was published in 1890 and these lines were put on his gravestone as directed by him:

This be the verse you grave for me:
Here he lies where he longed to be;
Home is the sailor, home from sea,
And the hunter home from the hill. (Poets, 2020).

nightshirt slipped on, all tucked in. I was now a little sleepyhead, counting sheep. But there was no need as I was now going to sleep until the cows came home. There were now kisses but no longer carbolic bloaters from Mrs Jones. The voices all blurred into one, becoming softer and softer, fading into nothingness.

# 24

# THE GLORIOUS FIRST OF JUNE

Immediately after Ashey, I played with my new engine and coal truck for hours on end. I also relived the Master of Arts' memorable race with jumps made of books. The water jump was made with a big book by Captain Portlock[144] from the Royal Navy. It was just right as it was all about the sea and it was wide enough for the water jump which brought about the downfall of Warner King. I used Gramp's ivory dominoes as the horses as they made the racing easy with their numbers. I would toss them along the front room floor being careful that the Master of Arts' domino always won and that the Warner King domino always fell at Captain Portlock's water jump. I became the crowd, the jockey, the horse, the starter and the bookmaker shouting the odds of sixteen to one for Master of Arts and two to one for Warner King. Gramp pretended to have a bet, always picking the form horse, Warner King, just for fun, making his face look all disappointed when it fell. Granny would then call us for tea saying in the same breath to Gramp that his trousers would soon go at the knees if he played many more race games. This made him smile, all pleased with the happy thought.

Within a few days the excitement of Ashey faded. My constant repetitions ended with hardly a person in the village not knowing of my good fortune. The butcher laughed with delight asking me to pick a winner from the daily paper, calling out the names. I picked Blue Fire, which was a wonderful name. 'At five to one,' the butcher said, 'with a large field, it's in with a chance!' It won and when the butcher arrived the next day he was, as Gramp said, 'as happy as a sand boy,' giving me sixpence for my tip. After he left there was a

---

144 This is the book by Captain Nathaniel Portlock (1748 -1817) and George Dixon (1748-1795) published in 1789 entitled *A voyage round the world but more particularly to the north-west coast of America performed in 1785, 1786, 1787 and 1788 in the King George and Queen Charlotte.* Captains Portlock and Dixon formed a partnership called the *King George's Sound Company* to develop the fur trade (Robson, 2020).

shout from the kitchen. It was Granny. 'My Godfathers, the butcher's let me have an extra piece of steak for my money as well!' exclaimed Granny.

'Which shows what comes of Blue Fire,' observed Gramp. 'Pon my puff,' he added, 'we're lucky to have such a tipster in the family and such a sportsman for a butcher!' I could hear by the way Granny hammered the steak on the kitchen table that this pleased her very much.

'My puff', Gramp informed everyone suddenly. 'Tomorrow is the Glorious First of June.'

The Glorious First of June, I remembered, was when Lord Howe defeated the French Fleet off Cape Ushant.[145] I had learned about this battle many times before from my father as we lay on the front couch before we caught a bird, falling asleep in the Sunday afternoon quiet. This great never-to-be-forgotten battle was always included again and again with the other stories, usually the last one before we entered the land of nod.

Safe in port, in the old shed, I had three ships I'd made with pieces of wood supplied by Gramp. I had used a lot of string for the rigging and a lot of burnt matchsticks for guns of the line. Each ship had a poop deck[146] as well. I trailed my wooden ships behind me on a piece of string, particularly over the high grass of the lawn which was the sea. The ships rolled first one way and then the other, sometimes nearly capsizing when the grass was very high as that meant the sea was very rough. It was great fun in this garden sea facing the dangers of the deep and from the coast when the onshore bonfire volcano was erupting. Then I put on all sails to bear offshore, standing hoveto, to rescue people from the rocky beach. If Gramp raked the bonfire with the old garden fork, the volcano really did erupt, sending flames into the air, as volcanoes do, with sparks falling all around, with rocks of charred paper falling around the ships that could kill a man. It was very dangerous then.

---

145    The British Channel Fleet under Admiral Lord Howe attempted to prevent a French grain convoy sailing from the United States. It was being protected by the French Atlantic Fleet, commanded by Rear-Admiral Villaret-Joyeuse. The two fleets fought in the Atlantic about 400 nautical miles west of the French island of Ushant on 1 June 1794. Lord Howe defeated Admiral Villaret-Joyeuse but the grain got through to France (Payne, 1979).

146    A poop deck forms the roof of the cabin in the aft part of a ship where the commanding superiors observe the work and navigational proceedings.

My three ships were Nelson's *H.M.S. Victory*, Drake's *H.M.S Golden Hind* and of course my smallest ship, fluttering like a bird, Sir Richard Grenville's galleon *Revenge*.[147] In honour of the Glorious First of June I had a review of my ships in the Solent which was the garden path just outside the back door near the honeysuckle. The ships were dressed all over with little paper flags secured from mastheads, poops' stays and rigging. This meant much hard work cutting out the little flags and colouring them in with my crayons. The largest flags were the Union Jack from the top masts and the White Ensigns flying from the poops. So both Granny and Gramp helped cut out the flags of all shapes and sizes copied from a book called *Modern Seamanship*.[148] I coloured them in and secured them with Granny's strongest button cotton to the string rigging ropes. When we had finished, the Union Jacks and the White Ensigns flew proudly from the mast heads and the poops.

Just before bedtime, my three ships were finished and dressed completely all over for the great review the next day on Saturday, it being a non-school day. Granny, Gramp and Mummy proclaimed that my ships looked the picture of England's greatness, making me long for the day when I was grown-up to join the Royal Navy and a fighting ship to sail the seven seas.[149] My three ships were safely anchored in the old shed as the evening embraced

---

147   Admiral Horatio Lord Nelson (1758-1805), Sir Francis Drake (c.1540-1596), Sir Richard Grenville (1542-1591).

148   *Modern Seamanship* was the standard professional and pleasure boater's bible for over eighty years. It dealt with ship handling and safety. It was first published in 1901 and its eightieth edition was published in 1988. It was written by Rear Admiral Austin Melvin Knight, U.S. Navy (1854-1927) (Geni, 2016).

149   The origins of the phrase 'Seven Seas' goes back to ancient times. 'In Greek literature [...] the Seven Seas were the Aegean, Adriatic, Mediterranean, Black, Red, and Caspian seas, with the Persian Gulf thrown in as a "sea." In Medieval European literature, the phrase referred to the North Sea, Baltic, Atlantic, Mediterranean, Black, Red, and Arabian seas. After Europeans "discovered" North America, the concept of the Seven Seas changed again. Mariners then referred to the Seven Seas as the Arctic, the Atlantic, the Indian, the Pacific, the Mediterranean, the Caribbean, and the Gulf of Mexico. Not many people use this phrase today, but you could say that the modern Seven Seas include the Arctic, North Atlantic, South Atlantic, North Pacific, South Pacific, Indian, and Southern Oceans. However, our oceans are more commonly geographically divided into the Atlantic, Pacific, Indian, Arctic, and Southern (Antarctic) Oceans.' (National Ocean Service, 2020).

the night and dissolved into the Glorious First of June in the quiet of the sleeping village.

After helping Gramp, as usual, first thing in the morning with the birds, I arranged my ships outside the back door in a perfect line, the *Victory* of course being head of the line. It was a glorious June day too and I couldn't imagine a first of June being anything other than like this. Gramp sat on the upturned feeding bucket piping the King[150] in the uniform of an Admiral of the Fleet aboard *H.M.S. Victory* as I stood to attention. *God Save the King* had just started when who should appear around the corner, where the garden path ended and the honeysuckle began, but old Mr Cooper[151] the milkman. At once he placed his milk can down with a clang and stood stiffly to attention. When *God Save the King* was over, Mr Cooper sat down on the top of his milk can with his eyes all creased at the corners. 'Well! It's the first time in all my born days I've had the *King* played for me, and that's a fact,' he said looking towards Gramp with a smile.

'I'm sorry Mr Cooper,' I said. 'We didn't really play *God Save the King* for you. I hope you don't mind but Gramp was playing it for the King who had just been piped aboard *H.M.S. Victory*.'

'Is that really true young man?' asked Mr Cooper, looking puzzled.

'Yes,' I replied. 'You see, it's *The Glorious First of June* today when we defeated the French fleet in a great sea battle and this is the Solent review to …'

'Honour it!' Mr Cooper exclaimed falling over his aitch.

---

150   Nelson's *HMS Victory* was launched in 1765 and so the King at the time was George III (1738-1820) who reigned from 1760 to 1820. If the King inspected the Fleet he would wear the uniform of an Admiral of the Fleet and be piped on board as a sign of respect. Here Gramp is pretending that the King is inspecting the Fleet and so is piping him on board with his brassy whistle-pipe.

151   This is Walter Edward Marks Cooper (1871-1939) who shared his milk round with his brother William Richard Marks Cooper (1880-1960) delivering milk for the Woodlands Dairy. They lived together at *The Bays*, New Road, Wootton. Sadly, Walter died of his injuries during his milk round on 22 August 1939 when he and his milk cans were accidentally knocked down by the Wootton District Nurse Miss King as he was crossing the road. It appears from the inquest that this may have been due to his poor eyesight. According to his obituary, he was a Sunday School teacher at St. Edmund's Church and St. Mark's Church, was a man of sterling character, very fond of children, a non-smoker, practically a total abstainer and collected for many deserving causes (Isle of Wight County Press 26 August and 9 September 1939).

'Yes! That's right, Mr Cooper,' I said, 'and that's the *Victory*,' pointing to the ship, 'with the King aboard.'

'Ah! Now I'm beginning to understand what it's all about,' Mr Cooper said, inspecting each ship in turn almost as if he was the King, I thought. 'And I see,' he added, 'they are dressed all over for the great occasion.'

'That's right, Mr Cooper,' I agreed with pride.

'Then I think,' Mr Cooper said, turning to Gramp, 'we should have *Rule Britannia* and *Land of Hope and Glory*.'

'Quite right,' replied Gramp. So we had *Rule Britannia* and were halfway through *Land of Hope and Glory* when who should arrive but the butcher. The butcher, noticing Mr Cooper and the ships dressed all over, realized the importance of the occasion. So he stood looking very serious, with his feet together and his meat-plate tucked into his left side as if it was a navy hat. When Gramp ended *Land of Hope and Glory*, the butcher said, 'I think we should have it again, only this time we will sing the lines.'

'That's right,' Mr Cooper said, getting up from his can. 'If we sing it will fit the great occasion and then the crews will join in!'

'Of course,' said the butcher.

So Gramp played *Land of Hope and Glory* again. Mr Cooper started to sing in a beautiful deep voice, his beard moving with the music with its grey-whiteness glinting gold in the sun. The butcher's voice rose high above Mr Cooper's to be joined by Granny whose head appeared through the open kitchen window singing like a boy alone in church. Far across the sea-lawn from over Jolliffe's hedge came another voice, the voice of old Mr Jolliffe himself, rising and falling in the onshore breeze. It was a little behind the others but, as Gramp said afterwards, it made us mightier yet!

'My that was good,' the butcher said, handing the price-ticketed meat through the window to Granny.

'It was that,' said Mr Cooper. 'I wouldn't have missed the review for worlds,' whispering in the butcher's ear the loudest whisper I'd ever heard. He was so close to the butcher his beard tickled his face. 'It's the review of the fleet with the King. It's *The Glorious First of June* today,' Mr Cooper added.

'Why of course it is!' the butcher said looking at me. Then inspecting the ships with pleasure, he said to my pride, 'One of the best reviews I've ever attended for many a day,' and then continued walking down the path to his small meat van whistling *Rule Britannia.*

'Well young man,' Mr Cooper said. 'I shall have to be on my way too. Can't let even a naval review keep everyone waiting for their milk or I'll be in trouble.' Mr Cooper filled Granny's two pint milk jugs with his measure from his milk can giving a little extra drop to each jug making Granny smile with pleasure.

'Mr Cooper,' I started. 'Where did you, where did you fight in the last war?'[152]

'Oh, I was not strong enough to fight young man. I had to stay at home to take people their milk but my brother, the other milkman who does the other half of the village, was in the trenches.'

'In the trenches,' I said. 'He must have been brave!'

'He was that,' said Mr Cooper.

'Do you mean Mr Cooper the tall milkman in the white coat and yellow face with a red nose? Is that really your brother?'

'He is that,' said Mr Cooper with pride.

'You mean Mile Cooper is your brother,' I exclaimed, looking at Gramp in amazement.

'Well I'm jiggered,' said Mr Cooper, thinking as hard as he could. 'My brother called Mile Cooper! I've never heard that before. Never!'

Meanwhile, Gramp, shaking his whistle-pipe against the end of his fingers to remove the spittle, explained, 'We call your brother Mile Cooper within the family because when he sees you coming a mile away he starts a conversation!'

'Of course, Mr Starks. Come to think of it, that's true enough!' Mr Cooper smiled. 'When you see him next, Peter, ask him about the last war. But if you do some will have their milk near dark I'll be bound!'

---

152  The First World War.

Mr Cooper took up his can turning to go, then put it down again and standing to attention, saluted the fleet.

I returned my ships to the old shed, Gramp saying there had never been a review quite like it. But by now I was thinking of Mile Cooper. I must ask him about the war I thought. I'll catch him on his round on the other end of the village as soon as I could.

On the next Saturday morning I slipped out down the village hill in search of Mile Cooper. I hadn't gone far when a long way in the distance I could see the white coat and the two milk cans glittering in the sun like a diamond in Mummy's ruby ring. Mr Cooper disappeared for a moment through a garden gate to reappear coming slowly up the hill. There was a strong wind blowing in my face when all at once the booming voice of Mr Cooper reached me. 'Morning Peter.' I knew my voice couldn't reach Mile Cooper, but I shouted out cupping my hands, 'Good morning Mr Cooper.' He put down his milk cans, shouting back as if he'd heard. 'Just going in here a minute,' disappearing between two hedges.

By the time he'd reappeared I was within a stone's throw. Mr Cooper shouted to me about the weather and I shouted back agreeing with everything. At last we stood side by side as the milk cans were safely placed by Warne's, the baker's[153], gatepost. Mr Cooper took my hand which he always did, completely enclosing mine in its roughness as we shook. After Mr Cooper had asked about Gramp and had enquired if the birds were laying well, I managed to ask, 'Did you really fight the Germans in the last war, Mr Cooper?'

A look of complete happiness spread all over Mr Cooper's face at this question, the yellow of his face clearing into a whitish pink, as he made himself comfortable on the iron railing of Warne's fence.

'Yes, I fought the Germans, Peter!' Mr Cooper began. 'Four long years of it, in and out of the trenches. I'd be a rich man if I had a pound for every shot I'd fired!'

---

153 'Frank Greenham Warne had his bake house behind his house, called Clovelly, about halfway up the hill. He was already a baker, living at Wootton Bridge when he married Louisa Williams at Gatcombe in 1894. In 1905, three years after being widowed, he married Frances Wickendon at Binstead. Like the butcher and the grocer it was expected that the baker would deliver the bread straight to the door.' (Gosden, 1998, p. 23).

'Did you kill any Germans with your sword, Mr Cooper?' I asked expectantly.

'We didn't have swords, only short pieces of steel called bayonets fixed to the end of our rifles. When we went over the top of the trenches charging the Germans and stuck a bayonet in a German's belly, he'd yell like old Bennett's pigs at the top of your garden on a killing night!'

Mr Cooper didn't say anything for a moment while he collected his thoughts so I climbed onto the iron railing beside him making myself comfortable. Then he said, 'One day I must have killed a dozen, some I shot and some with the bayonets. Paid a shilling a day we were, which made it about a penny a dead German. That's all we got, a shilling a day.'

It was the first time I'd met anyone, outside my history picture books or when catching a bird on the couch, who had killed a man. Mr Cooper didn't look fierce; in fact he didn't look as if he could ever be angry, yet he'd killed all these Germans.

'It was the poor horses I was sorry for', Mr Cooper began again. 'You see, they didn't know what it was all about. It was terrible to hear them when they were wounded.'

'Were you ever wounded, Mr Cooper?'

Mr Cooper rolled up his coat sleeve. 'I've still got some bits and pieces of shrapnel in me. Can you see these little black marks? Mind you, most of them have gone now.'

I looked and touched the little black marks.

'I had a touch of gas as well. That was the worst. I get a cough every winter. It's what makes me face yellow so they say.'

I'd heard Gramp talking about how they used gas in the war, so I understood. The black marks were fascinating. I touched them again, feeling real war, making my fingers tingle with excitement.

'Was no good Peter. I hope you never see one, but if it comes, well, you see, it's your country.'

The road sweeper walked slowly by with a measured step, as if, Gramp would say, he was at Queen Victoria's funeral. His white shirtsleeves were furled like topsails gleaming in the sun. 'Good morning, Will,'[154] he called with a smile at me.

Mr Cooper didn't see or hear him as, almost talking to himself, he said, 'Here I am, home in a land fit for heroes to live in, they said. Give me a milk round and cows. They can keep their war. I can't grumble. I'm one of the lucky ones.'

Mr Cooper must be a hero, I thought, thinking of him being back home on the land with his cows fit for heroes. So I asked, 'Are you a hero, Mr Cooper?'

'Bless you, no Peter! I'm no hero. Heroes were men who got the VC and things for being brave'.

'But you were very brave killing all those Germans.'

'No Peter! That was only doing what I had to do. It's when you do more than you have to, then you're brave.'

Mr Cooper straightened himself and picked up his cans. As he turned to return down the hill, he smiled. I looked after him. He'd gone quite a way from where I stood when he looked back and shouted, 'Goodbye, Peter.'

'Goodbye,' I echoed.

He walked on, putting down his cans to turn again, shouting, 'Don't know what your Gramp will say, me, talking about the war.'

'He won't mind,' I shouted.

I started to walk back up the hill, stopping several times to look at Mr Cooper walking slowly with his cans. It was a beautiful day. I ran the rest of the way home from Wootton Lodge corner. When I talked to Gramp later he said some wonderful things about Mile Cooper, saying he was really very, very brave and kind as well. This was just as I had thought.

---

154  This is William Richard Marks Cooper (1880-1960) listed in the 1921 census as working at Woodlands Dairy and living with his brother Walter at *The Bays*, New Road, Wootton (Wootton Bridge Historical, 2015). He would have been 34 at the start of the war in 1914, 38 in 1918 and around 44 when my father knew him in 1924.

# 25

# ANOTHER MISADVENTURE
# WITH VICTORIA

Victoria called on her way home from afternoon school for me to go out to play. It was another beautiful day in one of the best summers Gramp could remember.

'Let's go to the bluebell wood,' Victoria said, which was in a part of the grounds of Fernhill[155] off Packsfield Lane.[156] It was a beautiful, lovely clearing in the copse[157] made very exciting by a noticeboard which, I knew, read 'Trespassers Will Be Prosecuted', with a gamekeeper always about on the lookout for trespassers. As we were leaving, Mummy called, 'Don't forget you have your new shoes on. Don't kick any stones. Perhaps you'd better change them. Your memory's like a colander!'

'I won't forget', I replied.

We walked up the road to Packsfield Lane with our arms around each other's waists. Within a few minutes we were crawling through a well-worn gap in the hedge into the copse leading to bluebell land. Soon we reached

---

155   Thomas Orde Powlett, 1st Baron Bolton built Fernhill House shortly after the purchase of the estate in 1790. At the time of Peter and Victoria's misadventure, the owners were Major C. G. Brodie and his wife Mrs Brodie J.P. As mentioned earlier, their son was married to Peter's nursery school teacher of Hillgrove House. Major Brodie died in 1933 and the house burnt down in 1938 (Gosden, 2000, pp. 28-9). 'To my mind, it must have been heavenly to wander in splendid solitude across the fields to the lake itself, savouring the beauty of it all, for in those days all this land stretching down to the bridge at Wootton belonged to Fernhill, thus making it one of the most beautiful estates on the Island' (Wilson, 1976, p.1). 'This was a very lovely house and was some way off the main road, down a long drive with wooded countryside all around it. They had their own little chapel just inside the gates and when St. Mark's Church was built [the chapel] was used by the Mothers' Union' (Snow, 1986, p.31).

156   'The lane was a clear road for some one hundred yards and then there was a copse. All the way down this there was a pathway to the farm by the railway […]. It was called Packs' Field' (Snow, 1986, p.32).

157   Peter refers to this elsewhere as 'Brodie's Copse' as the owners were the Brodies.

the clearing filled with bluebells. It was almost as if we were on the edge of a picture book heaven: the soft grass under our feet felt like a wavy cloud and the little stream rising and falling over the stones and tree roots sounded like heavenly music. We stretched ourselves by the stream, resting our elbows on the cool grass with our chins in our hands, watching our world.

A bumble bee droned its way into a bluebell, making a grumbling sound as if to complain that other bees had been there before him.

'Isn't he big,' Victoria said. We smiled, hands touching.

'Look,' I whispered.

A hare sat on the edge of the clearing, paws somehow going over the back of his head, giving his long ears a good wash. The hare was joined by another to play a game of 'It'[158] or so it seemed. They rushed at each other, stopped, touched each other with a paw, jumped back then jumped one over the other to begin again, ending up running this way and that. We couldn't stop laughing at this unbelievable circus.

'I feel like Alice in Wonderland,' Victoria said. It was just like fairyland, I thought. The white rabbit would arrive at any moment muttering about his gloves or the Mad Hatter's tea party would begin right before our eyes.

'Let's pretend this is the garden through the door,' Victoria exclaimed, 'and let's pick some bluebells and daisies. I'll make you a bluebell chain if you'll make me a daisy chain.'

We busied ourselves picking handfuls of bluebells and daisies. We then sat down to make our chains, pausing for a moment to watch a large hairy caterpillar, with its back going up and down, hurrying on its way to nowhere. High up in the treetops, out of sight, wood pigeons cooed incomplete sentences, and, if you really stopped to listen hard enough, you could pick out the thrushes' and blackbirds' voices in this non-stop other world of song. Victoria paused from her daisy-chain making.

'Keep guard,' she said. 'If you see the silly old gamekeeper coming start to whistle.'

---

158   Also known as Tag.

Victoria disappeared out of sight behind a tree. My thoughts returned to Ashey races and the tune *When the Red, Red Robin Comes Bob, Bob, Bobbin' Along* which Gramp had taught me to whistle. I started to whistle the tune with all my might. At once a red-faced Victoria appeared whispering expectantly, 'Where's the silly old gamekeeper?'

'Don't know,' I said, adding another daisy to my chain.

'But you whistled!'

'Sorry, Victoria, I forgot.'

'You forgot!' she screamed, hammering my chest with her fists. 'You silly thing. I've wet my pants because of you!'

She disappeared, saying between clenched teeth, 'Don't you dare forget this time!'

I didn't and in a moment she was back. I must have been forgiven for she fixed the bluebell chain around my neck, hurrying me to finish hers, which needed more daisies because of their shorter stems.

With my chain finished, and safely around Victoria's neck, it was time to leave. As we started to run, my foot caught in a tree root, sending me over and over with blood on my knee. It hurt quite a lot but, thinking of Mile Cooper, I didn't cry, until Victoria said, 'Look at your shoe!'

My new shoes, I thought, afraid to look, knowing Victoria must have discovered something terrible. I then looked and began to cry, rubbing my eyes with my knuckles. The sole of my right shoe had broken away with the toes of my little white socks looking through.

'My new shoes,' I said between gasps of tears. 'Your new shoes,' Victoria joined in, starting to cry showing that she understood my feelings.

All at once she stopped crying and pulled my arm. 'I think I can save you,' she said.

The shock of this sudden and unexpected news made me stop crying too, going all hiccups in excitement.

'If we hurry down the hill to Harry Wavell[159] he'll fix it. He can fix anything,' she added.

159  Harry Wavell (1896-1960) is listed in the 1911 and 1921 Census as living in Red Road (Wootton Bridge Historical, 2015). He was the son of William George Wavell (a carter) and

*Permission kindly given to reproduce the image from Hilary Lloyd's Postcard Collection. Photo circa 1910. Out of copyright and in the public domain.*

With this happy thought my hiccups vanished. We left, running as fast as my shoe would let me, then walking, then running until we were near the bottom of Wootton Hill. We then turned into Red Road and went through a white gate into a front garden, passing the house's side back door going into the back garden. Victoria led the way to a chicken house where the noise of a lot of hammering, together with men's and children's voices, reached us. Victoria knocked on the chicken house door. Everything went all quiet till a voice called 'come in', the 'come' starting low down going high up on the 'in'.

Two men and three children about my own age sat on a school form-seat, which nearly went along the whole length of the chicken house. In the corner, on an old kitchen chair, sat one of the happiest and mightiest men I'd ever seen. His white shirt was undone at the neck because his neck was too big for a shirt. His bare arms with rolled-up sleeves reminded me of the low-down apple branches on our old Bramley that you could swing on. His face on top

---

Fanny Glasspell. 'When I was young a cobbler lived there. He was a cripple, but he was a good mender of shoes etc. When I was older I would stand and watch him. That way I got to be able to mend my own shoes sometimes' (Snow, 1986, p.23).

of his shirt was all brown like his arms, and his hair was jade black like Auntie Aggie's[160] jade beads. He smiled at me from a mouth full of protruding nails. In all my little life, I had never seen anyone or anything quite like it. He was surrounded by boots and shoes, hammer in hand, looking at an old boot. Between his knees he held a round piece of wood with an upturned iron shoe looking out, on which he suddenly fixed the old boot, sole up. He placed a lovely shiny piece of leather on top of the boot sole which he fitted all over. He smiled at me again from his mouthful of nails and I knew at once he was one of my best friends.

I watched, fascinated, as nail after nail from his mouth was hammered straight and true into the browny leather sole, the edges being smoothed with a rough-looking file and then made black, like the rest of the boot, with a strange-looking tool. It was the first time in my life I had ever seen a shoemaker at work. It was an unforgettable delight. My new found friend tossed the boot to one of the men, sitting on the form, who was smoking a long clay pipe and wearing clothes covered in bits of straw.

'There you are, Brother', he said to the clay-pipe man.

'Times are 'ard. Pay me on pay day. I'll do t'other sole next week when you can spare the time.'

The clay-pipe man put the boot on his bootless foot. 'Thanks 'arry,' he said.

The job finished, my shoemaker friend was at once invaded by Victoria and three other little girls who clambered all over him, one settling on each arm and two on his lap. I was completely forgotten amid the laughter and hugs but, at last, Victoria remembered and smiled at me. Jumping down she said, 'This is my friend Peter.'

Harry gave one big smile of white teeth now replacing the nails in his mouth. His hand still holding the hammer, he put it among the other tools on an old upturned box and then stretched his hand out towards me. 'Pleased to meet you, Brother.'

I didn't quite know what to say. One thing I knew. There must be some mistake. I only had one brother. Besides, the clay-pipe man was a brother as

---

160   Aunt Agnes Ellen Morris (1863-1936).

well, which seemed to make things more complicated than ever. My thoughts tumbled over themselves. His hand was warm and moist from all that hard work. I was wondering what to say when I remembered Granny saying, if you didn't know which fork or spoon to eat with you should wait and see what the others were using. And if you didn't know what to say when meeting anyone you couldn't go far wrong if you gave the same reply, so I said, 'Pleased to meet you Mr er, Mr er Brother.'

'Harry,' he said laughing and releasing my hand. 'I'm Harry Wavell, Brother. We're all Brothers aren't we?'

The straw-bits-covered man, with the new sole, removed his clay pipe with a jerk, replacing it with a fag, saying in between, 'That's right, Harry.'

'Well, it's like this,' said Harry lighting his pipe again. 'It's like this, Peter. All of us are brothers and sisters 'aint we?' turning his head to the boys and girls leaning against the shed. They all answered with a very loud 'Yes' and the three men on the bench moved their heads up and down looking very important. But I still didn't understand and wished Gramp was sitting next to me. He would have explained it to me. Gramp always said, 'If you don't understand anything Peter don't be afraid to ask,' so I said, 'I'm sorry, but I don't understand how you are all my brothers and sisters 'cause I'm sure I would have had to know all about your birthdays, 'cause I always give my big brother Morris a present.'

This caused my friends, leaning against the chicken house, to giggle with smiles from the three men as we waited, while Harry pressed the matchbox on the top of his pipe, puffing huge clouds of sore-throat smoke towards the roof. 'You have your brother don't you, Peter?' asked Harry through the drifting smoke.

'I love him, but I didn't love him much the other day when he told Granny I'd forgotten to wipe my shoes and I'd left mud on the front room carpet and Granny gave me a hard smack.'

'Yes, and I had a smack the other day and was put to bed before bedtime when my brother told my parents I had broken one of their best cups,' Victoria said, adding, 'Brothers can be horrid sometimes.'

'And so can sisters,' a little boy said who was about my age.

'Yes, but if one of your brothers or sisters was hurt, say by falling out of a tree and breaking a leg or something, wouldn't you be very unhappy?' Harry asked looking from one child to the other.

'I know I would,' said Victoria. 'And so would I, and so would I,' all of us added.

'So you see,' said Harry, 'you really do love each other, all of you, and when I call people Brother, Peter, it means I love them like a brother. God made us all brothers and sisters and told us to love one another and that's what we've got to do. We must all do things for each other and help one another because it's in doing and helping that makes us loving.'

'So there you are!' Harry exclaimed. 'Now what can I do for you, Brother?'

Victoria answered quickly in one breath. 'Peter has his new shoes on. He was running along and fell over a tree root. It's broken his shoe. He didn't cry when he fell down, only after when he saw his shoe!'

'I can see you've both been crying from them dirty marks round yer eyes. No need fer that. We can't 'ave people cryin' in the world can we, Brother?' Harry said, nodding to the clay-pipe man's agreement.

'Then we shall 'ave to do somethin' about it Peter,' Harry said turning to me. 'Let's 'ave a look at yer shoe.'

Harry inspected my shoe first one way and then the other, running his eye along it. Oh dear, I thought, oh dear!

'Well,' he announced, 'it's faulty workmanship and no mistake.'

Much to my amazement he found a large needle with thick black cotton and started to sew. He didn't sew for long, finishing off cleaning my shoe with a piece of rag.

'Give me t'other shoe Peter,' he said cleaning that as well and then, looking very pleased with himself, he placed them on my feet with a final wipe. He then poured some water from an old wine bottle into a small galvanised bowl, tearing off a piece of rag from the old rag on the floor.

'Come you two jokers,' he said giving Victoria's face a wash and then mine, leaning back in his chair with pleasure.

'There you are, both fit to go before a queen. Your shoe is better than new,' Harry observed, smiling at me.

I bubbled over with thanks, but how could I pay for my shoe? The clay-pipe man was going to pay next week, but my Ashey race winnings had gone. The more I thought about it the worse I felt. I could feel my face burning redder and redder. While Harry was looking at me I could see his smile slowly going until his face was all fixed and wondering about the money.

'I'm just a thinking what's biting you, Brother,' Harry said, leaning forward at me. 'Whatever can the matter be this time?'

'Mr Wavell, I mean Harry,' I stammered. 'I'm afraid I've no money left. Can I save up and pay you next year?' I blurted out, surprised I'd managed to ask such a favour.

Harry swayed backwards and forwards in his chair with great shakes of laughter. The other man, who hadn't said a word so far, laughed so much he had to stand up, while the clay-pipe man choked and spluttered over his pipe so that I thought he would burst. The little girls with Victoria shook with laughter, though what could be so funny about me not having any money I could not understand.

'Whoever heard,' said the quiet man, sitting down again, 'of anyone asking to pay next year!'

'Well, I never did!' said Harry, repeating again, 'Well, I never did!'

'He's a regular Isle-of-Wighter,' said the quiet man, waving a hand in my direction. 'You can tell that. He's a long-headed one!'[161]

I felt my cheeks burn again with this news. I didn't think my head was longer than Victoria's or anyone else's. I would have a look in the mantelpiece mirror at home. Perhaps if it was long it would get shorter when I got taller, I thought. I certainly hoped it would. I'd ask Gramp about it.

Harry continued to smile, running his hands through his hair. 'No charge fer a little job like that, Brother. We must 'elp each other, fer a little 'elp's worth a pound of pity!'[162]

---

161 Shrewd.

162 This is the same proverb as 'A little help is worth a deal of pity' or similar to 'Actions speak louder than words'.

Harry groped around on his worktable, as I was busy with my thanks, finding a flat tin box with some matches inside, saying to himself, 'Funny, thought I'ad one,' closing it with a tiny snap.

'Peter, I expects you would like to do a little job for me.'

'Oh, yes please, yes please,' I replied feeling very, very important.

'Then run up to old Mother Johnson's.[163] Ask 'er fer a twopenny Wood fer Mr Wavell. You'll be back before I'm 'alf way there on me crutches with this old leg of mine,' giving his left leg a slap, which for the first time I noticed was all twisted, resting over his right knee.

I didn't know the shop but Victoria did, so she ran with me all the way until we came to Mother Johnson's in the High Street, just across the road from the corner of Red Road. When we pushed open the door, a bell clanged, just like the Newport fire engine's bell. On one side of the shop there were a lot of old books on shelves, which Victoria informed me you could borrow for a halfpenny. Some of the books were amongst the sweet jars. Mrs Johnson, who was wearing a blue dress and had her hair parted in the middle, appeared from a door at the back of the shop with her washtub-arms, dripping, taking up a lot of the uneven shop floor, with her head bent enquiringly.

'Please may I have a twopenny piece of Wood for Mr Wavell?' I asked, the twopence disappearing into a shiny red box as Mrs Johnson wiped her hands on an old towel from the counter. To my great surprise and concern, Mrs Johnson handed me a green paper packet, open at one end, with five cigarettes looking out, reminding me of Gramp's Dr Blossers. 'Mrs Johnson,' I hesitated, 'but Mrs Johnson, Mr Wavell wanted a twopenny piece of Wood!'

Mrs Johnson bent forwards and then back, hands on hips with a look of disbelief on her face, starting to go 'ho! ho! ho!' in a voice like a man's. Then recovering she said, 'I sees you 'aven't started to smoke yet. Them's Woodbine

---

163 '[The] sweet-shop was owned by a little old lady named Mrs. Johnson. She wore steel-rimmed glasses and did her hair in a bun, and she would sell you a half pence of raspberry-drops or a farthing strip of liquorice, or a packet of sherbet with a pipe of liquorice to suck it through, or a half pence of bullseyes. You could get chocolate of course, 2d a bar, or a large bar for 6d in old money' (Snow, 1986, p.27). Alice Johnson ran the sweetshop after her husband James Johnson died in 1927. She also lent out books at tuppence a time [although Victoria says it was half a penny] (Gosden, 1998, p.22).

cigarettes. That's a twopenny Wood!' handing us two large pieces of broken chocolate for being kind, making us very happy.

On our return to Harry, we found him alone but for the smoke cloud from the clay pipe which made a little heaven under the sloping roof.

'It's just about time I called it a day,' Harry said when I handed him the cigarettes, turning over the face down alarm clock from his wooden workbox to check the time. 'But I'll just enjoy one of them Woods before I go in fer me tea,' he added.

Harry got up with the help of a crutch under his left arm. He then opened the chicken house door and stood, with his one good leg on the broken-ash path, leaning against the little chicken house. Lighting his cigarette, he closed his eyes, creating, every now and again, a blue-grey puff of happiness. The air was still with no movement in the quiet. We stood, thrilled, embraced by Harry's delight of smoke rings following one another, reaching up to the big blue sky until they were lost in nothingness.

'You know, Brother,' Harry said suddenly to me, between smoke rings, 'I'm a millionaire!'

'A millionaire!' I exclaimed, remembering a millionaire was someone very, very rich like the man in Gramp's song *The Man Who Broke the Bank at Monte Carlo*.[164] Gramp would never believe it when I told him. I could just see his face and hear him say, 'Pon my puff. Well, that beats cockfighting and shows what comes of mending boots and shoes!' and Granny would be sure to say, 'My Godfathers, a millionaire!'

'Yes!' Harry continued. 'What more could a man want. Me, me own master, outside me own chicken 'ouse, with me smoke rings an' you two kids fer company, in lovely old Wootton, on a summer's day with the Mill Pond shining through them fruit trees. I'm a millionaire!'

---

164 This was a popular British music hall song written in 1892 by Fred Gilbert. The song was inspired by the gambler and confidence trickster Charles Wells who won over a million francs at the Monte Carlo casino using the profits from previous fraud, though he died penniless in 1926 (Genius, 2020). Perhaps this is the moral point of this reference. Lyrics: I've just got here, to Paris, from the sunny southern shore; / I to Monte Carlo went, just to raise my winter's rent. / Dame Fortune smiled upon me as she'd never done before, / And I've now such lots of money, I'm a gent. / Yes, I've now such lots of money, I'm a gent.

Turning down the wick of his paraffin lamp, as I was about to leave, Harry said, 'Young man, pull down the outside shutter for me or I shall have to visit the chimney sweep tomorrow and have my throat swept.' This was one of the funniest things I had ever heard.

When I arrived home late for tea with nothing said, I told Gramp about our visit to Harry Wavell's, though I was careful not to mention the shoe. Gramp's eyes shone just the way I knew they would when I told him about Harry being a millionaire with, 'Pon my puff. Well, that beats cockfighting and shows what comes of mending boots and shoes!' But I was wrong about Granny for she was so surprised she couldn't even say 'My Godfathers!'

Some days afterwards, Gramp said, 'You know, Harry made a very good job of your shoe, Peter!' Fancy Gramp knowing this, I thought, and when I asked him how he knew he smiled and said, 'A little dicky bird had whispered it in my ear early one morning when you were still sleepybyes, and the little dicky bird had heard it from the white blackbird who knows everything.'

# 26

# A WALK WITH GRAMP TO ARRETON: A MUSE ON GOD, 'MAUD' AND 'THE DAIRYMAN'S DAUGHTER'

This Sunday morning was wonderful. The birds had been fed and the pleasant smell of bacon lingered on over our last cup of tea. Gramp lit a Doctor Blosser's, blowing out a scented world between sips of tea. Either side of the living room window, open top and bottom, Granny's summer lace curtains talked to each other, making a rustling conversation. They nodded every now and then to the large wooden curtain rail as the wind from the lawn twisted them sideways as if the wind were fluttering its wings. From the top of the garden a pullet boasted a laid egg, some rooks were holding a meeting in Brodie's trees and, from our garden, every bird was in song.

'My puff. Pon my puff,' Gramp said, 'it's a nice day for the race and no mistake.'

This made me excited for I knew Gramp had something in mind. I also knew it didn't mean Ashey races either but the human race (with Mrs Jones' dropped aitch). Whenever Gramp said it was a nice day for the race, he had a plan, and it was certain the plan would be carried out.

'Where are we going? What are we going to do Gramp?' I asked all in one breath, climbing onto his knee.

'I've been thinking. If we smarten ourselves up a bit we could leave with plenty of time to walk to Down End with a stroll on the downs with something to wet our whistle at Arreton. There's a Pig and Whistle[165] near the church,'[166] Gramp said looking pleased at the happy thought.

---

165   The White Lion.

166   St. George's Church, Arreton.

*The Dairyman's Daughter's Cottage © C M Lansley*

'What shall I wear? What shall I wear?' I shouted, jumping down from Gramp's knee, thinking all Pig and Whistle.

'Your fawnish shorts and shirt, Ashey race shoes with white peaked cap and I'll wear my blue-serge suit with high-crowned hat, not forgetting my best silver-knobbed stick,' replied Gramp. 'And we'll both look as smart as a bandbox, won't we?' added Gramp tickling me under the chin.

Within two shakes of a duck's tail I had given my face a freshener with one wipe of Granny's scented face flannel from the cold tap, leaving my bird-feeding clothes in a heap upon the bedroom floor. With Mummy saying sleepy 'yes' and 'nos' in all the wrong places, I jumped into my summer Sunday clothes making sure my Ashey white hat sat on the back of my head like a jockey. Liking myself in the old wardrobe glass, I rushed from the bedroom before Mummy could gather her wits.

Downstairs in the living room, I waited impatiently for Gramp calling repeatedly, 'Are you coming, Gramp?' until I could see Gramp's blue-serge legs through the stair banisters, which filled me with such joy I turned summersaults on the floor, bouncing onto my feet like a jack-in-the-box when Gramp entered. Gramp looked at himself in front of the overmantel mirror, adjusting his high-crowned hat. I could tell he was excited about our trip from the way he patted his hat first one way and then the other, smiling all creases, his blue eyes twinkling like glass marbles. Gramp turned round, smoothing the silver knob of his walking stick, throwing it into the air with happiness and catching it like the band leader at the fete. He then hit the dining room table with his stick, in pleasure, making me glad for Gramp that Granny was having a Sunday lie in. This made our trip more exciting with no one to wave us goodbye or tell us to be careful or to mind how we go.

I tingled from head to toe thinking we were like two ships going to war with sealed orders into an unknown adventure, just like Uncle Harry on his submarine in 1914. Noiselessly, we slipped out of the back door into the perfect day, Gramp picking a snow-white pink for his buttonhole from the pinks that edged the gravel path, the carnations and pinks being his favourites, I knew. Granny had told me one day that Gramp loved them because they reminded him of ladies in dancing dresses. Gramp swung his stick, giving it a little twist at the end of each step, his eyes talking and laughing whenever he looked down at me, which he did very often with a squeeze of my hand. From many open kitchen doors you could hear the sound of breakfast things, while a little further along the road, just past the church, stood white-rolled-up-sleeve-suited Mr Freeman, leaning on his gate, puffing sweet-smelling smoke in a bluey cloud from his long clay pipe. Removing it with a smile of pleasure, he said, 'A nice day for the race,' before Gramp could even say it. Gramp raised his high-crowned hat, adding that it was good to be alive, taking great big breaths to prove it.

Gramp and Mr Freeman talked at once of horses and their luck, as I knew they would. Mr Freeman said, with a lowered voice, that he had had a lucky week with three long-priced winners, which made me give my arm a pinch to remember to remind Gramp that Mr Freeman hadn't had a lucky week after all. Yesterday, Mrs Freeman had told Gramp that her hubby (which she'd explained to me afterwards was really Mr Freeman) was down on his luck with three short-priced losers. I couldn't be mistaken I knew, because I had felt so sorry at the news, thinking of poor Mr Freeman having such luck. At the same time, I had a little giggle at Mr Freeman being Mrs Freeman's hubby, because I thought it meant 'hobby', which sounded so funny. When I told Granny we had met Mrs Freeman's 'hobby', Granny and Gramp nearly choked. Gramp said he didn't think Mr Freeman could be much of a hobby to Mrs Freeman after all these years, which made me decide to ask the butcher the difference between a hobby and a hubby when he came with next week's joint. He would know if anybody did, that I was sure, and I knew he would tell me even if he had to whisper it in my ear.

Should I remind Mr Freeman he'd really had three losers, I thought? In fact, I was just going to remind him, giving Gramp's hand a pull to let him know I was going to speak, when Mr Freeman's tummy started to make noises like a flickering oil stove needing filling. This made me laugh so much that Mr Freeman and Gramp had to laugh too, with Gramp saying, 'What's tickling?' Both of them wanted to know the joke until suddenly Mrs Freeman's voice called 'breakfast' from the kitchen door down the path. Mr Freeman disappeared for his bacon and eggs before we could say 'Jack Robinson', 'goodbye' or even 'good luck' which I thought was a pity.

'My puff. If ever a man needed his breakfast, Mr Freeman did,' said Gramp as we continued on our way. 'A few more tummies like that would have made a brass band. Just think of a baker's dozen of early morning Mr Freemans during prayers in a church service!' added Gramp with his face all twinkles.

The thought of Mr Freeman's tummy going plop, plop, plip, plop in church with, now and then, a gurgle, like the gurgle of Granny's washing up water going down the kitchen sink, made me laugh and laugh and laugh until I had to sit down on the grassy bank outside Mr Gutteridge's,[167] the builder and decorator, to recover.

---

167   The 1935 Kelly's directory lists Charles Reginald Guttridge, decorator, at 2, Florence Cottages, Station Road. The cottages were situated between St Marks & Gravel Pit Road on the same side. He married Ada Florence Sheath in 1912 at the United Methodist Chapel,

Mr Gutteridge, also all blue-suited with his hair parted more in the middle than the side, appeared from the bottom of his garden path. He was followed by his son George, known as Podge, who went to my big brother Morris' school. This reminded me of the smell of football, a journey to Cowes during a storm in the night and Mrs Jones at the old copper[168] on a Monday. I loved Cowes but Wootton, I knew, was best of all, especially on a Sunday morning when it was a nice day for the race.

Mr Gutteridge started to talk about God just as Mr Freeman talked about horses. Nearly every word, or so it seemed, began with God. Gramp's face remained very serious and Podge hardly breathed. God could do anything, or at least Mr Gutteridge thought so, and I could see from Gramp's face that he believed him, or if not quite, very nearly. God, Mr Gutteridge said, over and over again, could do anything. 'Ask, that's all you had to do. If only people would ask God,' said Mr Gutteridge. Everyone was thinking very hard about God. Gramp's face was all fixed and Podge was looking at his shiny boots while Mr Gutteridge looked at the blue, blue sky like Rhodie on the perch about to fly. Thinking as hard as I could about God, I thought about the church and Mr Freeman's breakfast tummy with him saying his prayers. I thought of his tummy going plip, plop, plop, plop until I had the giggles again, though I tried to stop. But the harder I tried to stop the more I giggled until I laughed and laughed making Podge go blue in the face trying not to laugh himself, twisting sideways like a worm just dug up from the garden, making me think his Sunday best trousers would split.

Meanwhile, Mr Gutteridge, who was wondering what it was all about, had a face all fixed with, now and then, a little smile. So, I then said, 'I'm sorry, I'm sorry Mr Gutteridge, but you see I was laughing about, about Mr Freeman's break, breakfast tummy,' which made Mr Gutteridge look very, very surprised. And then, between giggles, more twisting from Podge, twinkles from Gramp's eyes and a smile from Mr Gutteridge, I told him how

Quay St, Newport and they had two children, George Reginald in 1914 (known as Podge) and Florence Ada, 1919. As his occupation was decorator, he was probably a lay preacher on the Methodist Circuit.

168   The copper supplied hot water so maybe Mrs Jones was doing some washing or cooking.

Mr Freeman's tummy had gurgled as it called for its breakfast. But what I had wanted to know, as Mr Gutteridge was talking about 'asking God', was whether Mr Freeman's tummy would have stopped going plip, plop, plop if Mr Freeman had prayed very hard at early morning service for it to stop. Mr Gutteridge was a very clever man, I knew, and cleverer than Tom's father, who was only a Parson. Mr Gutteridge was a builder and decorator in the week as well as a Parson on Sundays, which meant he must know nearly everything. Besides, Gramp had said he'd made a fine job when he had decorated our hall a lovely blue, so I asked, 'Mr Gutteridge, do you think God could have stopped Mr Freeman's tummy from making noises if Mr Freeman had asked very hard?'

At this question Gramp looked the other way while Mr Gutteridge smiled and wiped his face with his pocket handkerchief, with Podge thinking of Mr Freeman's tummy all over again. Mr Gutteridge then took a deep breath, thinking so hard over this important question that he forgot he had his best suit on and sat down beside me on the grassy bank. After playing with his right ear for a few moments he said, 'Peter, do you think if you asked God to stop the Ryde to Newport engine making the noise of its puff, puff that God would stop it?'

I didn't need to think about an answer and said at once, 'But I wouldn't want to ask God to stop the engine going puff, puff Mr Gutteridge. It has to go puff, puff to work because it's a steam engine.'

Mr Gutteridge gave his leg a slap and jumped from the bank as if he'd been stung by a wasp, only he was all smiles. 'That's it Peter. The engine has to go puff, puff to work just as Mr Freeman's tummy has to make noises when it's needing its breakfast. It has to work hard too so God wouldn't stop the noises even if He was asked to, would He?'

'No, that's true,' added Gramp looking all-knowing. 'So you see, Peter, now you know God will only give you what you ask for if it's really necessary, just as Mr Gutteridge says.'

'Quite right,' said Mr Gutteridge, following Podge up the garden path, turning with a happy smile as he disappeared behind the laurel bush at the end of the path.

'That's what I like about Mr Gutteridge,' said Gramp as we continued our way along the gravel road. 'It's as good as going to church to meet him on Sunday. He always makes you think Sunday, and it's good for you to be Sundays now and again. You feel better for it, like a fire freshly lit after the sweep's been. Remember too Peter, when you ask God for anything and you don't receive it, it will be because God knows your works and you're better without it! Promise you'll remember this all your life,' Gramp added, giving my hand a little squeeze.

'I promise,' I said, hearing the distant sound of the puff, puff from the Newport shunting yard. I knew I would never, in all my life, ask God to stop the sound of the Ryde to Newport engine, for one of the happiest sounds in all the world was the puff, puff getting nearer and nearer when waiting for a train.

Only a little way up the road from Mr Gutteridge's, by Miss Shedden's[169] was White's petrol station. We were very lucky for just as we arrived by the locked metal oil-and-petrol-smelling cupboard, who should draw up in his car, with lovely brass lamps, but the Captain.

'Good morning, Mr Stark. Good morning young Peter,' said the Captain, jumping out from the car and raising his hat.

'Good morning, Captain,' Gramp replied, sweeping his high-crowned hat off and on, reminding me of my kite on a windy day.

The Captain took out a large gold watch from his inside watch pocket, holding it by its thick gold chain. He then pressed a button, high up on the gatepost, and from far in the distance we heard the sound of the bell.

---

169   Miss Mary Constance Shedden (1862-1938) lived at Wootton House for forty five years. She was the second daughter of Mr Roscow Cole Shedden, J.P., of Millfield, East Cowes, and sister of Sir George Shedden. She raised a considerable sum for the building of St. Mark's Church, provided the stipend for the incumbent for several years until the church was taken over by the Rector of the Parish Church, and provided it with an organ. While the church was being built she threw open a large room in her house for church services, as well as missionary and other meetings, and for many years she conducted classes for mothers and for young women. She also took a great interest in the Wootton Football Club from its formation and lent her field for their matches and practice, and provided them with a room for committee meetings (Isle of Wight County Press Archive, 1938).

'Just three minutes,' the Captain said to Gramp, leaning forward at the same time as holding the watch under my nose, placing his thumb by one of the minute marks.

'In three minutes Peter, when the hand reaches my thumb, Mr White will be here. He may even be quicker if he hasn't had breakfast, but when he arrives he'll say "Good morning Captain, sorry I'm late" wiping his forehead with a red and white spotted handkerchief.'

'Ah! I hear him running,' the Captain observed. Mr White's steps could be heard getting louder and louder. 'He's making good time too and that means it's before breakfast,' laughed the Captain.

Suddenly, a very breathless, red-faced Mr White appeared. The minute hand hadn't reached the Captain's thumb. 'There you are, two and a half minutes. You've beaten your record Mr White,' said the Captain sliding his watch into his pocket.

'Good morning Captain. Sorry I'm late,' replied Mr White regaining his breath, wiping his forehead with his spotted handkerchief just as the Captain had described.

I tingled with excitement as Mr White pulled out a long silver-coloured chain from his trouser pocket, with a ring at the end with many keys of all sorts and sizes. What magic secrets Mr White must have to own so many keys, I thought, as I watched him pick out the long thin key from the bunch to open the lovely oil-stained smelly door. Inside, there was a pump, just like a garden pump, only petrol would come out of it, I knew. On a shelf beside it there were three metal jugs.

'Two gallons, please,' said the Captain. Mr White filled the largest metal jug and took it with a funnel to the car, making himself look very important. Gramp and the Captain's glances at Mr White made him take very deep breaths to show just how important his petrol filling really was.

When Mr White had finished, the Captain said, 'I think I'd better have the two petrol cans on the running board refilled as well in case I run out.' So the two cans were taken from the running board, wiped several times by Mr White, filled and replaced. Mr White then made a note in a very oil-stained book, which hung from a hook inside the cabinet.

'Oil next time, Captain,' said Mr White.

'Next time,' replied the Captain. The fascinating cabinet was then closed and locked. One day, I thought, when I was grown-up and had a car, Mr White would open it for me. What a day that would be.

As soon as the Captain knelt down in front of his lovely brass carriage lamps, I knew what we were going to do. We were going to play the game of faces, which I had wonderful memories of the last time I met the Captain on the way to school. In the game, the Captain made his face ten foot tall and then flatter than a pancake in the reflections of the brassy lamps. At once I had the giggles which became all laughter as the Captain made his nose all nose in the brassy lamps and then his face all face. Gramp joined in with his high-brimmed hat, first looking all hat, then all brim, then all flat face and then again all hat. The Captain was funniest of all with his face going redder and redder and with him pulling his ears to make them even longer. Funnier still, perhaps, was Mr White, who stood without saying a word or a smile on his fixed face, until the Captain said, 'Come on Mr White, the better the day, the better the deed. Let's see your Sunday face!'[170]

Mr White, of course, had to obey the Captain. He went creak, creak, creak as he bent his knees to look into the brassy lamps. It seemed he didn't know how to smile for suddenly he gave one mighty laugh instead. This caused his false teeth to pop halfway out of his mouth making us almost jump out of our skins. This was followed by him snapping them back in with an angry crack, crack like a dog catching a bone. His face became all fixed again as if he'd never laughed in all his life, which was nearly too much for the Captain and Gramp who both gave loud 'ho hos' with many 'pon my puffs' too from Gramp until they both sat down on the running board to recover.

---

170   At this time, Sunday was generally considered to be a day of rest, with many people believing it was a sin to work. However, some work on a Sunday was unavoidable. Work done on a Sunday (the better day of the week) had more merit and virtue than work done on any other day (Daily Proverbs, 2019). This proverb may have been quoted verbatim in response to being admonished for working on a Sunday. Here the Captain is telling Mr White it's OK to play the face game even though it is Sunday.

The fun over, and although Mr White still wasn't smiling, the Captain made him look very pleased when he said, 'A jolly good sport Mr White. You're a jolly good sport for joining in. A real sportsman.'

Gramp nodded his head to this which I remembered to do too, trying not to smile, though I still wanted to laugh thinking of Mr White's teeth, which I knew I would never forget.

'Going far?' the Captain asked, Gramp getting up from the running board.

'We're out for a walk to Down End,' replied Gramp.

'Then let me give you both a lift as far as the Iron Church. I'm on my way to call on your Governess,'[171] the Captain added, smiling at me.

Once again I knew the delight of the soft, shiny, coolness of the beautiful high-backed seat of the Captain's open Rover. With several honk, honks and many waves to Mr White, we were on our way. 'Have a good breakfast Mr White,' I called out. Mr White smiled at last, which made me so happy for Mr White, who no doubt was thinking of his breakfast.

On our way, we journeyed down Station Hill with the Captain and Gramp raising their hats to the Sunday walkers who all smiled. At Homestead Cottages, just before the Station, there was a little sweet shop, with lace curtains which was closed, and next to it was the road sweeper's cottage, with its front and back doors and windows opened to catch the day's air. The road sweeper was outside with his white sleeves rolled up high and his Sunday best leathery-gold shiny braces. He stood there just like a king admiring the road he would sweep again the following day. He raised his Sunday cap with a loud, 'Good Morning Captain' and a 'Morning Mr Starks' to Gramp and a 'Morning Peter' to me, making me feel like a prince of some fairy court on the way to an enchanted castle. All the while, Gramp held onto my coat tails just in case I forgot where I was and tumbled out into the road.

Over the Station tunnel we raced, the Station far below with the platform deserted but for the dancing flowers. Unhappily for me, there was no sight of a train, but Mr Spinks[172] the Station Master was walking down the steep

171   He is off to visit Peter's teacher Miss McKerchar at Hillgrove School, Hillgrove House.

172   Henry George Spinks (1867-1942) was an Island railwayman for nearly 40 years. He served in the King's Royal Rifles and retired as sergeant. He entered the service of the I.W.

path to the platform with his watering can, on his way to quench the thirst of his coloured, scented world. Up the hill from the Station, we raced past the Woodman's Arms, all shuttered and quiet, until, with a jerk, we came to a stop at the crossroads with its Iron Church glistening in the sun. Once again I enjoyed the sweet bonfire smell of tobacco from the Captain's coat on being swept from the high-buttoned seat onto the road, with the Captain and his Rover disappearing in a cloud of dust to Hillgrove School. With his voice rising and falling above the noise of his engine, the Captain promised to send my love to Miss McKerchar, making me blush. Gramp's eyes glistened with bluish mist, which they often did when people made him happy.

We crossed the road to the Iron Church, its galvanised iron walls already hot from the sun, burning to the touch. We walked slowly towards the grave mounds, then quietly between the sleeping people. Gramp carefully removed some nettles and coarse grass from one overgrown grave, revealing some little, miniature red and white roses. In his whispering voice, which he used when his thoughts were so strong they had to speak, Gramp said, 'Come into the garden Maud,[173] for who knows, who sleeps so safely here,' the little red and

---

Central Railway Company at Cowes in 1895 and served at Newport, Freshwater, Yarmouth, and Newport Railway Company. In 1910 he was appointed stationmaster at Yarmouth, where he lost his right arm in an heroic effort to save the lives of two men who were unloading coal from a truck on a siding. He subsequently had charge of the Wootton, Havenstreet, Ashey, and Whippingham Stations. He retired in 1933, when he received a clock from the Company in appreciation of his 39 years' service and was personally congratulated by Sir Herbert Walker (then chairman of the Southern Railway Company). Despite his disability he was an accomplished billiard player (Isle of Wight County Press, 1942).

173    This refers to Alfred Lord Tennyson's poem *Maud*, published in 1855, written at his home Farringford House on the Isle of Wight. The profits from its sale enabled him to purchase the house in 1856 which he had previously rented. The poem became an overwhelming success with Balfe's parlour song *Come into the Garden, Maud* (1857). In the poem, the speaker tells of his father's suicide following financial ruin. Lonely and miserable, he falls in love with Maud, the daughter of the wealthy neighbour who led his father into bankruptcy. After he kills Maud's brother in a duel, the speaker flees the country; he goes mad when he learns of Maud's death but recovers his sanity through service in war. At the beginning of the poem, the speaker discovers a rose floating in a rivulet and believes Maud has sent it to him as a message to wait for her. In the Victorian period, the language of flowers was seen as a secret code for lovers to communicate their thoughts but the speaker consistently misinterprets their significance as symbols of deep love. He casts Maud as the messiah who will enable his resurrection but it expresses sexual undercurrents. The speaker's very presence in Maud's enclosed rose garden alludes to the *Song of Solomon* 4.12, in which Mary's womb is a "garden

white roses now lying couched in Gramp's palm. I almost stopped breathing, for I knew Gramp's thoughts would speak again of Maud.

Gramp raised a little red rose[174] from the others and said, 'The little red rose cries:

"She is near, she is near,"' and then, taking the little white rose[175], he said, 'And the white rose weeps: "She is late; she is late." The larkspur listens, "I hear, I hear."'[176]

Gramp paused, straightening himself, resting on his silver stick. 'Listen, listen,' Gramp said, and we both listened very, very hard.

'It seems almost as if Tennyson is here,' Gramp smiled. 'Yes! He must be, for I hear little fairy footsteps and, look, the red roses seem to be getting redder and redder.'[177]

I looked at the little roses, their bright splashes of red on the green mound seeming to become brighter and brighter as I looked with Gramp's voice saying, 'I hear her, I hear her.'

'She is coming, my own, my sweet;

Were it ever so airy a tread,

My heart would hear her and beat,

Were it earth in an earthy bed;

My dust would hear her and beat,

enclosed," reflecting both purity and female sexuality. The speaker's presence in her garden therefore becomes a violation, especially since he let himself in. The image of the speaker's decomposing corpse, creating new life in the form of blossoming flowers, suggests that he sees himself as a part of the garden, even after death. His relationship with the garden, both real and imaginary, are an expression of his own desire and are therefore an extension of himself (Swafford, Joanna (2020).

174   The rose denotes passionate and sensual love but also symbolises something ominous suggested by the self-absorption implicit in the nature of passion (Steffler,1980, p.22-52).

175   The white rose foreshadows death. It's colour, in the context of a weeping image, recalls the "death-white curtain" in Maud's bedroom window that instils a sudden horror and fear of death in the speaker (Steffler,1980, p.22-52).

176   From *Maud* Part I, XXII, X (Tennyson, 2006, p.206). The larkspur is neutral, only listening. The speaker is caught between feeling hopeful, sad, and trying to listen to Maud's footsteps.

177   The garden rose is of a deep red colour, signifying bashful shame (Swafford, 2020).

*St. Michael and All Angels Cemetery Gate © C M Lansley*

Had I lain for a century dead;'
'Yes!' Gramp whispered, lowering his voice to a very, very low 'Yes!'
'My dust would hear her and beat,
Would start and tremble under her feet,
And blossom in purple and red.'[178]

We moved away, hushed, through the path beside the graves, Gramp weeding as we walked, cutting the more overgrown nettles down with his stick. I wondered about the people and their cats, dogs and birds and how they fed and cared for them, how they collected the birds' eggs and visited Newport market. I gave Gramp's hand a squeeze and he squeezed mine back with a knowing look on his face, so I didn't speak, though I thought about the picture in the old Bible of all the graves suddenly opening and everyone

---

178    From *Maud* Part I, XXII, XI (Tennyson, 2006, p.206). The image of the speaker's decomposing corpse creating new life in the form of blossoming flowers suggests that he sees himself as a part of the garden even after death (Swafford, 2020).

waking up. I knew of course it was not like this because all the people were angels, as Gramp had explained when he told me about Mount Joy. But what a lot all the people would have to talk about if they really could wake up all at once and what a surprise for everyone in the village. I could just imagine the Butcher's face when he came for his orders if I said, 'What do you think happened, Butcher,' and he would say, 'I don't know, Peter,' and then I would say, 'Why, haven't you heard? All the people buried at St. Edmund's Churchyard woke up all at once on Sunday morning.'

'Not all at once!' he would say, and Granny would be sure to say, 'My Godfathers!'

I smiled at this thought as I got another squeeze from Gramp's hand. Perhaps he had been thinking the same thing, for he was smiling too.

We left the Iron Church with its sleeping Islanders, not bothering to return through the church gate but through a much worn path and gap in the hedge on to the road for Down End.[179] The road was dusty, with little protection from the now hot sun and, every now and again, Gramp would stop to sit down on the grassy banks to regain his breath, until at last we arrived where the road bent like an open safety pin,[180] with beautiful pinewood Christmas trees growing close to the road on either side.

'We will go into the pines and have a little rest,' Gramp said, his moist hand taking mine, leading me into the cool soft-smelling pine air to an old fallen pine tree, half covered in ivy. Gramp spread his white top pocket handkerchief and his white 'to be used' handkerchief on the tree for us to sit on, lifting me with his hands under my arms onto the old trunk. The air was alive with summer. High up, out of sight of the pine treetops, wood pigeons talked of where to go, over and over again. From the pines themselves, pine sheddings fell through the sun-glinted branches, adding to the soft carpet surrounding us, making a home for insects and beetles. They also provided a happy hunting ground for the robin that flew from nowhere to breakfast

179   This is Briddlesford Road.

180   This is the junction of Long Lane and Briddlesford Road at the mini roundabout outside Robin Hill Country Park.

at our feet, singing with delight after each wriggling course swelled his red-dened breast.

Gramp took several deep breaths and then took out his brassy whistle pipe from his inside pocket, running his fingers quickly over the holes, playing scales and then, because it was Sunday, *All Things Bright and Beautiful*, with the little red robin joining in. It perched on the end of Gramp's outstretched boot, head on one side with half closed eyes of happiness. After several tunes, Gramp ended with *When the Red, Red Robin Comes Bob, Bob, Bobbin' Along* just to please the robin, Gramp said. It must have pleased the robin for it flew around us, from Gramp's boot and back several times chirping with delight, only flying away towards the road as Gramp ended, like someone leaving the Village Hall after a concert.

'I think,' Gramp said, cleaning his whistle-pipe, 'it's time we were on our way but before we leave I'll tell you the story of *The Dairyman's Daughter* because she lived at Arreton.

'*The Dairyman's Daughter*,' I repeated, immediately smelling the lovely farmyard smell of cows, hearing the swish, swish of tails and the rattle of milk pails just before milking time, seeing the baked-hard farmyard in summer and the sound of hooves squelching mud on rainy winter days when it was nearly dark by half past three. With these delightful thoughts, I jumped down from the tree trunk, resting my head on Gramp's knee, saying, 'Begin Gramp, begin,' because a story was the happiest of all things, especially a farmyard story. Gramp cleared his throat, lit a Dr Blosser's and then said quietly, 'It's nothing like the stories you hear about pirates and things when you're catching a bird on the couch with your Dad. It's not exciting or anything like that. It's just a true story about a little girl who lived near here a long, long time ago. Perhaps, I'll tell you all about her another day.'

This was too much for me, or almost too much, to know that Gramp had a story ready, yet considered keeping it for another day, so I said, 'Please Gramp, tell me now. I don't really mind it not being exciting,' quickly adding, 'no I don't,' as Gramp looked at me with a 'mind not quite made up' look. 'Please, Gramp,' I repeated. 'Tell me all about the farmyard and *The Dairyman's Daughter*. Please Gramp, please, please!'

'Well,' Gramp replied, 'just because you said you don't mind it not being exciting, then I will.'

'As I was saying,' Gramp said, 'a long time ago, nearly a hundred and fifty years in the past, before you were born, a little girl, Elizabeth Wallbridge, lived with her parents, brothers and sister in a thatched cottage about two miles from here at Arreton. Her father did farm work for the farmers nearby and also managed a few cows of his own with a little dairy. When Elizabeth was about your age, she would help her father with the cows, clean them for milking, patter the butter[181] and help her mother with making the bread and cakes and keeping the little cottage clean and tidy. With all this she would still manage a few lessons in reading and writing from the Parson when he could, although this was not very often as he was very busy helping at other churches and visiting sick people on his horse.'

'When she was about eleven, she started to work in the large house nearby and when she was older she left home to work and live in one of the large houses quite a way from her home. Of course, being a pretty young girl she enjoyed herself as much as she could for a few years, but she later came home to look after her mother and father when they were old. At the same time she visited old and sick people and read *The Pilgrim's Progress*[182] and other books to them, Elizabeth being one of the few people who could read in the village in those days. In fact, her life was so good and lovely, with her kindness to all the villagers, that a friend of Queen Victoria's father, Mr Richmond,[183] who was a Parson at Brading Church, wrote a book about her called *The Dairyman's Daughter*.[184] It was read all over the world.'

'All over the world!' I repeated excitedly, for anything all round the world, or all over the world, always made my toes wriggle with anticipation, making

---

181   In the 19th century butter pats were used to shape butter into bricks, which were stamped with a wooden stamp or print to identify the individual farm dairies (Object Lessons, 2020).

182   This is a Christian allegory written by John Bunyan 1678.

183   Legh Richmond (1772-1827).

184   *The Dairyman's Daughter* was first published as a tract by the Religious Tract Society in 1814.

me think of explorers and icebergs. 'Where, where, Gramp?' I asked, tumbling over my words.

'In the palaces of Kings and even in North America in an Indian hut,' Gramp replied, adding, 'and about two million, and you know how large a million is, about two million of *The Dairyman's Daughter* were printed and sold. That means if you stretched them in a line from here towards Ryde, they would go right down to the sea and beyond, I expect, past the end of Ryde pier.'[185]

I tried to imagine all those books in a line from where we were to Ryde pier. That would be a funny sight. And then I thought of the Indian hut and I asked, 'Tell me all about the Indian hut, Gramp.'

'Perhaps, I'll tell you all about that on the way home,' said Gramp, jumping down off the tree trunk, 'but we must walk on or we'll never get to Arreton.'

---

185   In fact in 1828 its circulation exceeded four million copies in 19 languages (Leach, 2006. P.68). If laid side by side, they would certainly go beyond Ryde Pier. Peter and Gramp would have been amazed to learn that they would make forty seven lines of books between Arreton and Ryde (Arreton to Ryde is about eight miles or 63,360 inches. Divided by the average width of a book at six inches gives 84,480. Divided into four million gives 47.35).

# 27

# ST. GEORGE'S CHURCH
# AND THE SEA MARK

From the cool pine woods the heat from the dusty road shimmered against my legs. The rising and falling warmth brushed against my face until it carried the unforgettable smell of fresh horse dung from the still-steaming, picture book volcanic islands on the road.

'Pon my puff!' Gramp said, admiring the dung. 'A pity we're so far from our gate. It would be worth a dustpan and brush. But anyway, we have the oil man's horse, not to mention old Markwick's and the baker's, so we can't grumble. Come to think of it,' added Gramp, 'we're lucky for they always seem to go when they stop at our place. That's a wonderful thought and that's something we won't have when motors rule the day. All you'll get then will be oil marks from the engine outside our gate and fumes, pon my puff, enough to choke you, I'll expect. This dung is something which will make things grow but the oil and the fumes will only make the leaves wither and die before their time. I'm glad I won't live to see the day,' said Gramp, prodding the dung with the end of his stick. 'I don't suppose they'll be clever enough to make a motor car like a horse, I'll be bound,' said Gramp. I thought this was very funny as it made me think of the Captain's car with a tail. Gramp's eyes would go all twinkles when I told him and at Sunday teatime he would say, speaking more to himself, 'What a golden thought, cars with tails, and that's something Henry Ford didn't think of either!'

Slowly we walked up the slope, turning round the bend in the road away from the magic pine woods, Gramp needing all his breath. Then, in the distance, near the pine wood corner, but still out of sight, we could hear the sound of a horse and cart getting nearer. Gramp's eyes glowed with pleasure at this sound and he gave my hand a knowing squeeze as we stopped and waited. In a moment, a beautiful black horse appeared, harnessed to a four-wheeled dray, its wheels all yellow-spoked, complete with a jolly red-faced man who said, 'Woah back Beauty,' giving a pull on the reins, bringing Beauty to a stop. It reminded me of my story book *Black Beauty* as his ears moved with obvious pleasure at the unexpected sight of meeting two likely passengers.

'Going fer?' the happy driver enquired of Gramp.

'Out for a walk to Arreton,' Gramp said, breathing very hard to prove it.

'Jump up then,' said the driver, helping Gramp with a large hand, throwing Gramp the reins to hold onto at the same time. He then climbed down to lift me onto the seat beside him, while Beauty gave a tap, tap on the road with his hoof, bowing his head with contentment. In a moment we were on our way with a swish from Beauty's tail, making me, I was sure, the happiest person for miles around.

'Nice day to be breathin',' the driver said.

'Wonderful day,' Gramp nodded, taking a deep breath.

''Ave a piece of gum stick,' the driver said in a loud voice, pushing a large paper bag under my nose. 'An' I don't mean you Beauty,' he added. 'You'll get yours at Ashey an' not afore,' giving the reins a slap, slap on Beauty's back. Beauty raised his head to acknowledge the driver, getting in an extra clop, clop.

I selected a large broken piece of toffee from the bag, digging my teeth in with one large bite. I had quite a job getting my teeth apart but it seemed to me the best toffee I'd ever tasted. The driver looked at me with knowing delight, saying to Gramp, 'I knew he'd like it. Misses makes it every Friday for Beauty and me. Don't think we could get through the week without it, could we Beauty?' Beauty gave his ears a quick, 'That's right, that's right,' increasing his speed again with anticipation. 'Arreton's a nice little place,' the driver said.

'Yes,' said Gramp. 'It makes a nice trip from Wootton on a day like this. Going to call and wet our whistles at the Inn[186] near the church before we leave, but before that I want to take Peter,' nodding towards me, 'onto

---

186    The White Lion was a coaching Inn for over two centuries and still exists as a pub today. This is the pub Peter and Gramp would have known. It is not to be confused with the Dairyman's Daughter pub at nearby Arreton Barns rebuilt after a fire in 2001 (Isle of Wight County Press, 2002).

the Down to see the view and then to the church to see the Dairyman's Daughter. It must be nearly forty years now,' Gramp added, 'since I was in the churchyard.'

'Not so many today would know what you were talking about if you spoke of the Dairyman's Daughter,' said the driver. 'Leastways, that's what me thinks, yet when I was a kid we used to read *The Dairyman's Daughter* at Sunday school, stopping at the church on our Sunday school outings to see her grave. Tell you what, come to remember it, during the war at Arras,[187] there was this bloke who 'ad put 'is age back to join up who was old enough to be me Dad. Sentimental 'e was. He sent a couple of violets 'e'd picked in a letter to 'is old Mum when he was under fire. "Violets from Arras" 'e wrote on a bit of paper 'e'd pressed 'em in. Funny I should remember this now, first time in years. Well, he 'ad a little book with 'im. Ye guessed right,' he added, looking towards Gramp. 'It was *The Dairyman's Daughter*. I packed it up with his things when he,' and he glanced at me, 'when 'e was killed. 'Is old Mum 'ad written something inside to 'im but I didn't 'ave the 'art to read it. I just packed it up with 'is things but I always hopes she got them violets from Arras. It was a beautiful Sunday like this when 'e put them in the letter an' as the sun was leaving the day 'is number came up. 'E couldn't 'ave known a thing but I always remember 'is face fer suddenly 'e looked about a kid of eighteen again instead of over fifty. I always 'ad a feelin' 'e must 'ave seen the angels as they took 'im in.'

'Ah well, if I puts you down 'ere you'll be able to climb up the old grey path to the top of the Down. I 'opes to see ye on the way back. Nice 'avin' company,' the driver added. He helped us down onto the chalky white road and, with a flap of the reins to Beauty, they were away. But as he left I heard him say, ''Ow I 'opes his old Mum received them violets.'

Slowly we began to climb the worn, greyish-white chalk path, which wound its way to the top of the Down, reminding me of an old sea rope whitened and greyed by the sun, zigzagging along the side of the hill. Every now and then we stopped while Gramp rested until at last we reached a large

---

187  During most of the First World War, Arras was about 6.2 miles away from the front line. A series of battles were fought around the city in 1914, 1917 and 1918.

ASHEY SEA-MARK, ISLE OF WIGHT.

Looking over Ryde, to Spithead & Portsmouth

*Sea Mark on Ashey Down. From Sketches Of Scenes In The Isle of Wight by Geo. Brannon, 1832. Out of Copyright. In the Public Domain.*

stone pillar which Gramp explained, upon regaining his breath, was a Sea Mark[188], which had been there for nearly two hundred years. It was used by ships out at sea to mark their position. Gramp leant against the huge stone saying, over and over again, what a beautiful day it was. He then lifted me up to sit on his shoulders to give me an even better view of the sea.

'It's just how I remember it all those years ago,' Gramp said, 'though even more beautiful. Perhaps the years have increased its beauty, making it as if it's viewed for the very first time.'

'Look! There's Ryde Pier and a paddle steamer,' I said excitedly. Far away to my right, I could see Ryde pier, with a paddle steamer surrounded by white sea-foam, while here and there were sailing ships, reminding me of toy ships in my bath, with grey warships, glistening in the sunlit day, nearer the mainland shores of Portsmouth. Looking to my left, Gramp pointed out the River Medina, a silvery glass of blue, edged by white, increasing in size until it joined the Solent at Cowes amid a cluster of ships of all sorts and sizes. A little further out was a most beautiful ocean liner, all white, rising from the blue sea, the sun turning the yellow funnels into gold, its portholes shining like diamonds as it moved like a fairy queen towards the bigger sea for the Atlantic crossing.

'Toll for the Brave! The brave that are no more!'[189] Gramp said. 'Out there lies the *Royal George*[190] with the bones of her eight hundred men and all those

---

188   Brannon identifies this as the Sea-Mark on Ashey Down (Brannon, 1832, p.15). 'It was not unfrequently my custom, when my mind was filled with any interesting subject for meditation, to seek some spot where the beauties of natural prospect might help to form pleasing and useful associations. I therefore ascended gradually to the very summit of the hill adjoining the mansion [Knighton, now demolished]. Here was placed an elevated sea-mark: it was in the form of a triangular pyramid, and built of stone. I sat down on the ground near it, and looked at the surrounding prospect, which was distinguished for beauty and magnificence.' It was erected in 1735 by the Trinity Board (Richmond, 1829, p.23).

189   These lines are from the poem *On the Loss of the Royal George* by Thomas Cowper:

Toll for the brave— / The brave! that are no more: / All sunk beneath the wave, / Fast by their native shore. / Eight hundred of the brave, / Whose courage well was tried,/ Had made the vessel heel /And laid her on her side; / A land-breeze shook the shrouds,/ And she was overset;/ Down went the Royal George, / With all her crew complete (Cowper, 1782).

190   On August 29th 1782, the 100-gun warship *HMS Royal George* sunk whilst lying at anchor off Spithead, Portsmouth. She was heeled over for maintenance to be carried out which

years between. From across the Spithead at Pompy, your Dad and Uncle Harry sailed to battle, like hundreds of other brave men and, as you know, Uncle Will on *HMS Drake* didn't return. Remember her as you see the shiny shores of England. Remember the men who sailed from the Solent in the last war to France. Many returned but many remained forever gone like the men who sailed with Nelson and Drake. Yes, and men will sail again. Those unknown to us will go into unknown battles and so forever from freedom's fortress for freedom's cause, men will be sad in joy to leave and, for others, joy in peace to return along these Solent shores.'

The view, I thought, reminded me of one of Mr Jolliffe's miniature garden villages on fete days with nothing being left out. There were the little fairy-like houses, farm barns and churches with the spires of Ryde sparkling in the sun like steel knitting needles. Every now and then the sun reflected a blinding white light from the twisting and turning railway lines running between the towns and villages. Gramp called out each Down by their loving names, like old friends. A little to our left Gramp pointed to Mersley Down, while over towards all important Newport was Gramp's friend of his school days, Great Pan Down. The grandest of them all was St. Catherine's Down behind us to the south with the blue, white-edged sea rising and falling on sand, rock and stones making a glittering frame. On the Downs themselves there were sheep, here and there, quietly eating away the hours. The fields nearer the farms, with their cows, horses and woods, were all magic and all inviting. The most beautiful of all were the fields of wheat, barley, oats and

---

involved running some of the guns and provisions over to one side of the ship, causing the other side to rise out of the water. However, she soon took on water through her ports. Despite the captain attempting to correct the heel, the ship quickly sank. The death toll was estimated to be between six hundred and one thousand people including Rear-Admiral Kempenfelt. John Ker, a surgeon on board the Queen wrote, 'Every hour corpses were coming ashore on the beach, every hour the bell was tolling and the long procession winding along the streets'. The deceased crewmember's families struggled to reconcile the expectations of glory placed upon British sailors with the fact that their relatives had not died in battle. Relics from the ship became appropriated into material culture with miniature cannons, commemorative coins and snuffboxes made out of the recovered materials (Daly, 2017).

*Sea Mark on Ashey Down © C M Lansley*

meadows of hay, reminding me of a giant multicoloured rug made by Gran on a winter's evening.[191]

'It's time we wended our way,' Gramp announced slipping his silver hunter back into his waistcoat watch pocket, lowering me to the grassy Down.

'We have had some fine times here and no mistake,' Gramp said, looking below to the now deserted Ashey racecourse and railway station resting in the sun.

Slowly we turned leaving Ashey Down and its Sea Mark on this beautiful day, picking our way down the zigzag path to the road back along the way we had come towards Arreton. We hadn't walked far along the road when Beauty and our red-faced driver friend pulled up beside us. 'Nice to see you both again,' the driver said, helping us up and offering me a piece of gum stick in the same breath, smiling with pleasure. 'Expects it was well worth the walk on a day likes this,' the driver said.

'Worth a king's ransom,'[192] Gramp replied.

Gramp and the driver both appeared to be thinking of the king's ransom without words but nodding and smiling at each other knowingly, until after too short a time, for me, we arrived at the Inn near the church.

'Well 'ere we are 'an I won't be leavin' before time, so if you are going to the churchyard don't worry as there'll be plenty of time to wet your whistles 'fore we leave. I can give you both a lift back to Wootton on the way to the farm. It'll be nice 'avin' you as I've said before.'

With Beauty nose-bagged and tethered to a ring in the Inn wall and the driver greeted by friends from within, we walked to the lane around the corner which led to Arreton Church.

---

191 Richmond describes similar scenes from the Sea Mark: 'South-eastward, I saw the open ocean [...]. The sun shone, and gilded the waves with a glittering light that sparkled in the most brilliant manner [...]. Where I was placed, rose two downs, [...] both covered with sheep, and the sea just visible over the farthest of them [...]. In this point ships were seen, some sailing, others at anchor' (Richmond, 1829, p. 25).

192 This means a large amount of money. In the early Middle Ages it referred to the amount required to obtain the freedom of a king who was held prisoner (Phrase Finder, 2020a).

'Hundreds of years old,' Gramp said as we walked up the stony path. 'It's called the church of Saint George.[193] It's even mentioned in the Domesday Book,'[194] Gramp continued, which 'made my skin go all of a creep', as Mrs Jones would say, because I knew if anyone was doomed it was the most terrible thing that could happen to anyone. Yet, for a doomed church, it looked very, very strong to me, which was the reason, I supposed, it was still standing after all these years of being doomed. I'd ask Gramp all about it later, I thought, and I was sure the butcher would have something to say about it, for as Granny often said, the butcher had an answer for everything.

'We had better go inside first and say a little silent prayer,' Gramp said as he gave the slightly-open, heavy door a careful push. We entered, hardly breathing and, to make sure I made no noise, I walked on tiptoe. Gramp found some hard cushions for us to kneel on to say our little prayer. I prayed for Gramp as hard as I could and everyone at home, not forgetting Mrs Jones, the butcher and all my village friends. I remembered old Markwick's horse as well because I had heard Mr Markwick say, only the other day, he was afraid his old horse was not too well and feeling his age. I opened my eyes before Gramp, which I could well understand, as Gramp would know many, many more people to pray for, which I knew would take a much longer time. The windows were very beautiful with the outside light shining through the picture of Jesus Christ I knew so well. As I gazed at the window, I could see the light coming towards me, forming a cross of dancing dust edged with gold. During this moment, I had a feeling of happiness beyond happiness, so great, in fact, that if I hadn't been inside a church I would have shouted with joy. So, I closed my eyes again until Gramp gave me a little nudge and, with

---

193   The parish church of St George at Arreton was the Anglo-Saxon Minster church of the Isle of Wight, and still retains evidence of its Saxon origins in the 10th century west doorway and blocked window above. The church tower was added in 1299. The early Norman church consisted of a nave and chancel only. In 1160 a north aisle was added, followed in the 13th century by a south aisle, lengthening of the chancel, and the addition of a south chapel (Arreton Church, 2020).

194   Domesday is Britain's earliest public record. It contains the results of a huge survey of land and landholding commissioned by William I in 1085. Domesday is by far the most complete record of pre-industrial society to survive anywhere in the world and provides a unique window on the medieval world (National Archives, 2020).

a nod of our heads to the altar, we crept from the church without a sound, by the same big door into the daylight.

We followed the path of little stones by the side of the church. 'Let's see,' said Gramp, looking all around, 'Elizabeth Wallbridge[195] is somewhere opposite the church door. Yes, here it is. Here we are,' Gramp said, pointing to a grave with a stone covered with many words. We stood silently, hand in hand, breathing very quietly, until all I could seem to hear were the birds and the sleepy sound of the gentle wind rustling the uncut grass. Near to where we were standing now, Gramp explained that Queen Victoria had stood there when she was a little Princess visiting Elizabeth Wallbridge's gravestone. Her mother[196] had read her the story of *The Dairyman's Daughter* which was about Elizabeth. 'Do you remember, I told you about her when we sat on the old tree in the pine woods?' Gramp reminded me.

I thought of the pine woods, then of the Dairyman's Daughter, the farmyard, Gramp, the Queen who belonged to Gramp, and again of the young

---

195  According to Legh Richmond, Elizabeth Wallbridge's life until the age of 26 was 'of the most worldly character. Never immoral, she was wilful, proud, selfish and irreligious' (Richmond, 1829). Her life was, however, transformed by a sermon and she became very devout. Richmond conducted the funeral of her sister Hannah, and Elizabeth was buried alongside her. During Elizabeth's illness Richmond often visited her and their discussions inspired him to write *The Dairyman's Daughter* (Osbourne House, 2016). Elizabeth Wallbridge (1770-1801) died tragically young in 1801 of consumption, aged just 31. Her tombstone can be found behind the church, outside the north wall of the chancel (Ross, 2020). The inscription reads: 'To the Memory of Elizabeth Wallbridge, The Dairyman's Daughter, Who died May 30, 1801, aged 31 Years. She, being dead, yet speaketh. / Stranger! If e'er by chance or feeling led, / Upon this hallowed turf thy footsteps tread, / Turn from the contemplation of the sod, / And think on her whose spirit rests with God. / Lowly her lot on earth – but He, who bore / Tidings of grace and blessings to the poor, / Gave her, his truth and faithfulness to prove, / The choicest treasures of His boundless love, - / (Faith, that dispell'd affliction's darkest gloom; / Hope, that could cheer the passage to the tomb; / Peace, that not Hell's dark legions could destroy; / And love, that fill'd the soul with heavenly joy.) / Death of its sting dissarm'd, she knew no fear, / But tasted heaven e'en while she linger'd here. / O happy saint!- may we like thee be blest- / In life be faithful, and in death find rest!' (Brannon, 1832, p.13). The epitaph was written by the poet Mrs W. C. Bousfield, author of *Elijah* and *The Famine of Samaria* (Ward, Lock, 1926, p.88).

196  In the summer of 1831, The Duchess of Kent and her daughter Princess Victoria spent three months at Norris Castle on the Isle of Wight. A tourist to Arreton churchyard, on nearing the tomb of the 'Dairyman's Daughter', found a lady and a young girl sitting beside the mound. The girl was 'reading aloud in a full melodious voice the touching tale of the Christian maiden' (Hopkins, 1901, Ch.2). He found afterwards, on speaking to the Sexton, that the two ladies were the Duchess of Kent and Princess Victoria (aged twelve) (Osbourne House, 2016).

girl of longer than long ago whose story had made the little Princess so sad she shed a tear and made her such a great Queen. Did everyone have to be really sad before they could become great, I wondered? My eyes gently caressed the mound of the grave, to the headstone and beyond, far up to the tablecloth-blue of the sky. As I gazed, my little blue patch of sky became a farmyard with a cowshed leaning against a thatched cottage.[197] From within the cottage I could see the scrubbed-white table, a large window seat with a window sill holding a few books held up at one end by a large book, so large it must have been their Bible. I also knew there were two chairs placed by the window seat, waiting for the close of day to bring them into use, as described by Gramp.[198] From the cottage, my mind wandered outside into the farmyard and the cowshed where Elizabeth was busy milking one of the three cows in the tail-frisking, dim fading light. A squeeze from Gramp's hand brought me back into the warm sun from the dimly-lit farmyard, as we returned along the strong path to the road by the Inn, continuing our happy day.

I waited by the open door of the Inn while Gramp talked to the Cox's Orange[199]-faced smiling landlord who was waving in my direction. Gramp returned with permission for me to enter this paradise of men, blue smoke and laughter. We went to sit at the end of a long Sunday school type of bench, opposite the jolly driver, with his face all wrinkles and smelling of beer-breath. There was a lemonade for me, which had been coloured with a dash of beer, to give it body, whatever that was, by the man beside me. He had polished boots that were so shiny that I could see the reflection of my face when I looked down. I elbowed Gramp and pointed down at the boots, which made Gramp give a huge grin of delight. I knew that this more than pleased him as he lit a Dr Blosser's, which was a sure sign of agreement

---

197   The Dairyman's Daughter's Cottage is on the right hand side of the road going in the direction of Sandown at Hale Common. It is in the grounds of a campsite and is not open to the public.

198   'Everything wore the aspect of neatness and propriety. On each side of the fire-place stood an old oaken arm-chair, where the venerable parents rested their weary limbs after the day's labour was over. On a shelf in one corner lay two Bibles, with a few religious books and tracts' (Richmond, 1829, p.40).

199   Cox's Orange Pippin apple, which is orange-red in colour.

and pleasure. All at once and to my great concern, glassy-boots got up and said, 'Well, I think I'll go and splash my boots,' while another man with plough-field boots said, 'Think I'll join you Charlie.' The two men left while I wondered why glassy-boots would ever want to splash his lovely face-shining boots, though I could well understand the other man wanting to do so as he should have done so long before.

In a few moments they both returned, delighted to finish their beer, but their boots were just the same. I was wondering about this when glassy-boots bought some more beer, including Gramp, with more lemonade for me. Wonderful-boots smiled from one ear to the other, moving an old hat backwards and forwards on his head as if he had an itch, talking and laughing with Gramp, as if they had known each other for ever and ever.

'Think I'll go and see a man about a dog,' Gramp said, looking at glassy-boots.

'I'll join you,' said glassy-boots. Then to me he said, 'Don't you want to splash yer boots?'

I looked down at my shoes. 'Well,' I said, 'you see I only wear shoes,' which for some reason made the whole table shake with laughter. Plough-field boots then said, ''Ere, give me your 'and and come splash yer shoes!'

All at once we had fixed faces contemplating this important operation as we followed glassy-boots and six men from the table outside and round the corner. I became a little worried, for I knew Granny would have something to say if the water went through my shoes and made my socks wet. We entered a brick building[200] with water running down the black walls. It was then I knew that we were all going to 'go' against the black wall. This was nothing like the lovely washbasins of Newport Railway Station (with Gramp helping me with my buttons, for I always had one button that was very difficult). Soon we all started to 'go'. Everything was silent except for the sound of running water. But the running water was like steaming taps all running at the same time, and very smelly. Once we were all outside, in the sweet-smelling daylight, everyone started to laugh and joke, pleased to think, I suppose, that it was all

---

200   Known locally as 'The Splash House'.

over. Then, I suddenly remembered they had forgotten to splash their boots. So I took hold of glassy-boot's hand and asked, 'When are we going to splash our boots and my shoes?' looking up at the tilted hat. Glassy-boots looked down with a 'I don't know what' look and laughed like an old dog clearing his throat. Then everyone joined in, though I couldn't think why until he bent down, almost double, to whisper in my ear, 'We call it splashing our boots 'cause when you go in a public[201] you often splash yer boots, leastwise if yer not careful.'

Gramp then said quickly, 'When you want to "go" at Miss McKerchar's or when you are out with Granny, be careful not to ask if you can splash your boots! Promise.'

'I promise,' I said, feeling very grown-up as we returned to our drinks in the Inn. But one thing I must do. I must tell the butcher. I knew it would surprise him to know what 'splash your boots' really meant. He would be pleased.

To calls of 'time please' said over and over again by the happy landlord, we left the blue smoke to blink in the sunny day. Beauty was unhooked from the ring in the wall and the rosy-faced driver with beer-breath helped me up to sit next to him. After handing me the reins, while he helped Gramp to join us, we were soon on our way with happy 'goodbyes' and 'see you agains' and with much whip-waving Beauty gathered speed, neighing with delight at thoughts of home. The sound of the wheels on the dusty road and Beauty's hooves soon carried me into sleepyland until, with a jerk and a stop, we were home to the smell of lamb and mint sauce greeting us from the open dining room window. If there was one thing I loved above all else it was a mint sauce Sunday. I knew too that wherever and whenever I had mint sauce I would also taste this happy, happy day. And should I live to be older than Gramp, a mint sauce Sunday would find me just five years old with Gramp saying, 'It's a nice day for the race,' and our day would begin all over again and it would be mine and Gramp's forever.

---

201  The Gents'.

# 28

# THE BADGER, THE FERRET, THE HARE AND THE FOX

One day Mummy asked the oilman, 'Do you know of anyone who repairs shoes nearby as it would save me taking them into Newport?'

'Why of course,' said the oilman. 'Just take them down the hill to Harry. Peter will take them down, won't you?'

'Yes,' I said, and as I agreed I noticed Mummy looked rather concerned.

'Would it be alright for Peter, I mean?'

'Of course, Harry's wonderful with children. And Peter needn't worry about the journey. It's just straight down the hill. You then turn right at the corner, then take the first road on the left, and …' He then turned to me. 'And you have a tongue in your head Peter, don't you?'

'Yes, I'm sure I have,' I replied, and with this both Mummy and the oilman laughed so much I thought they wouldn't stop.

'Well,' continued the oilman. 'After you've taken the first turning on the left down the hill, you ask anyone and they'll tell you where Harry's house is. If the wind's blowing the right way, you'll 'ear 'im hammering. Just follow your nose.'

'Follow my nose?' I interrupted.

'Why of course. Walk straight on an' you'll see 'is 'ouse. It's the last but one before the school.'

'Tell you what,' said the oilman before I could say anything more, 'you can do something fer me if you would. I've a pair of Mr Jacobs' shoes which 'e asked me to drop in to Harry's fer repair. Would you take them in fer me as well?'

'Yes, and could I go this afternoon, Mummy?'

'I suppose you can,' agreed Mummy.

Sometime after three o'clock I set out alone for the great adventure of going down the hill. I knew my left and my right so it was quite easy. At the end of our road I turned right. Now I only had to turn left, I thought to myself, as I carried Mr Jacobs' shoes under my left arm and my little shoes under my right arm. I crossed the road at the corner as I went down the hill so I wouldn't forget to turn left. I could have asked one or two people passing me by, but I had made up my mind, I was going to find Harry's shoe house myself.

I could hear the sound of hammering getting louder and, at last, I stopped at a half-open gate and listened very hard. Yes, I was sure the hammering came from here. I walked up the long path and at last arrived at the back door. Suddenly, the door opened and an old lady asked, 'You wanting 'arry?'

'Yes,' I answered.

'He's up the garden,' was the reply.

I could hear some more hammering, so I walked up the path to the sound of hammering and children's laughter coming from the enclosed chicken house I remembered from my last visit with Victoria. I knocked on the door and a voice shouted 'hello' from within. I didn't say anything. 'Hello,' said the voice again. Timidly, I opened the door and walked in and then I started to cough. The man in the corner with shoes and boots all around him took the pipe he was smoking out of his mouth and said, 'I'm sorry, Brother, if this makes you cough. It gives me a sore throat.' With this, he stretched out his hand and said, 'Nice to see you, Brother'.

'Please, Harry, Mummy asked if you would repair my shoes,' handing them to Harry. Harry looked them all over.

'Kick a lot of stones?' he asked.

'Yes, I do. How do you know Harry?'

'That's a very sensible question young man. You see, I can see the marks where you have kicked the stones here. It's as easy as that and after you've worked for years repairing shoes you know a lot about a person without any-one telling you. Every shoe tells a story.'

Young man, I thought. I was now a young man. What a lot I would have to tell everyone when I got back home. Then I handed Harry Mr Jacobs' shoes. 'The oilman asked if you could repair Mr Jacobs' shoes. He forgot to leave them.'

Harry studied Mr Jacobs' shoes putting his finger into the hole on the bottom. 'Poor Mr Jacobs,' said Harry half to himself. 'I repaired these shoes six months ago and he forgot to pay me. Poor Mr Jacobs. He must be in trouble but I don't think he drinks. I wonder what the trouble is.'

Gramp would never have believed that, I thought. I don't think I had ever enjoyed myself so much apart from it being so smoky. Suddenly, a nicely-spoken man, sitting next to me, got up and touched the top of the paraffin bottle with his walking stick. Then he did it again. 'That's Mr Jacobs' trouble, Harry,' he said. 'Only he doesn't buy it in the village. He has it at home on the quiet.'

'Well, I'm blowed. I am surprised,' said Harry. 'Is that ever right?' said Harry again. 'Well, I've learned something this afternoon. It just shows we all have something to hear. Always count your blessings one by one young man,' Harry added, turning to me.

Just then a farmer, waiting for his shoes, changed the conversation and said, 'A badger will dig faster than a man. There's only one thing to do if you're after a badger and that's to entertain him.'

Harry laughed, taking nail after nail from his mouth as he hammered them into an upper held firmly on the last.[202] I looked at the farmer, wondering how anyone could entertain a badger and I started to giggle.

'What's got into the young shaver?'[203] asked the farmer looking at me with Gramp's eyes, all creased at the corners, making me feel happy and sad at the same time.[204]

'I was thinking,' I replied, 'how anyone would entertain a badger.' And, remembering Gramp again, I added, 'Would you play a tune on a whistle-pipe?'

Harry and the farmer rocked with laughter with tears making little smoky marks down Harry's face.

---

202  A last is a mechanical form shaped like a human foot used by shoemakers in the manufacture and repair of shoes (The Sneaker Factory, 2015).

203  Young lad.

204  Peter is feeling happy because the farmer's eyes remind him of his Gramp's but sad because this is not long after his Gramp's death in March 1929. So Peter is around ten years old.

'Well, it's like this, Brother,' said Harry. 'If you find a badger when he's gone to ground and you try to dig 'im out you'll be wasten ye time, for he'll dig faster than a man any day.'

'That's right enough, Harry,' agreed the farmer. 'And when it comes to entertaining a badger …' For a moment they both roared with laughter again before the farmer continued, 'When it comes to entertaining a badger, it means you send a couple of dogs in after him. Then, while they keep him occupied, the badger stops digging and that gives you the chance to dig him out.'

'And when you get to the badger, would he ever attack?' I asked.

Both Harry and the farmer sucked their pipes, filling the old converted hen house workshop with smoke, reminding me of the engine going through the tunnel at Wootton Station.

'For a young feller,' Harry said, 'that's a question!'

'Most people would say "no",' the farmer remarked. 'But as I've told Harry many times before, I always believe I was attacked by a badger once, and no one could convince me that that badger didn't mean business.'

'It happened this way,' the farmer explained. 'I was returning to the farm just round about dusk time. It was a beautiful evening and I had a wonderful time bagging a few rabbits over by Church Field. In fact, I had the dead rabbits slung round my neck. I must have looked like a walking rabbit and my ferret[205] was sound asleep in his box, hanging from my belt. I was just enjoying the song of the nightingale coming from the direction of the grove when, I had the fright of my life. At that moment, I was walking along a dip with high banks on either side. Suddenly, I saw a black something coming through the air straight at me. I had no time to aim, but I got a shot in and whatever it was, judging by the noise, it ended up in the middle of a blackthorn bush. I told my father when I arrived back at the farm and next day, sure enough, we found a dead badger in the bush. He was one of the biggest I've ever seen and must have weighed around twenty pounds. I'd shot him right between

---

205  Farmers use ferrets to help reduce the rabbit population on their land. The long, sleek animals are the perfect size to fit into a rabbit burrow and chase the rabbits out into a trap (Morton, 2016).

the eyes and couldn't have done better if I'd had all the time in the world to shoot him.'

Harry gave a little chuckle, which I had come to love and know so well since the death of my Gramp, as he said to the farmer, 'Brother, he was after you and no mistake, 'cause it could have been the smell of the rabbits and maybe he thought you were the biggest rabbit he'd ever smelt and seen!'

This gave me a bout of the giggles, in which Harry and the farmer joined in, though I didn't say how funny I thought it was for the farmer to smell and look like a rabbit. However, there was something about the farmer's ears that started me giggling all over again. Finally I asked, 'Why did you have a ferret in a box?'

'Ferrets are wonderful little animals,' the farmer replied.

'You're right, Brother,' retorted Harry, 'but you've got to know how to use them and not to feed 'em too well before you take 'em out or the little beggars will go to rest.'

'One day,' the farmer said to me, 'you must come out ferreting for rabbits with me.'

'Can I, can I?' I shouted, jumping up and down on the seat.

'Yes, but for now I'll answer your question about the ferret in my box. When you go out to bag a few rabbits you put your ferret down the hole. If you have a good ferret it won't be long before the rabbits come out of their holes, hell for leather, as the saying goes. You then let fly with your gun and, if you're a good shot, you should have enough rabbits to feed you for a month of Sundays.'

'That's it Brother,' said Harry, 'but if you have a lazy ferret or one that's been used for rats, it's no good.'

'True,' answered the farmer, 'for a rat is different from a rabbit. A rabbit will just wait to be bitten if it's cornered but a rat will fight back. A ferret that is used for rats will keep biting the rabbit as if he were fighting a rat and that's no good.'

I was thinking of the rat holes under the old iron shed, wondering if I could borrow the ferret, when Harry said, 'Tell the young man about the rats in the pig sty and the time when a ferret ate his way out through nine rabbits.

That a be a good story for him to tell when he's old enough to visit the Pig and Whistle.'

'Yes please,' I said. 'Tell me about the rats in the sty and the rabbits.'

'Well, of course, as you know, Brother,' said the farmer, 'you are bound to get rats some time or other, and the farmer who tells me he doesn't is no farmer. Well, we had a regular colony of rats under the sties. The rats used to come out and fill their bellies from the pigs' troughs. I'd seen them at dusk and dawn, more than once, and, of course, it would have been dangerous to have put poison down or set traps, so the only thing was to use a ferret.'

'Just by a stone slab, which must have weighed about a ton, there was a rat hole,' the farmer continued. 'So, I puts the ferret down the hole and, after a short time, up come rats from all over the place. I must have shot about a dozen. But the ferret was still down there and there he stayed. I puts my ear to the hole and hears a rustling noise. "There's something going on down there," I said to my son who was helping. So, we went back to the farm and, with a long iron bar, we managed to lift the slab, and there was the rats' run. And sure enough, there was a rat with the ferret—he was a size! They were both all covered in blood. Both of them had bitten each other near the neck and both were hanging on. I hits the rat over the head and kills it. The vet came and treated my ferret, the finest ferret I'd ever had, but in a week he was dead in the cage. It wasn't from the actual bite but the poison from the rat's teeth that had killed him. A rat is about the worst thing you could ever be bitten by.'

'Yes, Brother, the worst thing at any time.'

'At any time,' repeated the farmer.

'Tell him the story of the hare,' said Harry.

'Yes, go on,' I insisted. 'Tell me about the hare.'

'Well all these stories are a little tall, but I can tell you they're as true as I sit here,' said the farmer. 'And I'll also tell you about the sly old fox. And if you tell me animals don't think, well, I can tell you, animals think alright!'

'Go on about the hare first,' I said, 'and then the fox.'

The farmer continued. 'When I was a youngster, a little older than you, I was out ferreting with my father. This ferret somehow not only raised a hare but had jumped on his back and was riding him like a jockey. The hare stopped for a moment and let out a kind of scream and then ran like an express train straight for a five-barred gate about one hundred yards away. The hare needn't have run at the gate. It could have bolted across the fields or through the hedge, but, no, it ran straight at the five-barred gate. Suddenly, it shot right underneath the last bar with a sound like a shot going off. There was my father's best ferret dead, dead as a doornail, with its head all smashed in. Mind you, there was a lot of hare fur around the place. But if you asked me, that hare worked it all out when it stopped to think for a moment. Nothing would ever persuade me or my father that the hare didn't plan to kill that ferret that way.'

I was truly having a wonderful time as Harry said, 'Now tell him about Mr Fox.'

'Yes, and here's one that convinced me again that animals know what they're about right enough. I was in bed as a lad, just getting over measles, and the hounds were meeting at the corner of Church Road that morning. From all the commotion I heard, I knew they were coming my way, and I jumped out of bed just in time to see the old fox come through the hedge with the hounds only a short distance away, and I knew I would see the kill. Not on your life, for the old fox jumped straight into the water butt in the farmyard, and there he was, with just the tip of his nose looking out of the water. The hounds went all round the yard and so did the huntsmen but they didn't see the fox. After a time, they went away and then, and only then, did the sly old fox sit up. And then, with a quick look around to see if the way was clear, the fox jumps out of the butt and, after a good shake, ambles away with all the time in the world. To this day, I've never seen a fox with such a smile on his face as that one.'

Harry then handed me my shoes, putting the money in his old tobacco tin, which he always used for that purpose. To many hearty goodbyes from Harry and the farmer, I ran off and walked up the hill for my tea. When I arrived home, Granny informed me that the Vicar had looked in for tea. With a mouth full of cream bun, the Vicar waved a hand at me and, after saying, 'Yes, I'd love another cup,' he asked, 'And how is Harry, Peter?'

'Very well. I have just taken my shoes and poor Mr Jacobs' shoes to be repaired.'

'Poor Mr Jacobs?' the Vicar repeated.

'Yes,' I replied. 'And there was a nice man visiting Harry who knows what Mr Jacobs' trouble is.'

'Really,' said the Vicar. 'Now I wonder whatever that can be.'

Mummy and Granny looked at me with very worried looks. I thought this must be about poor Mr Jacobs. I wondered if I ought to say any more. The Vicar thought I should as, helping himself to another cake, he asked, 'Now what can Mr Jacobs' trouble be about?'

I felt very important. This was really a great day. 'Well,' I said, 'Harry looked at a hole in Mr Jacobs' shoe and said, "Poor Mr Jacobs. He must be in trouble"' and then … I stopped for a moment as Granny was making faces at me.

'Ah,' said the Vicar. 'And then?'

'And then a very nice man got up from the bench and touched the top of Harry's paraffin bottle with his walking stick twice and said, "That's Mr Jacobs' trouble, Harry."'

Mummy and Granny looked very funny. Mummy looked down on the floor, and Granny completely forgot what she was doing, for instead of handing me the plate of cakes to take one she suddenly put one into my hand. The Vicar was coughing and when he stopped he said to me, 'Just a crumb going down the wrong way.'

Somehow, neither Granny nor the Vicar seemed to worry much about Mr Jacobs' trouble, whatever that was, as they all started talking about other things. I don't think Mr Jacobs' trouble could have been quite as bad as Harry thought or the Vicar would have worried about it too. After the Vicar had gone I told Granny and Mummy all the stories about the badger, the hare and the fox, over my egg and toast. But how I missed Gramp and the many things I would have liked to have asked him. I am sure he would have enjoyed the story of the fox most of all.

# TWENTY FIRST BIRTHDAY RETURN TO
# WOODSIDE VILLA

The blackness became lighter in its greyness. The curtains moved with the dawn wind, stronger now than when I'd walked up the hill. The alarm rang loud and strong and in my alcoholic ears of final parting it recalled an engine racing through a darkened tunnel without any light.

The day was here. That day no human hand could stay. The looked-for-ward-to day of manliness had arrived with the voice of Granny saying, 'Here's a nice cup of tea for you,' and a kiss on either cheek with 'God Bless you to see you safely home my dear.' And Granny was eighty-six years old.

The friendly smell of bacon and eggs followed her through the door as I sipped my tea. I found after all these years that the bathroom looked different; it was strange in its nakedness of electric light[207] waking me from this dream. It must be fun to be a child. It would be fun to be a child with Vickie again and race down the hill together to the old Mill Pond; to strip off unashamed in the secret bushes and plunge into the icy depths that took the breath away and raced the heart; to throw mud and sand; to hold hands and laugh as we acclaimed each other, climbing the old tree to our treehouse within its leafy bower until it was time to run up the hill to be late for tea and free to say 'see you tomorrow by the ivy tree'. Now it was long ago but it would be fun to pretend, to pretend I didn't have to go; fun to pretend to go to the old tree and wait for Vickie. But the days of pretence were over. This was real. This

---

206   This ending to the book was not part of the original manuscript and was probably not intended to be included. It was discovered on some loose sheets of paper among Peter's notebooks. Although it brings the book to an abrupt end, Peter's thoughts on his return to Wootton after about sixteen years are a poignant indication of the strength of his emotional attachment to his childhood memories. Peter's twenty-first birthday was on 7 May 1940 so this was probably referring to this day or the day after.

207   In his childhood days the hall was lit by the oil lamp and the bedrooms by candle light.

*Peter in tropical uniform during WWII © C M Lansley*

was war.[208] But my tears were for yesterday, mixing with the strong shaving soap of today, recalling my moistened Teddy Bear and Vickie, bouncing onto my bed in the early morning: Vickie smelling of a mother's care, all powdery, of soap and scented lilac in her hair.

---

208   World War II 1 September 1939 – 2 September 1945. So on his visit home, Britain had already been at war for eight months.

*Annie Ethel (Mummy), Harriette (Granny) and Peter (aprox 21 years old) © C M Lansley*

# PETER STARK LANSLEY (1919-1999)
# A SHORT BIOGRAPHY

**7 May 1919**: Born Nursing Home, 41 Queens Road, Buckland, Portsmouth. Parents: Percy Lansley and Annie Ethel Morris Lansley (née Stark).

**4 September 1919**: Christened at Whippingham Church, Isle of Wight.

**1920-1923**: Lived at 2 Cypress Terrace, Adelaide Grove (now 69 Adelaide Grove), East Cowes, Isle of Wight.

**1924-1945**: Permanent address at 1-2 Woodside Villa (6-8 Station Road), Wootton.

**1930-1933**: 32 St John's Road, Newport, Isle of Wight. Lived there with Percy, Annie Ethel Lansley and Harriette Stark while Peter was at Grammar School, Newport, Isle of Wight.

**September 1937 – July 1938: Wireless College, Calmore, Southampton**. Trained for the Marconi International Marine (Merchant Navy) to become a Radio Officer at sea. At time of war the Merchant Navy was controlled by the Admiralty under the authority of the Royal Navy.

**September 1938 – September 1939: Municipal College Portsmouth**: Three year Higher National Certificate (HNC) equivalent course in Radio Engineering. Only one year completed as interrupted by outbreak of war. The Municipal College became Portsmouth Polytechnic and then the University of Portsmouth. Peter's early days at the college coincided with the Prime Minister Neville Chamberlain's 'Peace in Our Time' Munich agreement with Hitler in September 1938 which averted war at that time. Prior to this agreement, Peter remembered the digging up of the parks in the City of Portsmouth for air raid shelters and the sandbagging of buildings as war seemed a foregone conclusion. Whilst there, in view of the emergency, Peter called in at the Royal Navy Recruiting Centre, Portsmouth and offered his services, but he was advised to continue his course pending the outcome of peace or war.

**12 September 1939**: Just over a week after war was declared, on 3 September 1939, Peter received a letter dated 12 September 1939 from the Wireless Telegraphy Board, Admiralty, London, from the Wireless register (in which he had enrolled in the Spring of 1939) stating that in view of the fact that he already held a PMG/Radio Officers Certificate and that there was a most pressing need for Radio Officers at sea he should contact the Marconi Wireless Marine Service.

**30 November 1939**: Special Certificate of Proficiency in Radiotelegraphy (Issued by the Postmaster General). After a three months' refresher course, Peter obtained his Special Certificate of Proficiency in Radiotelegraphy at the British School of Telegraphy, London. Peter was therefore qualified to enter the employ of the Marconi Company and was told to report to their depot in East Ham, London.

**17 January 1940**: Joined the Merchant Navy on the staff of the Marconi International Marine Communications Company Ltd., as Radio Officer and proceeded to sea on board *M.V. Port Hobart*.

**19-20 October 1940**: While serving on *M. V. Wandby* as 2nd Radio Officer, his ship was sunk by enemy action off the coast of Iceland. The sinking of *M. V. Wandby* was part of one of the biggest convoy disasters of the war. *M. V. Wandby* was in convoy HX79. Sixty three ships were lost during the night of 19-20 October 1940. The German U-boat aces Kapitänleutnant Günther Prien, Heinrich Bleichrodt, Joachim Schepke and Engelbert Endrass were responsible. The official account can be found in *The Battle of the Atlantic: The Official Account of the Fight Against the U-Boats 1939-1945*, H.M. Stationary Office, 1946, pp.22-3, and *The Battle of the Atlantic* by John Costello and Terry Hughes, Collins 1977, p.110. Peter's ship *M.V. Wandby* was torpedoed at 23:22 hours during the period of a full moon on 19 October 1940 and sank on 21 October. The ship was on route from Victoria British Columbia and was carrying a cargo of 1,700 tons of lead and zinc and 7,200 tons of lumber.

Over the next six hours, thirteen ships were torpedoed, six by U-47 alone. None of the attacking U-boats were damaged. Throughout the day a large escort force of 11 warships also gathered to provide cover. It suffered major losses from a U-boat attack and, with the attack on convoy SC 7 the previous day, represents the worst two days shipping losses in the entire Atlantic campaign. Peter was rescued by *H.M. Tranler Angle*, one of the convoy's escort vessels. Along with other survivors, Peter was landed at Belfast, arriving in England in early November 1940. The crew of 34 were all saved.

**21 March 1941**: Certificate of Proficiency in Radiotelegraphy. Issued by the Postmaster General.

**July 1941**: Released from Merchant Navy to take up temporary shore appointment due to illness resulting from the sinking of his ship.

**11 August 1941**: H.M. Signal School, Lythe Hill House, Haslemere, Surrey. Appointed to Admiralty Signal Establishment as Temporary Laboratory Assistant in the Admiralty Scientific and Technical Pools. Duties included the design and production of Wireless Telegraphy apparatus in H.M. ships together with pure Radio Research. Peter served firstly in S5 Section and later in G1 Section Laboratory under its head, G. M. Wright (G.M. Wright was Head of the Radar Countermeasures Group and Chief Scientist. By 1943 he was responsible for drawing up the signal plans for D-Day ).

**December 1942**: Certificate of Proficiency for Radio. Issued by I.C.S. London.

**6 July 1943**: Released by Admiralty as pronounced medically unfit to serve at sea due to War Service Disability.

**July 12 1943**: Commenced as ground Radio Officer on staff of British Overseas Airways Corporation (B.O.A.C.) and posted to Bristol.

**September 1943**: Proceeded overseas with R.A.F. draft. Posted to Cairo (Egypt), Leopoldville (Belgian Congo), Lagos (Nigeria), Khartoum (Sudan),

*Peter Stark Lansley 4 April 1946 aged nearly 27 years © C M Lansley*

and thence to B.O.A.C.'s base at Half Die at Bathurst in the Gambia, West Africa.

**10 January 1944**: Appointed Radio Inspector (temporary) on home staff British Airways and took up duties at Filwood Broadway, Bristol preparatory to being posted to Croydon Airport.

**4 April 1944**: As health improved, and as Peter wished to take an active part in the war, he volunteered for sea service. He was passed medically fit by the Merchant Navy Officer's Pool Doctor at Leadenhall Street, London.

**20 April 1944**: Left B.O.A.C. and placed on staff of Siemens Wireless Marine Co. of Woolwich for duties as Radio Officer in the Merchant Navy.

**20 May 1944**: Joined *Gloxinia* at South Shields as 1st Radio Officer but fell ill.

**23 May 1944**: Admitted to the Merchant Navy Rest Home for Merchant Seamen at The Riding Allendale, near Newcastle.

**3 June 1944**: Recovered and joined *S. T. Empire* Roger as Radio Officer in charge on Articles for the Liberation of Europe.

**15 August 1944**: Proceeded to North of England to stand by for another ship.

**4 September 1944**: Appointed 1st Radio Officer for operations on *Empire Newfoundland* which he understood were to be part of the anticipated action against mainland Japan. After inspecting the aerials in heavy rain, Peter caught a severe chill resulting in his having to receive treatment at the Ministry of Pensions Hospital, Gateshead. Officers and men of the combined services and the Merchant Navy received treatment there.

**3 October 1944**: Discharged from service in Merchant Navy by the Merchant Navy Pool Doctors as being 'Physically unfit for further sea service'.

**October 1944 – June 1946**: After a period of recuperation, Peter became a student at the School of Radio Engineering, Regent Street Polytechnic, Regent Street, London.

**June 1946 – 8 January 1978**: Following his training at the Polytechnic, Peter joined the Ministry of Aviation in June 1946 serving at various Civil Aviation establishments throughout the United Kingdom, the Channel Isles and the Isle of Man. This included Prestwick Oceanic, located in Birdlip Gloucestershire. This was the North Atlantic Radio Telecommunications Link (NARTEL) Control Station with world-wide cover for aviation from the UK at this time. Finally, Peter served at London Air Traffic Control Centre, Heathrow, until his medical retirement on 8 January 1978.

**11 June 1999**: Peter died on 11 June 1999 and his remains were scattered at his home in Alverstone Garden Village, Isle of Wight.

**Medals for War and Civilian Service**

- **The 1939-45 Star**: Merchant Navy personnel qualified upon completion of 180 days of service with at least one voyage made through an operational area.

- **The Atlantic Star 1939-1945**: The Atlantic Star was awarded for six months service afloat in the Atlantic or in Home Waters within the period from 3 September 1939 to 8 May 1945. Merchant seaman qualified for the award of the medal on condition that the 1939–1945 Star must have already been earned. They were required to have served in the Atlantic, Home Waters, North Russia Convoys or the south Atlantic.

- **The France and Germany Clasp 1944-1945**: The France and Germany clasp would have been awarded for operational service between D-Day (6 June 1944) and V.E. Day (8 May 1945) at sea in the North Sea south of a line from the Firth of Forth to Kristiansand, in the

English Channel or in the Bay of Biscay east of longitude 6° West in direct support of land operations in those countries.

- **The War Medal 1939-1945**: a campaign medal which was instituted by the United Kingdom on 16 August 1945, for award to citizens of the British Commonwealth who had served full-time in the Armed Forces or the Merchant Navy for at least 28 days between 3 September 1939 and 2 September 1945.

*Peter rowing on the Isle of Wight 1961, about 42 years old © C M Lansley*

- **The Ministry of Pensions, The King's Badge for Loyal Service**: The King's Badge is a large silver lapel badge issued to servicemen by the Ministry of Pensions during the Second World War who, as a result of their injuries, had been discharged from active service. As well as members of the armed services, merchant navy and fishing fleets qualified.

- **The Imperial Service Medal 5 March 1976**: Peter was presented the medal by the Chairman of the Civil Aviation Authority, Lord Boyd Carpenter on behalf of Her Majesty the Queen. On his retirement Peter had worked for the Civil Aviation Authority for approx. 34 years making this a total of 40 years' service for his country.

*Peter Stark Lansley's plaque on the memorial wall at Ventnor Botanic Gardens © C M Lansley*

# REFERENCES

Abelard (2008). 'Brer Fox, Brer Rabbit and the Briar Patch.' Available at: <https://www.abelard.org/brer_fox_brer_rabbit_briar_patch.php> (Accessed on 23 January 2020).

Albert, Samuel (2020). 'There Is A Green Hill Far Away: Story Behind Hymn and Lyrics.' Available at: < https://www.christianmusicandhymns.com/2015/06/there-is-green-hill-far-away-story.html> (Accessed on 29 January 2020).

Allett, Paulene (2020). The Copper Water Boiler: 'The copper which supplied hot water in Victorian and early 1900s houses.' Available at: <https://www.1900s.org.uk/copper-water-heater.htm> (Accessed on 7 February 2020).

Almroth-Wright (2014). 'Hampshire and Isle of Wight: Island Grand National: And they're off!' Available at: <http://www.bbc.co.uk/hampshire/content/articles/2009/03/27/iow_grandnational_feature.shtml> (Accessed on 1 March 2020).

Andrews, Cath (2019). 'Wyandotte Chickens: the Sophie Loren of the Poultry World.' Available at: <https://www.raising-happy-chickens.com/wyandotte-chickens.html > (Accessed on 23 October 2019).

Arreton Church (2020). 'Arreton Church: The Church of St George'. Available at: <https://wealdanddownlandchurches.co.uk/arreton-church/> (Accessed on 8 April 2020).

Barratt (2020). 'Barratt's Sweets: Our Story'. Available at: <https://barratts-weets.co.uk/our-story/> (Accessed on 29 May 2020).

Bay of Biscay (2020). 'Traditional Sea Shanties & Sea Songs: The Bay of Biscay, Oh!' Available at: <http://www.traditionalmusic.co.uk/sea-shanty/Bay_of_Biscay_Oh!.htm> (Accessed on 12 January 2020).

Biography, Your Dictionary (2019). 'Robert and James Adam Facts.' Available at: <https://biography.yourdictionary.com/robert-and-james-adam> (Accessed 12 October 2019).

Brannon, George (1832). *Sketches of Scenes in the Isle of Wight*. Wootton, Isle of Wight: G. Brannon; London: Westley and Davis.

British Library (2020). 'Collection Items: Black Beauty'. Available at: <https://www.bl.uk/collection-items/black-beauty-animal-tales-space> (Accessed 27 February 2020).

Carols (2017). 'Christmas is Coming'. Available at: <https://www.carols.org.uk/christmas_is_coming.htm> (Accessed on 4 April 2020).

Chandler, Selena (2017). 'Basketry Then and Now'. Available at: <https://everydaylivesinwar.herts.ac.uk/wp-content/uploads/2017/08/The-Orsett-Basket-Works-Essex-Selena-Chandler.pdf> (Accessed 23 February 2020).

Chandler, Victoria (2019). 'The ultimate guide to Stir-up Sunday 2019.' Good Housekeeping. Available at: <https://www.goodhousekeeping.com/uk/christmas/christmas-countdown/a550045/ultimate-stir-up-sunday-when/> (Accessed on 12 November 2019).

Cosy Hen Company, The (2019). 'Light Sussex.' Available at: <https://www.cosyhens.co.uk/page_2321792.html> (Accessed on 10 November 2019).

Cowper (1782). *On the Loss of the Royal George*. Poetry Foundation. Available at: <https://www.poetryfoundation.org/poems/44029/on-the-loss-of-the-royal-george> (Accessed on 8 April 2020).

Cryer, Pat (2020a). 'The variety of Victorian and Edwardian Kitchen ranges.' Available at: <https://www.1900s.org.uk/kitchen-ranges-variety.htm> (Accessed on 7 February 2020).

Cryer, Pat (2020b). 'House lighting with oil lamps in the early 1900s and in Victorian times.' Available at: <https://www.1900s.org.uk/oil-lamps.htm> (Accessed on 9 February 2020).

Daisy Daisy (2020). Available at: <https://nurseryrhymescollections.com/lyrics/daisy-daisy.html> (Accessed on 12 January 2020).

Daily Proverbs (2019). 'Proverb of the day : The better the day, the better the deed'. Available at: <http://dailyproverbs.us/2019/08/31/proverb-of-the-day-the-better-the-day-the-better-the-deed/> (Accessed on 2 April 2020).

Daly, Scott (2017). 'The sinking of HMS Royal George and its importance in British Naval Culture'. Port Towns and Urban Cultures. Available at: <http://porttowns.port.ac.uk/the-sinking-of-hms-royal-george/> (Accessed on 8 April 2020).

Definitions (2020). 'To Muffle the Oars'. Available at: <https://www.definitions.net/definition/to+muffle+the+oars> (Accessed on 6 May 2020).

Disused Stations: Wootton, (2019). Available at: < http://www.disused-stations.org.uk/w/wootton/index.shtml> (Accessed on 12 October 2019).

Dolly Gray (2020). 'Vintage Audio - Goodbye Dolly Gray.' Available at: <https://firstworldwar.com/audio/goodbyedollygray.htm> (Accessed on 12 January 2020).

Dream Astro Meanings (2020). 'Dreams About Birds – Interpetation and Meaning'. Available at: <https://dreamastromeanings.com/dreams-about-birds-interpetation-and-meaning/> (Accessed on 15 March 2020).

Ennever, Barry (2019). 'Albert Midlane, hymn writer (1825-1909).' Available at: http://www.ennever.com/histories/history4739.php (Accessed on 8 December 2019).

Foresters Friendly Society (2019). 'Our History.' Available at: <https://www.forestersfriendlysociety.co.uk/about-us/our-history/> (Accessed on 23 November 2019).

Geni (2016). 'Admiral Austin M. Knight'. Available at: <https://www.geni.com/people/Admiral-Austin-M-Knight/6000000000875277647> (Accessed on 3 March 2020).

Genius (2020). 'The Man Who Broke the Bank at Monte Carlo - Fred Gilbert'. Available at: <https://genius.com/Fred-gilbert-the-man-who-broke-the-bank-at-monte-carlo-lyrics>  (Accessed on 18 March 2020).

Gosden, Hilary (1998). *A History of Wootton Bridge: Part Two: The High Street*. Newport, Isle of Wight: Burnt House Publishers.

Gosden, Hilary (1999). *A History of Wootton Bridge: Part Three: The Old School*. Newport, Isle of Wight: Burnt House Publishers.

Gosden, Hilary (2000). *A History of Wootton Bridge: Part Four: Fernhill*. Newport, Isle of Wight: Burnt House Publishers.

Gosden, Hilary (2002). *A History of Wootton Bridge: Part Five: Inns and Ale Houses*. Newport, Isle of Wight: Burnt House Publishers.

Happy Chicken Coop, The (2019). Available at: <https://www.thehappy-chickencoop.com/leghorn-chicken/> (Accessed on 13 November 2019).

Herman, David (2020). *AJR Journal/February 2020*.

Hopkins, John Castell (1901). *Queen Victoria: Her Life and Reign*. Toronto: The Queen Publishers.

Isle of Wight County Press Archive (1924). 'Saturday December 6 1924 – advertisement.' Available at: <http://archive.iwcp.co.uk/> (Accessed on 27 February 2020).

Isle of Wight County Press Archive (1928). 'Saturday November 17 1928.' Available at: <http://archive.iwcp.co.uk/> (Accessed on 25 January 2020).

Isle of Wight County Press Archive (1928). 'Saturday November 26 1932.' Available at: <http://archive.iwcp.co.uk/> (Accessed on 25 January 2020).

Isle of Wight County Press Archive (1928). 'Saturday February 18 1967.' Available at: <http://archive.iwcp.co.uk/> (Accessed on 25 January 2020).

Isle of Wight County Press Archive (1928). 'Friday May 14 1993.' Available at: <http://archive.iwcp.co.uk/> (Accessed on 25 January 2020).

Isle of Wight County Press Archive (1938). '19 March 1938.' Available at: <http://archive.iwcp.co.uk/>   (Accessed on 28 March 2020).

Isle of Wight County Press Archive (1939). 'Saturday 26 August 1939.' Available at: <http://archive.iwcp.co.uk/> (Accessed on 13 March 2020).

Isle of Wight County Press Archive (1939). 'Saturday 9 September 1939.' Available at: <http://archive.iwcp.co.uk/> (Accessed on 13 March 2020).

Isle of Wight County Press Archive (1942). 'Saturday 31 January.' Available at: <http://archive.iwcp.co.uk/>   (Accessed on 28 March 2020).

Isle of Wight County Press Archive (1945). '24 February 1945' and '3 March 1945'. Available at <http://archive.iwcp.co.uk/> (Accessed on 27 April 2020).

Isle of Wight County Press (2019). 'Popular Isle of Wight Grand National and Ashey Scurry are Back -23 March 2019'. Available at: <https://www.countypress.co.uk/news/17522557.popular-isle-of-wight-grand-national-and-ashey-scurry-are-back/> (Accessed on 1 March 2020).

Isle of Wight County Press Archive (2001). 'Thursday April 12 2001.' Available at: <http://archive.iwcp.co.uk/> (Accessed on 10 April 2020).

Isle of Wight Rifles (2020). 'Princess Beatrice's Isle of Wight Rifles.' Available at: <https://isleofwightrifles.org.uk/index.php> (Accessed on 29 February 2020).

Jackson, Mark (2010). 'Divine Stramonium': The Rise and Fall of Smoking for Asthma.' *Cambridge Journals Medical History. Med Hist. 2010 Apr; 54(2): 171–194.* Available at: https://www.ncbi.nlm.nih.gov/pmc/articles/PMC2844275/ (Accessed on 6 January 2020).

Lansley, Charles Morris (2018). *Charles Darwin's Debt to the Romantics: How Alexander von Humboldt, Goethe and Wordsworth Helped Shape Darwin's View of Nature.* Oxford: Peter Lang.

Leach, Alexandra N. (2006). 'The Dairyman's Daughter: From Yesterday to Today', Chapter 4, 65-74. *From the Dairyman's Daughter to Worrals of the WAAF.* Edited by Butts, Dennis and Garrett, Pat. Cambridge: Lutterworth Press.

Lewis, Dave (2020). 'Clari, or the Maid of Milan, operetta'. All Music. Available at: <https://www.allmusic.com/composition/clari-or-the-maid-of-milan-operetta-mc0002356876> (Accessed on 28 April 2020).

Longdon (2018). 'What are the lyrics of Land of Hope and Glory and what do they mean?' Available at: <https://www.classicfm.com/composers/elgar/lyrics-land-of-hope-and-glory/> (Accessed on 2 March 2020).

Longfellow (2020). 'Henry Wadsworth Longfellow: A Maine Historical Society Website.' Available at: https://www.hwlongfellow.org/poems_poem.php?pid=296 (Accessed on 9 January 2020).

Lyrics (2020). 'When the Red, Red Robin Comes Bob, Bob Bobbin' Along.' Available at: <https://www.lyrics.com/lyric/9585732/Doris+Day/

When+the+Red+Red+Robin+Comes+Bob-Bob-Bobbin%27+Along> (Accessed on 29 February 2020).

Lyrics (2020). 'Bye Bye Blackbird'. Available at: <https://www.lyrics.com/lyric/15776095/Peggy+Lee/Bye%2C+Bye+Blackbird> (Accessed on 29 February 2020).

Lyrics (2020). 'Keep the Home Fires Burning'. Available at: <https://www.lyrics.com/lyric/5583359/%5BChorus+%26+Orchestra%5D/Keep+the+Home+Fires+Burning+%28%27Till+the+Boys+Come+Home%29> (Accessed on 29 February 2020).

Macquarie (2014). Macquarie Dictionary Blog: Archives. 'Forgotten and Misunderstood Phrases.' Available at: https://www.macquariedictionary.com.au/blog/article/88/ (Accessed on 11 January 2020).

McKerchar Index, The (2019). Available at: https://www.mckercher.org/TheIndex?personID=I764 (Accessed on 23 December 2019).

Merriam-Webster (2020). 'Portmanteau.' Available at: <https://www.merriam-webster.com/words-at-play/types-of-baggage-luggage/portmanteau> (Accessed on 30 January 2020).

Met Office (2020). 'Red sky at night and other weather lore.' Available at: <https://www.metoffice.gov.uk/weather/learn-about/weather/how-weather-works/red-sky-at-night> (Accessed on 3 June 2020).

Morton (2026). 'Ferrets helping farmers to beat the rabbit problem.' Available at: <https://www.theland.com.au/story/3854308/ferreting-about-for-a-rabbit-fix/> (Accessed on 14 April 2020).

National Archives, The (2020). 'Domesday: Britain's finest treasure'. Available at: <https://www.nationalarchives.gov.uk/domesday/> (Accessed on 8 April 2020).

National Ocean Service (2020). 'What are the Seven Seas?' Available at: <https://oceanservice.noaa.gov/facts/sevenseas.html> (Accessed on 3 March 2020).

News, The (2019). Available at: https://www.portsmouth.co.uk/lifestyle/heritage/the-epitome-of-chic-1-2477036 (Accessed on 13 December 2019).

Object Lessons (2020). 'Butter Pats & Print, Victorian, Original.' Available at: <https://www.objectlessons.org/work-and-innovation-victorians/butter-pats--print-victorian-original/s64/a942/> (Accessed on 5 June 2020).

Old Scottish Genealogy (2019). Available at: <https://www.oldscottish.com/school-leaving-certificates-mcintosh-mclean.html> (Accessed on 22 December 2019).

Opera North (2018). 'The Merry Widow in a Nutshell.' Available at: <https://www.operanorth.co.uk/news/the-merry-widow-in-a-nutshell/> (Accessed on 16 November 2019).

Osbourne House (2016). 'Queen Victoria's childhood visits to the Isle of Wight'. Available at: <https://www.facebook.com/notes/osborne-house/queen-victorias-childhood-visits-to-the-isle-of-wight/1251016784930908> (Accessed on 9 April 2020).

OU (2019). 'Ariel's Song.' Available at: <http://www2.open.ac.uk/openlearn/poetryprescription/ariels-song.html> Accessed on 23 November 2019.

Paddle Steamers (2019). Various sources available at: <https://woottonbridgeiow.org.uk/psryde.php>; <http://www.kingswearcastle.co.uk/Withdrawn48.htm>; <https://en.wikipedia.org/wiki/Solent_Sea_Steam_Packet_Company>; <https://www.redfunnel.co.uk/en/corporate-info/about-red-funnel/red-funnel-history/passenger-vessel-archive/> (Accessed on 18 November 2019).

Pagat (2019). 'Card Games: Banking Games.' Available at: <https://www. pagat.com/banking/> (Accessed on 15 November 2019).

Payne (1979). 'The Battle of The Glorious First of June, 1794'. Available at: <https://www.navyhistory.org.au/the-battle-of-the-glorious-first-of-june-1794/> (Accessed on 2 March 2020).

Phrase Finder, The (2019). 'The meaning and origin of the expression: On the QT.' Available at: <https://www.phrases.org.uk/meanings/on-the-qt. html> (Accessed on 26 November 2019).

Phrase Finder, The (2020a). 'The meaning and origin of the expression: A king's ransom.' Available at: <https://www.phrases.org.uk/meanings/a-kings-ransom.html> (Accessed on 13 April 2020).

Phrase Finder, The (2020b). 'Pig and Whistle'. Available at: <https://www. phrases.org.uk/meanings/pig-and-whistle.html> (Accessed on 4 June 2020).

Poets (2020). 'Requiem. Robert Louis Stevenson'. Available at: <https:// poets.org/poem/requiem> (Accessed on 29 February 2020).

Rabbitmatters (2020). 'Brer Rabbit.' Available at: <http://www.rabbitmat-ters.com/brer-rabbit.html> (Accessed on 23 January 2020).

Richmond, Rev. Legh (1829). *Annals of The Poor: Containing The Dairyman's Daughter, The Negro Servant, And Young Cottager*. London: John Hatchard and Son.

Robinson, Roger (2012). 'Young Sam Butler and the origins of modern running: His Athletic and Illicit Exploits as a Fox and a Hound.' Available at: https://www.joh.cam.ac.uk/young-sam-butler-and-origins-modern-running-his-athletic-and-illicit-exploits-fox-and-hound (Accessed on 10 January 2020).

Robson (2020). 'Nathaniel Portlock and George Dixon's Expedition' Available at: <https://www.captaincooksociety.com/home/detail/nathan-iel-portlock-and-george-dixon-s-expedition> (Accessed on 2 March 2020).

Ross, David (2020). 'Arreton, St George's Church'. Available at: <https://www.britainexpress.com/counties/wight/churches/arreton.htm> (Accessed on 8 April 2020).

Ruger, Rebecca (2018). 'The Codd Neck Bottle'. Beach Combing. Available at: <https://www.beachcombingmagazine.com/blogs/news/history-the-codd-neck-bottle> (Accessed on 5 May 2020).

Schmoop University (2020). 'Song of Hiawatha Analysis.' Available at: https://www.shmoop.com/study-guides/poetry/song-of-hiawatha/analysis (Accessed on 9 January 2020).

Secondhandsongs (2019). 'Charleston.' Available at: <https://secondhand-songs.com/work/122988/all> (Accessed on 16 November 2019).

Sibley, Patricia (1983). *Isle of Wight Villages*. London: Robert Hale.

Sillito (2010). BBC News Magazine. 'Haitch' or 'aitch'? How do you pronounce 'H'? Available at: <https://www.bbc.co.uk/news/magazine-11642588> (Accessed on 3 March 2020).

Smith, Kasandra (2015). Backyard Chicken Coops. '5 Reasons to Love Rhode Island Chickens.' Available at: <https://www.backyardchickencoops.com.au/blogs/learning-centre/5-reasons-to-love-rhode-island-red-chickens> Accessed on 17 November 2019.

Sneaker Factory, The (2015). 'About Shoe Lasts.' Available at: <https://www.sneakerfactory.net/2015/01/shoe-last/> (Accessed on 14 April 2020).

Snow, Victoria (1986). *Wootton Bridge & Whippingham on the Isle of Wight*. Devon: Arthur H. Stockwell.

Songhall, (2020). 'Harry M. Woods'. Available at: <https://www.songhall.org/profile/Harry_M_Woods> (Accessed on 29 February 2020).

Steffler (1980). 'Stone, Flower and Jewel Imagery in Tennyson's Maud'. Unpublished MA Thesis. NcMaster University, Ontario.

Swafford, (2020). 'Songs of the Victorians: Obsession and Instability in Tennyson's Maud'. Available at: <http://www.songsofthevictorians.com/tennyson/analysis.html> (Accessed on 27 March 2020).

Tennyson, Alfred Lord (2006). *Selected Poems*. Selection, Introduction and Notes by Ruth Padel. London: The Folio Society.

Townsend, T.W. (2020). 'Isle of Wight - Pubs and Inns with a literary connection: Shanklin, Crab Inn.' Available at: http://www.homesteadbb.free-online.co.uk/ilowi.html (Accessed on 9 January 2020).

Ward, Lock (1926). *The Isle of Wight. Twenty-first Edition* – Revised. London: Ward, Lock.

Wiktionary (2019). Available at: https://en.wiktionary.org/wiki/out_of_the_mouths_of_babes (Accessed on 31 December 2019).

Wilson, Doris Georgina (1976). *Fernhill House*. Available at: <https://woottonbridgeiow.org.uk/fernhill/index.php> (Accessed on 19 March 2020).

Wootton Bridge Historical (2015). 'Genealogy: 1921 Census report.' Available at: http://woottonbridgeiow.org.uk/1921census.php (Accessed on 2 February 2020).

Wootton Bridge Historical (2015). 'The Inns of the Village 1775 – 1985.' Available at: https://woottonbridgeiow.org.uk/Inns.php (Accessed on 17 November 2019).

Wootton Bridge Historical (2015). 'James Andrew Hendy – 1942.' Available at: <https://www.woottonbridgeiow.org.uk/hendyja.php> (Accessed on 1 February 2020).

Wootton Bridge Historical (2015). 'St Michael and All Angels'. Available at: <https://woottonbridgeiow.org.uk/stmichael.php> (Accessed on 28 March 2020).

Lightning Source UK Ltd.
Milton Keynes UK
UKHW021237090421
381718UK00005B/91